FABULOUS BEASTS AND DEMONS

WITHDRAWN

Fabulous beasts and demons

by Heinz Mode

Phaidon

Phaidon Press Limited, 5 Cromwell Place, London SW7 2JL
Distributed in the United States of America by Praeger Publishers, Inc.,
111 Fourth Avenue, New York, N.Y. 10003
First English edition published 1975
Originally published as *Fabeltiere und Dämonen*

ISBN 0 7148 1642 6
Library of Congress Catalog Card Number: 74-5582

Printed in the German Democratic Republic

Contents

Tritons

Griffin. Title-page to the
Triumphal Procession
of Emperor Maximilian

'NOT ONLY will the curious subject, the entertaining purpose and the colourful fictions which are here reported in a convincing and truthful tone prove attractive, but so will the humorous allusions in these stories to some of the old poets, historians and philosophers, who have written of many wonderful and fabulous things and whom I would have named were it not for the fact that in reading this book you will doubtless know who they are.' (1)

With these words a great writer of antiquity, Lucian, in the introduction to his *True History*, refers to our subject. They can also be applied to the present book, which includes many fabulous things without in any way implying the existence of all that appears here. Its purpose is rather to give an idea, by choosing examples from the enormous variety available, of what the human imagination has invented and illustrated in visual form. We shall not deal with all the marvels imagined by the human mind, but only with those composite creatures which are termed monsters: new beings, of which it can be said with certainty that they are neither 'god-created', nor extant in nature, but that they are entirely products of the human imagination and have received their outward shape from human hands. Thus we define a 'monster' as a new shape resulting from a combination – usually in visual form, but sometimes only in words – of characteristic components or properties of different kinds of living things or natural objects. It is therefore characteristic of the 'monster' that it does not occur in nature, but belongs solely to the realm of the human imagination, and also that its shape forms an organic entity, a new type capable of life in art and in the imagination.

In the history of civilization and in popular belief there are numerous notions of this kind. Forms found in nature are varied, are interchanged completely or in part, mixed and isolated, expanded and contracted, coarsened and refined, and thereby become monstrosities, synthetic creatures, abstractions – creatures new in form and content, whose origins lie clearly in the perception of natural forms, but whose final shapes must be considered as imaginary and extant solely in the human imagination. This relationship between origin and end-product distinguishes these notions – our monsters – from others, whose origins – geometrical, abstractly constructed forms – are as far removed from nature, as imaginary, as the end-product derived from them. The latter develop a life of their own no longer related to reality and, being pure abstractions, lack any human value or significance. But the 'monsters', which are indeed fantastic but are largely rooted in nature, in reality, never lose their links with the world of men. Angels and devils, demons and kindly genies, giants and dwarfs, fire-breathing dragons and winged horses carrying heroes – all are composite creatures which have been given visual form.

It cannot be sufficiently emphasized that our brief, systematic and historical treatment of the various types of monsters will be centred entirely on artistic representations. A good deal has already been written on the subject, but the writers were concerned with other problems: with questions of belief and disbelief, with explanation and justification of supposed errors in the observation of nature. Belief in angels and devils can still be professed even when it is denied that they have wings and horns, tails and goat's feet, or when these features are accounted for by some scientific theory. Scientific discussion of our subject often leaves artistic creation and its intrinsic value out of account. The dragon as described in literature and depicted in the fine arts remains a fabulous creature even when traced back to snakes from strange countries or to finds of prehistoric bones and fossils. Sirens with the bodies of birds or fish-tails cannot be accounted for by referring to human or animal malformations and abortions.

Even in classical antiquity attempts were made to trace the notion of the centaur, a combination of a horse's body with the head and torso of a man, back to a blurred observation of nature: horse and rider closely united in silhouette against a bright background.

In a lecture given in 1901 on 'The gods of Greece and human deformities' a modern gynaecologist, Professor Schatz, offered a different explanation for the centaur. It was, he said, to be traced back to deformed humans born with too many legs. He went so far as to express the hope that in the not too distant future every respectable treatise on Greek mythology would contain a chapter discussing the relationships between human deformities and the Greek gods. Other medical men, like Eugen Holländer in his book *Wunder, Wundergeburt und Wundergestalt* (Wonders, Strange Births and Strange Shapes), published in 1921, were critical of such explanations, though Holländer himself adopts throughout a moralizing attitude and condemns the extravagances of belief in miracles in connection with the interpretation of deformities as devil-shapes. Charles Gould (2) in 1886 had traced the dragon, the sea-serpent, the unicorn and the phoenix back to supposed natural forms, and in 1939 the much more circumspect Othenio Abel (3) adduced considerably more material from natural history, but still only posed the question why notions stemming from the Orient should also turn up in Germany, there to find acceptance and credence.

In his own way Lucian, whom we mentioned at the beginning of this chapter, pokes fun at the monsters found in travellers' tales of the ancient world, but he would presumably also have smiled at some modern attempts at explanation. For despite all his scepticism on questions of faith, his satires show that he knew very well how to appreciate the value of artistic imagination. Horace (4), too, gives his opinion on this problem:

Suppose a painter to a human head
Should join a horse's neck, and wildly spread
The various plumage of the feather'd kind
O'er links of different beasts, absurdly join'd,

1 Decorative animals in an illuminated manuscript. From the Book of Kells, Eighth century A.D. Trinity College, Dublin

Or if he gave to view a beauteous maid,
Above the waist with every charm array'd
Should a foul fish her lower parts enfold,
Would you not laugh such pictures to behold?

This is an undisguised attack on this sort of artistic composition, an attack taken up by art critics like Vitruvius, who deplores the taste for monstrous creatures and characterizes them as the decorative products of pure fancy, portraying things which do not exist, cannot exist, and never had existed (5). A natural philosopher like Diderot in his *Essai sur la Peinture* is, as one would expect, suspicious, even hostile to everything imaginary in art. But even an orthodox Christian like the reformer Bernard of Clairvaux (1091–1153) in the course of criticizing the excessive architectural ornamentation of medieval churches, inveighed against the representation of monsters:
'What is the meaning of these obscene monkeys and raging lions? And of the horrid centaurs, the wild men, the blaring huntsmen? Here you see many bodies joined to one head and there many heads on one body. There a beast drags a horse dragging half a goat after it, here a horned animal is the forepart with a horse forming the hindquarters. Everywhere there is a profusion of the most varied forms, as motley as they are astonishing, so that people prefer to read in stones rather than in books and spend the whole day gaping at every detail of these oddities instead of meditating on their prayers.' (6)
At the same time this passage illustrates the extent to which the Christian Church had taken over the ancient monsters in its visual repertory.
One could cite many more authors, rationalist as well as religious, who arrived at similar conclusions. But there are enough writers – and not always the worst – who deal decidedly less critically with these monsters. Thus Pausanias, in his account of his travels through Greece, shows himself to be no sceptic. He asserts that he has seen tritons, one of which was exhibited in Rome as a great wonder:
'The hair on their heads has the colour of the skin of marsh-frogs and one cannot tell one hair from another: the ample body bristles with fine scales like the fish Rhínè (a kind of shark). Under their ears they have gills, a nose like a man's but the mouth wider, and teeth like a wild animal; their nails are like mussel-shells; below the chest and stomach they have a dolphin's tail instead of feet.' (7)
Pausanias goes on to expound his views thus:
'Thus one should be neither too hasty in forming an opinion nor incredulous in things that occur rarely; and therefore I believe in winged snakes, even though I have never seen any, because a Phrygian brought a scorpion to Ionia which had wings just like locusts.' (8)
On this point Otto Keller wrote in his standard work on *Die antike Tierwelt* (Animals in Antiquity) (9):

2 Hieronymus Bosch: The Temptation of St Antony. Detail. F. van Lanschot collection, Hertogenbosch

'Though the evidence of fossils and ancient legends has led many people to infer that winged snakes once existed at the same time as men, one cannot be too emphatic in warning against such fallacious conclusions.'

Enough of controversy. Whether or not winged snakes really do exist or did formerly exist, we come back to the same point as in all disputes connected with the subject: the creatures here defined as monsters exist with certainty only in the realm of artistic representation, viable creations of the human imagination that have lasted not days, weeks, months or years, but thousands of years.

This statement contains an indication of what the following pages will seek to discuss and illustrate in detail. It may at first appear surprising that monsters had not already received their visual shape in the imaginations of the earliest human communities but that the conscious creation of such creatures is a product of the earliest known civilizations, as far as we can now tell, in the period around 3000 B.C. The first pictorial records of monsters are to be found in that period in Egypt and Mesopotamia and, perhaps a little later, in India, in the civilizations of what is called the ancient Near East. The representation of monsters was later to reach its most flourishing period in classical Greece, in ancient Italy and to a lesser extent in the Roman period, after two thousand years, during which the Hittite, Syrian, Iranian and also Cretan-Mycenaean civilizations kept the monster alive.

Monsters spread farther towards South-East Asia via India and towards the Far East not only by that route but also via Iran. It was roughly during the florescence of classical antiquity that China became, like India, a centre of monster-creation. Thus the westward spread is matched by an eastward one, and both proceeded from the same centre in the Near East. The further diffusion in westerly and North European directions runs chronologically parallel to the spread of ancient civilization and can be roughly placed during the last two thousand years.

In Europe a new peak is later reached in the Romanesque and Gothic art of France, Germany, Italy, Spain and England. Older monster types are to be found in Celtic civilization, and also in the Slavonic East of Europe. Here the ancient oriental images penetrated into the North and West through the mediation of Central Asiatic nomadic tribes, as a tributary to the main stream, which started in classical times and flowed from East to West and from South to North. The peoples of the Eastern Mediterranean

Because of their symbolic significance, monsters are favourite motifs in heraldry

and of Iran, who had been converted to Islam, played an important intermediary role in this. Civilizations built upon the world-religions, Buddhism, Christianity and Islam, contributed much to the diffusion of monsters. While Buddhism confined itself essentially to Asia, and Christianity at first conquered Europe alone, Islamic culture became an important connecting link between these continents and also between them and Africa.

We shall repeatedly note that Islamic art, commonly thought of as hostile to representational art, takes up almost all the well-known monster-types and transmits them through textiles, carpets, pottery, miniature carving and miniature painting. An even greater part was played by Islamic literature, and in particular by the famous *Arabian Nights*. Illustrators of this collection of fairy-tales, adventure stories and travellers' yarns, both in the Orient and Occident, have never tired of inventing new shapes for the genies and dragons, winged horses and other monsters. In his *Cosmography* the celebrated Qazwīnī devoted a special chapter to creatures of wonderful shape (10).

It may have been noticed that no mention has yet been made of ancient America nor of ancient Africa, the South Seas and Australia. That these areas may in fact largely be left out of the account is due to a fact already stated: namely that the idea of monsters arises at a relatively late stage of cultural development. The ancient American civilizations do show some rudimentary – perhaps independent – composite forms, but these are for the most part ill-defined and it is often difficult to distinguish between monsters and human figures masked or disguised in animal skins. Ideas of magic, totemistic customs, and animistic equation of different natural spheres may have led to some of the ideas underlying the shapes that interest us here. But it seems that these never brought about a true creation of new beings in a distinct visual form. For this reason we shall largely have to leave out these areas of civilization if we want to keep to our subject, though in individual cases reference will be made to possible connections. The observation that monsters were not created originally by the so-called 'primitive' peoples, as one might have expected, but are in fact to a large extent the product of highly developed civilizations is surprising enough. Even more startling, perhaps, is the fact that the literary tradition lags far behind the visual repertory. Anyone not familiar with the subject might think there were monsters

enough in ancient and modern literature, especially in fairy stories and legends. It is true that many works of literature contain names which go back to the monsters of classical antiquity, but there is seldom a detailed description of such figures as dragons, griffins and sphinxes, since they are either assumed to be known, or it is left to the reader to imagine them for himself, sometimes with the help of the odd hint, such as 'fire-breathing', 'speaking in a human tongue', or 'borne on mighty pinions', etc. It should be added that by no means all ghosts and spectres, fabulous animals, fairies and demons appear as composite monsters. A much older tradition seems to have visualized such ghosts and spectres, even gods, in the normal shapes of men or animals, but endowed with special powers not discernible from their outward shapes. These powers enable them to change their shape from human to animal and back again, to make themselves invisible, to move freely on land, in water or in the air, and so on. These transformations play a large part in old fairy-tales; ghosts have the power to slip into a dead body and thus take shape – but never the shape of a monster.

We are dealing here with processes of intellectual development and with notions which stem from the above-mentioned forms of thought associated with magic and animism, in other words from the ideologies of a society not yet split into classes.

Though at first sight it looks as though the opposite were true, the Stone-Age images and those of Africa and the South Seas, which imitate nature, are in fact more primitive than the monsters of the Ancient Orient, the ancient Egyptian and Hindu idols, and the fabulous animals seen on Romanesque capitals. In Stone-Age representations the natural form is clearly recognizable, but contemporary man, when he saw them, associated them with powers, unrecognizable to us, which in their natural shapes were nevertheless supernatural, incomprehensible, and therefore all the more terrifying. From this point of view the origin of monsters in the early civilizations is a process of rationalization, of making those powers palpable and visible; and hence, ultimately, also the beginning of a rational struggle against such terrifying figures. It looks very much as though the artists, the painters and sculptors, by embodying vague notions in well-defined images, made an essential contribution to the demystification of nature: for they gave shape, at the same time, to the counterparts of those images, their equally terrible conquerors, and in addition they exposed all these things to public view and thereby to the criticism and ridicule that soon followed. We have long known that the fine arts have often played the important role of revealing what is hidden behind unspoken thoughts and mysterious words. This is also perhaps the reason why most religions intent upon their function are hostile to the use of images so long as they are strong enough to put up resistance, and why on the other hand the process of profanation and de-sanctification sets in with, or at least is strongly encouraged by, the visual representation of religious ideas and figures.

These ideas, which can only be outlined here, are contrary to those such as have been put forward by Wilhelm Wundt in his *Völkerpsychologie* (Psychology of Peoples) (11).

He interprets this process in a more linear, more theoretical way, and without taking account of the pictorial evidence revealed by archaeology, the latest results of which were probably not available to him. Thus he was unaware of the great caesura in social development which took place with the rise of the earliest civilizations, that is, with the rise of class society. He sees the process as inherently mythological, as a change in the conception of the divine towards what is human, from animal to hybrid (our monsters) and from hybrid to man (12).

Let us return once more to fairy-tale and its relationship with myth. The visual representations can be analysed with the help of the archaeological evidence, which ranges from the Old Stone Age via numerous intermediate stages to the developed civilization of the ancient Near East, where we find the first unmistakable monster shapes. But it is only in the latter phase, and within the same territorial limits, that written records begin. The approximate date 3000 B.C. may be taken as a starting point.

Primitive stories or fairy-tales, probably for the most part simple animal stories based on totemistic and animistic notions, must have existed long before this date. They are now superseded by two new developments, both of them connected with a change in social structure. One of these developments can be inferred from written sources and may therefore at first appear to be earlier: myths in written form. For the other development we possess only indirect evidence. But it seems certain that the artistically more advanced fairy-tale proper now also begins to evolve from the primitive elements, parallel with the myth. Of course, since it was orally transmitted, we have no direct evidence of its existence in early times. Nevertheless, the substance of such fairy-tales as well as their artistically more advanced form make it clear that, like the myth, they must be assigned to the age of class society. The social relationships reflected in these tales presuppose this class society, or – to put it perhaps more accurately – its direct and clearly recognizable preliminary stages; just as the divine kingdoms transferred from terrestrial to celestial and subterranean realms must have corresponded with political structures that actually existed.

But when we examine the part played by monsters in fairy-tales and myth respectively, we find a significant difference. Fairy-tales are dominated by magic and by changes of shape. These features are, of course, also present in myth, though not so prominently: here the conception of the divine is dominant and – perhaps caused or at least strongly encouraged by pictorial representation – is more and more strongly individualized, not least in those hybrid or monster shapes discussed by Wundt. It is tempting to present these differences in the form of a historical sequence, which would look something like this: firstly primitive (animal) tales of uncertain antiquity, the products of a classless society; secondly fairy or wonder tales originating during the great revolutions which immediately preceded the earliest class society; and thirdly the products of a fully developed early civilization. Geographically the same limits, already noted, apply to the second and third stages, while a more universal distribution must be posited for the first. Chronologically, the date mentioned, 3000 B.C., can only apply to the third stage; the second must be placed immediately before it, whereas a longer interval had elapsed between the first stage and the second.

As has been pointed out, such a sequence cannot be proved rigorously from the archaeological sources so far available because fairy-tales, in the main, have been handed down orally and have only been recorded in comparatively recent times. But if we take an example such as Grimm's collection of fairy-tales, we find witches and devils, animal-princes and swan-maidens, giants and dwarfs, but hardly any composite monsters. Where dragons and other unnatural animals occur, they are hardly ever characterized as monsters, and even in the traditions of popular belief the goblins and sprites, fiends and witches are mostly vague spectres and are only rarely described as palpably monstrous shapes. In these tales, too, there are heaven and hell, intermediate realms of demons and fairies, magical changes of shape, but no clearly defined and fully described types of monster. Oriental fairy-tales, for a long time closely connected with myths, and told along with them, and thus more strongly influenced by them, are an exception. It is therefore a reasonable inference that the oriental fairy and wonder-stories are older in form than the corresponding popular tales of Europe, even though in some respects the latter may appear more original and less contaminated.

The tradition of both fairy-tale and myth has continued until today and has been taken up and adapted again and again in literature and the visual arts. It is very significant that most monster shapes found in twentieth-century art are still derived from the mythical creatures of the Near East and classical antiquity and that some of these composite creatures, while undergoing considerable changes in significance, have retained their shapes, almost without modification, for thousands of years. Superimposed upon this continuity – which runs parallel to the development of class society during about five thousand years – there have been certain periods with a marked predilection for developing ever new, above all pictorial, monster types. These new waves were prompted by the needs of two religions, the later, or Mahāyāna, Buddhism and medieval Christianity as it adapted itself to paganism. In the infernal, demonic phantoms of Chinese and Japanese painters, in the animal and monster fantasies of Romanesque and Gothic architectural sculpture and book-illustration, monsters in new, strongly individualized forms proliferate. However, in contrast with the ancient mythical shapes, they were mostly short-lived. The immediate successors to this new world of European monsters were the thousands of spectral figures in the work of Hieronymus Bosch, visually realized nightmares adapted to the world of vigorous popular fancy, much nearer to fairy-tale than to myth. We find something similar in the immediate past, and even, sometimes, in our own day, in the monstrous creations of some Surrealists, and also as the device of politically committed artists to create pictorial symbols of political and social forces – often to characterize the sinister, the violent, and the inhuman.

Here again it is less the fantasy and tradition of myth which are at work than the subliminal continuity of that primitive mode of thought, magic and animistic, which has come down to us in the fairy-tale. The shapes of monsters are always based, ultimately, upon observation of nature, and it is this fact, in turn, that accounts for their astonishing vitality. On the other hand what is characteristic is the exaggeration and mixing of shapes, the combination of the qualities, abilities and powers of various natural beings into one composite figure, a process which can only be achieved in the human imagination. In it the most impressive parts of various animals were those that were most widely used. That is why the mighty pinions of birds of prey, the horns of wild bulls, the fangs and claws of the great cats, and the sting of the scorpion are so often found as conspicuous components of these monsters. The ruling castes of early times often adopted similar power symbols: the ancient oriental ruler claimed a crown of horns for his head-piece or mounted a lion-throne. At times he is shown surrounded by monsters, which are looked upon as the embodiments of his attributes.

We must now see how all these very diverse shapes can be satisfactorily arranged. First of all, following what has been said so far, we can distinguish three groups: first, those monsters or fabulous creatures which are well defined in shape and have a name familiar from history and literature, like the griffin and the centaur, the dragon, the unicorn and the sphinx etc. These figures, mostly of animal shape, are generally found in classical or Germanic mythology, and some of them, like the unicorn and the dragon, later found their way into Christian iconography.

Many-headed monster. Title vignette of 'The Political Showman at Home'. London, 1821

A second group, consisting of images which are well known though nameless, is typified by the Evangelist symbols, such as the winged bull and the winged lion, but also includes such heraldic motifs as the double-headed eagle. The third group, the one richest in forms, is made up of the distorted, spectral products of the imagination, such as one sees in endless variety on medieval capitals, in the paintings of Bosch, in Japanese drawings, and also in Surrealist drawings. Whether named or anonymous, these shapes are usually only hidden details in modern art, discreetly concealed and subordinate to some more realistic subject matter, except in some pictures with a deliberately classical, romantic or satirical bias. In the work of some artists, such as Bosch, Goya or Kubin, the playful exaggerations or visionary combinations are used as devices to screen all that is natural and real.

These three groups, however, do not provide a satisfactory basis for clear arrangement and a closer analysis. For this a systematic investigation of shapes is more useful. Such an approach, it is true, tends to neglect the function or significance of each type, but permits a more clear-cut division of separate forms and their combinations. A judicious use of formal criteria suggests a division into five categories, which can themselves be further subdivided.

I. Monsters with a human body or with an animal body in a markedly human posture, with an animal head or some other features of animal origin. This category can be termed 'animal-man'. It comprises devils, angels, satyrs and minotaurs, and also the many animal-men of the ancient Near East which show the same characteristics. It also includes demons with or without wings and the numerous Egyptian divinities represented as men with animal heads. Animals shown in human posture can also be placed here since, although they are not composite in shape, they represent kindred notions. This is the earliest of our five categories – including Egyptian divinities and Sumerian animal-men – and is also, in modern art, numerically the largest if we include the animals in human posture, which are found so frequently in modern book-illustration.

II. Monsters with an animal body, or in unmistakable animal posture, combined with a human head, a human chest or other purely human features. For this category we propose the term 'man-animal'. It includes some of the best-known types such as the sphinx, the centaur, and the siren with the body of a bird or of a fish. In the ancient Near East and in South, South-East and East Asia this category was popular, particularly in the Nāga and Kinnara figures, which have snake and bird bodies but a human chest and head.

The first two categories, then, comprise man-animal combinations. This is also the case with some forms in category IV, which likewise make use of human as well as animal shapes. But the important difference is that the former are new, pictorially viable creations, whereas the latter, as we shall see below, are merely whimsical decorative conglomerations or reduplications, even though they, too, are understood as entities in their own right.

III. Monsters made up of parts (body and head) taken from different animal species or with other animal features added. Into this category come the griffin, the dragon, Pegasus and numerous other winged animals, and also the marine creatures with fish-tail and animal-body. This category can be put under the heading 'animal-monsters'. Most figures of this type have repeatedly been said either to occur in the world of nature or to result from a slight error of observation. The essential feature is the absence of human components.

IV. This category includes monstrous figures and combinations with deliberate reduplication or simplification, and also those with exaggerated enlargement or reduction of physical features, of limbs, heads and bodies. In some cases animal and human parts are combined, in others the natural shapes are merely modified. Small deviations from nature can be found in the unicorn, the one-eyed Cyclops, and in many monsters described in old, fantastic travel-tales – the one-legged, the long-eared, the mouthless, and so on. But this category also includes the many-armed or multiple-headed Indian divinities and the East Asian and medieval European freaks (grylli) with faces on their stomachs. In addition, as indicated previously, there are

Lamassu. Monumental figure from Nimrud-Kalchu, ninth century B.C.

3 Fabulous Creatures in a Children's Picture Book by F. J. Bertuch: Centaur; Chimaera; Greek Sphinx; Egyptian Sphinx; Gryllus; Siren. Mode collection

4 Fabulous Creatures in a Children's Picture Book by F. J. Bertuch: Harpy; Griffin; Satyr; Giant or Titan; Sea-Horse; Nereid. Mode collection

5 Fabulous Creatures in a Children's Picture Book by F. J. Bertuch: The Roc Bird; Basilisk; Phoenix; Unicorn; Boramez or Scythian Lamb; Dragon. Mode collection

7 Apse frescoes in St James in Castelaz

6 Fighting Monsters. Apse fresco in St James in Castelaz (Termeno), South Tyrol

9 Conventional Monsters: Dragons and Sphinxes with bird-bodies. Ornamental engraving by Agostino Veneziano. Museum für Kunsthandwerk, Leipzig

8 Centaur on Cretan seal

10 Griffin, Siren with fish-body and two tails, Lion-headed Bird and other Monsters.
Carvings on a wooden chest from Lower Saxony, about 1300. Staatliche Museen, Berlin

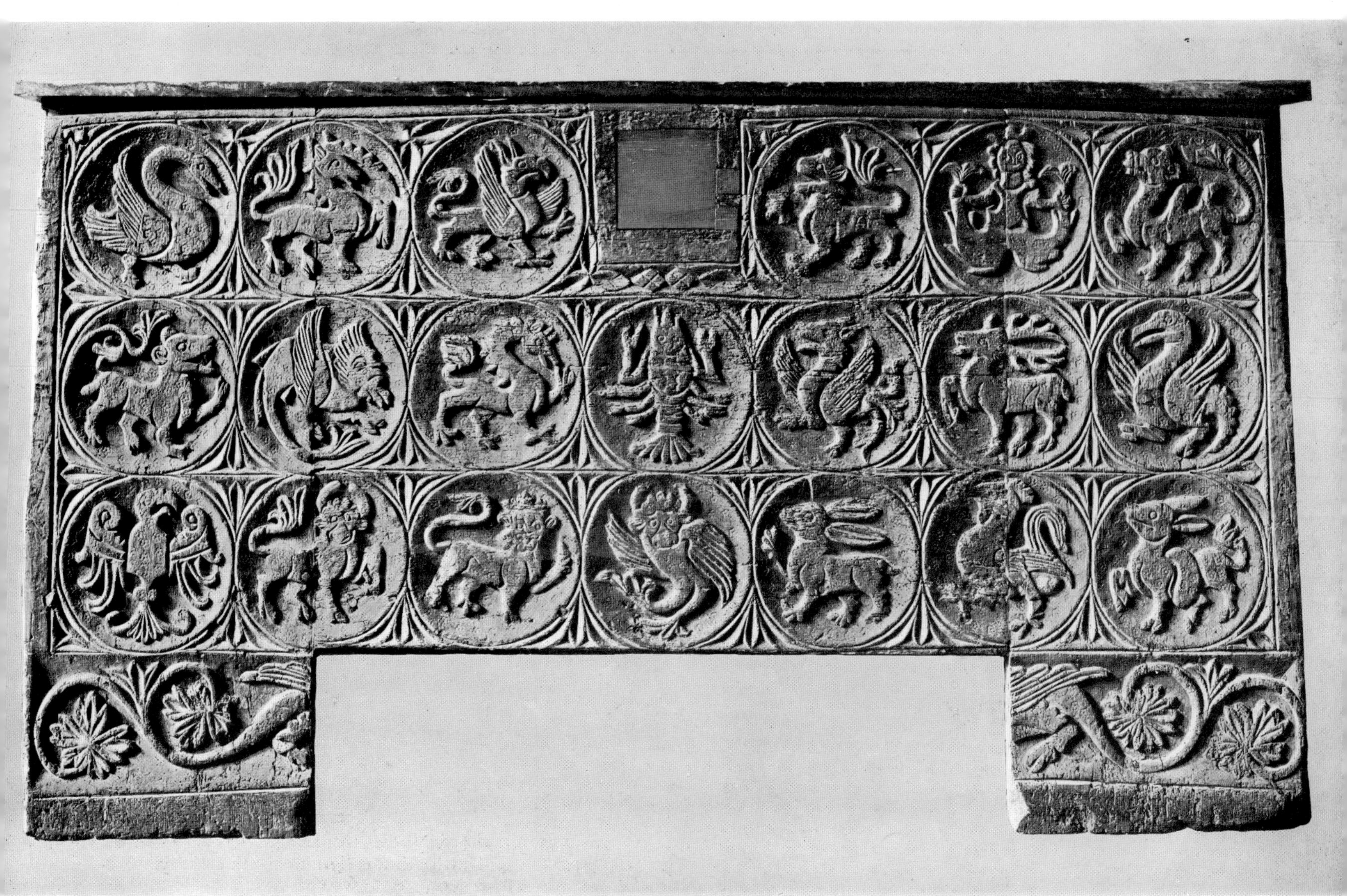

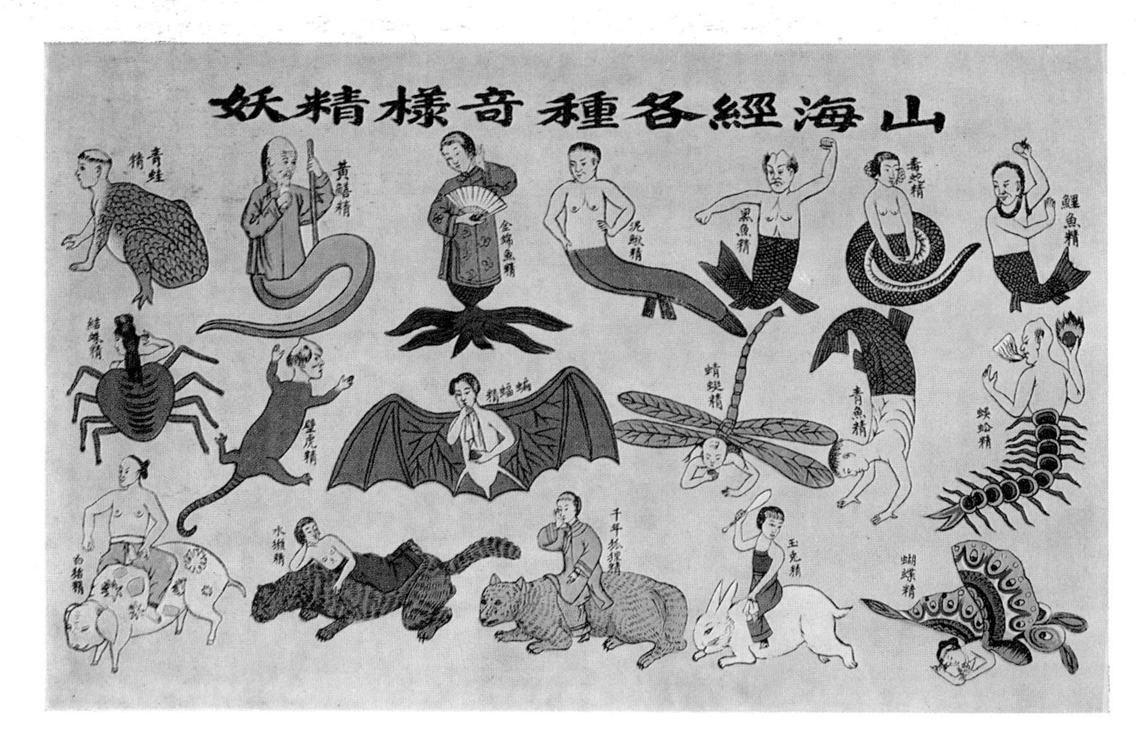

11 Metamorphoses: Insects, Serpents, Fishes and other Animals. Chinese. From Doré, Researches

12 Chinese Demons. From Doré, Researches

13 Sixteen Man-Animals of various shapes. Dutch print, early nineteenth century. Tobler collection, Amsterdam

No. 29. Wel kind'ren! wat zoudt gij nu meer wenschen? Deez' Beesten lijkene hier wel Menschen.

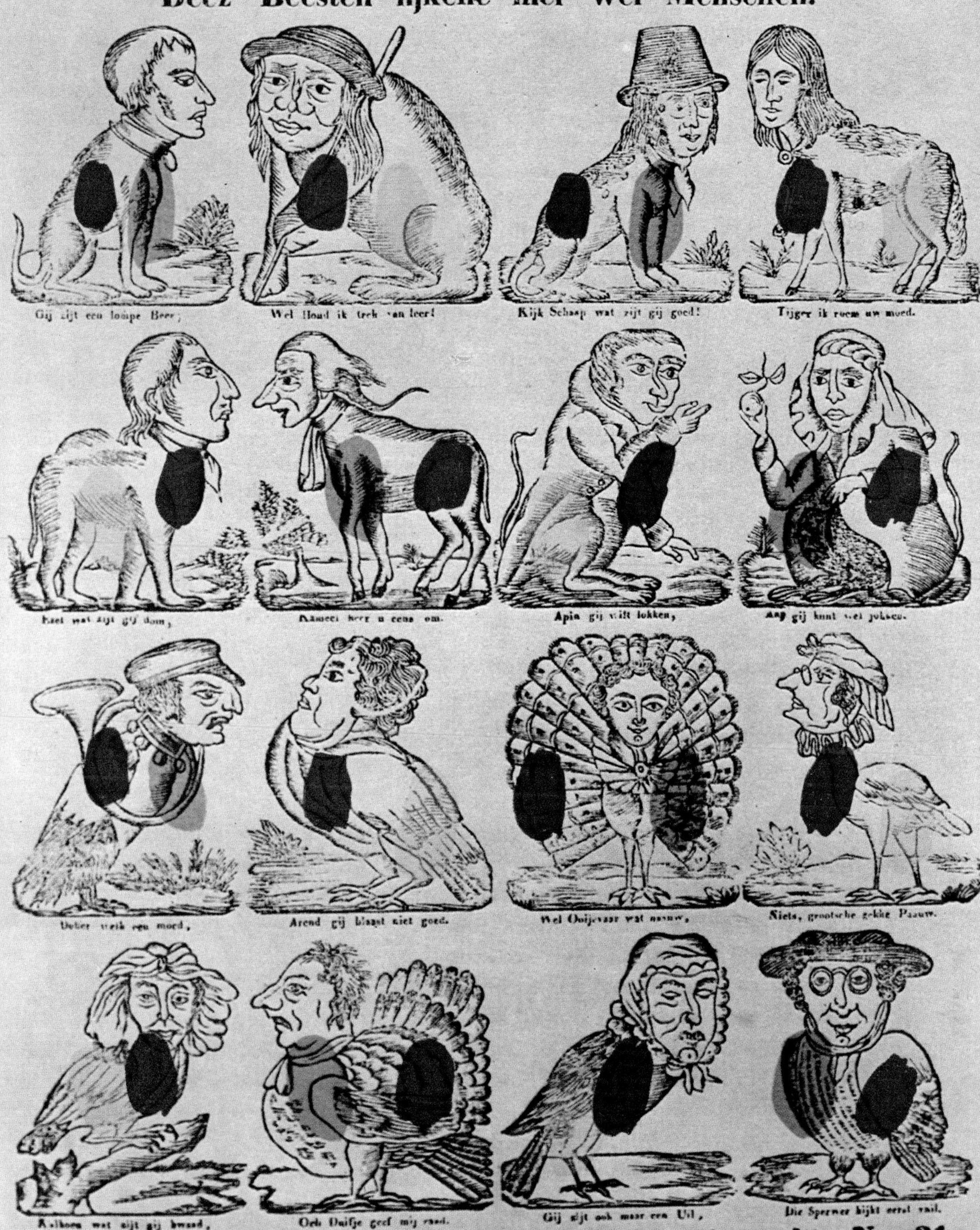

Te Amsterdam, bij J. J. Bollemij, op de Leliegracht, No. 21.

14 Symbols of the Evangelists:
The Vision of Ezekiel by Marc Chagall, 1934.
Staatsbibliothek, Munich

15 Devil. Engraving by David Newreti. Nuremberg, 1717

17 Aquarium of Mermaids, by Carl Marx, 1964. Private collection

16 'The Animal of our Time' by Josef Scharl, 1933. Put together from parts of various animals

the heraldic combinations, many of which appear already on early Mesopotamian seals, such as double-bodied animals, or even four or more animal bodies ending in a single head. It is difficult to find a general heading for this category; they could be termed 'Reduplicated or Simplified Shapes and Combinations'. On the fringe of this group are creatures which do not quite fit this definition, such as dwarfs and giants, or even witches of larger-than-life size. This category as a whole is very extensive, includes many precisely defined figures, and borders on the field of fantastic ornament.

V. This is the smallest but perhaps the most interesting category. Natural phenomena or man-made objects are given human or animal features and turned into new entities, often with only small, symbolic changes. From the ancient Near East we know water-men, mountain-men and tree-men, and also the sword in the shape of a man and the ship in the form of either a man or an animal.

Monsters in our sense of the term do not include objects which have only some animal components, such as thrones with lion's feet or other articles of furniture with animal feet. Extremities in the form of human or animal heads were favourite motifs in medieval art, both in architectural ornament and on the decorative borders of illuminated pages. But here, in the endless repetitions, the original magic content has been lost and there is hardly any creative impulse at work, so that such shapes are only loosely related to our subject. The real monsters in this fifth category can be defined as 'Man-made Objects and Natural Phenomena in the Shape of Living Beings'.

Pegasus. Engraving by Jacopo di Barbari

Wild man and unicorn.
Playingcard by the Master E.S.

Within each of these categories, which are to be a framework for the systematic analysis of types, we could make numerous further distinctions, based principally on particular parts of the animal or human body. Or we can single out favourite animals such as bull, lion and horse, eagle and snake, scorpion and fish, tiger and elephant – these last found mainly in Asia. Water, air and earth can be symbolized by animals or by characteristic parts of their bodies, while fire and light are often added to head or body in the form of rays or of haloes shaped like a solar disc. In the metamorphoses which form part of Greek myths, and which are known mainly from literary sources, insects symbolize fire, while fish, snake, and bird are the animals of water, earth, and air respectively.

Of the various parts of animal bodies, wings (mostly eagle's but also bat's), horns, bird's claws and lion's paws, boar's tusks and hair twisted in the form of snakes are those commonly used. The horse's hoof or goat's foot and particularly the tail of demons and devils, and the fish-tail of sea-monsters, also deserve special mention.

Finally reference must be made to the enormous variety of artistic means used in representing these fabulous creatures. Painting and sculpture, relief and seal-engraving, textiles and other crafts, above all folk art, early book-illumination and modern book-decoration, in a word, almost all branches of visual representation in every possible technique and material offer examples in such profusion that we shall not be able to do more than give a representative selection and point out the major relationships. Anything approaching completeness is beyond the scope of this study. The term 'fabulous beasts', which is often used, suggests that they are not found in nature, but it does not make clear that their parts conform to the laws of anatomy and that they *appear* to be capable of natural existence. They are therefore more accurately described as 'composite' or 'mixed creatures', a term already used in 1912 and perhaps even earlier. The word 'hybrid' is not entirely appropriate. In English and in the Romance languages the term 'monster', which stresses the terrifying aspect of these imaginary creatures, is commonly used. Another word in this field, 'teratology', is a purely medical term applied to the study of physiological monstrosities.

In her important work *Heilige und dämonische Tiere* (Sacred and Demonic Animals), Wera von Blankenburg distinguishes between fabulous animals (basilisk, dragon, phoenix, griffin, unicorn) and composite creatures (centaur, siren, eagle with lion's head and other combinations of animal parts). This distinction, however, appears to be too arbitrary, and I prefer to follow the usage of orientalists and archaeologists and to retain the comprehensive name 'composite creature' (or 'monster').

We shall try, on the one hand, not to lose sight of the specific role of monsters in the repertory of artistic motifs, nor of the almost inexhaustible opportunities for expression that they have supplied, with the result that the best representations show how they could be successfully adapted to ever-changing purposes down to our own times. On the other hand, we cannot write a comprehensive history of monsters in art, even though the subject is common to all periods. This is a task which can hardly be undertaken at present because systematic preliminary studies of many types and single figures do not yet exist. Despite our rough and ready division into chapters we shall try and adapt our treatment to the character of this strange world of new shapes and creations by attempting to remain as flexible and many-sided as our subject so as to mirror its infinite variety, and by following it down remote paths. We shall have to bear in mind the wide-ranging historical developments and the need for a systematic arrangement; within this framework we shall illustrate the wealth of fantastic creatures with examples from the art of as many peoples as possible.

EEN from the front it looked just like a German: a narrow snout, continually in motion, sniffing at everything it came across, tapered like that of our pigs to a round five-kopek piece; the legs were so thin that the bailiff of Yareskov, had he had them, would have broken them with his first jump in the Cossack dance. From the rear, however, it looked just like the provincial attorney, for hanging down behind it had a long, pointed tail just like that of a modern evening dress jacket, only the goat-leg and the snout, the little horns on the head and the fact that it was no whiter than a chimney-sweep, showed that it was neither a German nor the provincial attorney, but simply the devil.' (13)

Bull-Men and Satyrs, Angels and Devils

Here the devil is described sarcastically, but almost exactly as illustrations show him, with some animal characteristics appended to an otherwise almost human form. Similar figures had appeared, though not under the same names, in the early art of Sumer and Egypt. Enkidu, the bull-man, is known from the Gilgamesh epic; his body was covered with long hair, he grazed with the gazelles and drank with the cattle. In the early texts he is never stated explicitly to be of monstrous shape, but the features and habits described in those words could hardly be conveyed visually except by giving him such a shape when it was intended to distinguish him from the animals surrounding him as well as from human beings, whom Enkidu was to meet later.

The Mesopotamian seals of early dynastic times show such bull-men in many variations. There are bulls upright in human posture, whose face is almost human but is crowned with horns; human bodies with bulls' heads; and finally bulls in their normal form but in the upright, human posture. Whether the varieties are given a single name is not very important (14), for these monsters found on seals, and also on some reliefs (Plate 33) and as sculptures in the round, speak for themselves; but they also raise a basic problem – the relation between the literary model and a contemporary illustration.

When the illustrator of a fairy-tale tries to depict a speaking tree, how else can he do it than by giving it human features – arms, perhaps, or a human head growing out of the trunk or the boughs? In one of Goethe's poems a bell comes waddling across the fields: some illustrators have equipped the bell with feet, though there is no mention of these in the poem. Over and over again it becomes evident that a poet needs only to throw out a hint to awaken associations, whereas the painter or sculptor must be more explicit if he is to convey visually what is intended but is only hinted in words. If this is true of direct illustration, it applies even more to images which are independent works and isolated from any written context. A bull grazing among gazelles or drinking with other cattle at a watering-place – who would think of relating him to an epic unless there were some visible clue? Suppose, now, that a purely human figure were placed in the same context, the information conveyed is immediately altered so as to suggest a shepherd or a wanderer who has lost his way. This example shows clearly that something so peculiar, taken from myth or fairy-tale, is almost impossible to represent except in monster-form, unless a figure has identifying attributes or the scene is so unique and well known as to be immediately recognized by the spectator.

The bull-man Enkidu in the epic is a mythical figure, destined by the gods to be Gilgamesh's companion and share in his heroic deeds. It can be inferred from the myths and the mythological images of early Mesopotamian civilization from Sumerian times onward, but even more clearly in the later Babylonian and Assyrian periods, that winged men and other monsters with human traits represented the powers of guardian spirits, which are denoted by the ritual title of *kerub*, a word derived from Akkadian 'karabu' (to pray, to bless) (15). The great *kerubim*, or better, *lamassu*, are monumental statues whose function was to guard the Assyrian palaces. They belong to the second of our five categories because of their animal posture. But since they owed their significance to their function as guardian spirits they seem to have been associated with the animal-men, such as the bull-man, the bird-man and the lion-man. Most writers, however, refer to them as bull-headed, bird-headed and lion-headed demons. In Christian iconography the cherubim are winged guardians of Paradise, the second highest in the hierarchy of angels. But some passages in the Bible show clearly that these figures also had animal characteristics, for example Ezekiel I, 4–11:

'And I looked, and, behold, a whirlwind came out of the north, a great cloud, and a fire infolding itself, and a brightness was about it, and out of the midst thereof as the colour of amber, out of the midst of the fire.

Also out of the midst thereof came the likeness of four living creatures. And this was their appearance; they had the likeness of a man.

And every one had four faces, and every one had four wings.

And their feet were straight feet; and the sole of their feet was like the sole of a calf's foot: and they sparkled like the colour of burnished brass.

And they had the hands of a man under their wings on their four sides; and they four had their faces and their wings.

Their wings were joined one to another; they turned not when they went; they went every one straight forward.

As for the likeness of their faces, they four had the face of a man, and the face of a lion, on the right side: and they four had the face of an ox on the left side; they four also had the face of an eagle.

Thus were their faces: and their wings were stretched upward; two wings of every one were joined one to another, and two covered their bodies.'

The original tetramorph, as described here in Ezekiel, later developed into four independent entities, the well-known symbols of the Evangelists, with the lion and the bull retaining the figure of man-animals. But the cherub-angel with human face and usually four wings became a permanent motif in Christian art (Plate 19), and thus has preserved, in his composite shape, a type whose origins go back to the developed civilization of the ancient Near East.

No matter how strange it may appear, a similar derivation also applies to the second main figure of Christian art – the devil. As a fallen angel, Lucifer is from the beginning not essentially unlike the angels in general and is one of the beings created by God. Like the angels, he was invariably represented by artists as a composite creature with animal characteristics (Plate 28 and 30). The forms of both angels and devils are usually traced back to Greek models; angels to the goddess Nike (Plate 29) or to other winged human figures, devils to the satyrs (Plate 26), the demonic followers of the god Dionysus, who are portrayed with horse's or goat's legs and tails. But this derivation accounts only for the later part of their history, since both the winged shapes and the animal-men of Greek art can in turn be traced back to ancient Near Eastern models. The fact that the legs were not always borrowed from the same animal species is just as characteristic for these early periods as the previously noted double significance of the Mesopotamian angel and devil prototypes as messengers and agents of the gods and as guardian spirits.

Devils. Woodcut from Vintler, *Buch der Tugend.* Augsburg, 1486

However desirable it may be to link our monsters with definite names and concepts, and thereby to make them more understandable and memorable, it is clear from the little that has so far been said that this aim can hardly be realized. There was an almost universal migration of motifs, and forms, once created, were often adapted to new subjects. This formula is basically non-reversible. While forms were relatively conservative, with a tendency to stagnate, their significance was continuously changing under the influence of social and ideological developments. The devil – an expression which first appears in Greek as 'diabolos', i.e. slanderer – has, it is truly said, many names, and he is in no way a monopoly of those religions which are codified in scriptures. Buddhism, for example, tells of the temptation of the Buddha by the Evil One, Mara, who uses not only terrifying demons but also his fascinating daughters as allies against the Buddha's virtue. Indian and East Asian artists have illustrated and portrayed such hellish horrors in no less vivid and monstrous forms than their Christian counterparts (Plate 51). In the Jewish-Christian sphere the devil's family makes its appearance in some popular legends. In one of these his grandmother outsmarts him, makes him seem ridiculous, and thus shows who cracks the whip in the underworld. In Islamic tradition, too, there was the belief that Shaitan had a wife and nine sons, each of whom fulfilled a different function.

In the Old Testament Satan plays only a subsidiary role (16); in the New Testament this name alternates with the Greek 'diabolos'.

The Bible speaks of similar figures which also stem from ancient Mesopotamian concepts, such as the demon Asmodeus (17), who has been compared with Pazuzu, a monster-figure conceived for the most part as human, but with wings, horns, lion's paws instead of hands, and bird-claws instead of feet. There is also Abaddon, the

Prince of the Furies, King of the demoniacal Locusts (18), the Angel of the bottomless pit. Even though he is not expressly described as a monster, the hosts of locusts which he leads are so described in Revelation 9. 7–10:
'And the shapes of the locusts were like unto horses prepared unto battle; and on their heads were as it were crowns like gold, and their faces were as the faces of men.
And they had hair as the hair of women, and their teeth were as the teeth of lions.
And they had breastplates, as it were breastplates of iron; and the sound of their wings was as the sound of chariots of many horses running to battle.
And they had tails like unto scorpions, and there were stings in their tails: and their power was to hurt men five months.' (19)
The names Beelzebub, Mammon and Moloch, though different in origin, are still current and these figures are often identified with the devil. Very often we find conceptions of the devil associated with the idea of a demon, but this word also is derived from the Greek 'daimon', which originally signified impersonal forces and powers whose influence could be observed but not explained. But while Satan or 'diabolos' has not been transferred retrospectively to ancient Mesopotamian civilization, this has been done with the demon. Even works of reference include under this heading good spirits, the guardian spirits already mentioned, and malignant forces, as terrifying visions of natural phenomena and of night, but also as embodiments of physical

Bull-man.
André Masson: A Contented Priest

and psychological diseases (20). On Babylonian reliefs, the fever-demon, Labartu, is represented as a woman with the head of a lion or a panther, donkey's ears and bird's legs, suckling a wolf and a pig. Other figures with animal heads on human bodies are Utukku, Asakku and Māmītu, the last having a goat's head, and the 'Devastator' and 'Devourer' described in the Ras Shamra texts as having bull's horns and the hump of a buffalo but a human face. Such terrifying monsters are also known from Egyptian sources. In the *Book of the Dead* there are names such as 'Bloodsucker', 'Bonebreaker', 'Gut-eater' and a demon described as a corpse-eater has the head of a crocodile, the rump of a hippopotamus and the body of a lion (21). Etruscan art also seems to have been rich in such animal-man figures. It has not only winged demons, known as lasi, resembling angels, but also an underworld figure with wings and the beak of a bird of prey (22).

Personification of all these forces and powers probably took place only gradually. This is suggested by the fact that, before societies were split into classes, demons could hardly be distinguished from spirits, those bodiless beings which were believed to inhabit, and to give life to woods, fields, mountains, or even single trees or stones. Later, in the context of myths, these demons tended to gather in groups, e.g. as aerial spirits or as bringers of disease, and to become increasingly subordinate to clearly individualized gods. But it would be quite mistaken to think that belief in gods curbed, let alone superseded, belief in demons. On the contrary, demons and spirits became even more popular, for it was specially in folk-poetry, fairy-tale and legend that they came to supplant the gods.

A good example of this development can be found in the satyrs. Originally they were demons associated with a specific locality, which they animated and personified. Then they were visualized in human shape, but with certain animal features, and still inhabiting their old dwelling-places. Later on attempts were made to divest them of their animal shapes and to make them more fully human, especially in Roman art. What is interesting and characteristic of their changing significance is the adoption of the traditional Greek form, while their local origins were forgotten. The form of the Greek satyr, a creature of woods and mountains, served as model for the Roman faun, who was the visual embodiment of the old Italic field and harvest spirits.

Greek satyrs and Roman fauns have been mentioned only to suggest how the ideas of a personified demon developed. But the Greek personifications themselves, and the visual forms they assumed, can hardly be explained without reference to Mesopotamian and Aegean models. Here again, it is rather the forms, and not their significance, which influence the later types. Our information about the function of Mesopotamian animal-men is fragmentary. Mention has already been made of the guardian spirits and of some evil demons whose names we know. Although some gods, too, are depicted in the shape of monsters, Mesopotamia offers the prime example of an artistic tradition in which the gods were originally represented in human form.

18 The Archangel Gabriel as Ruler of the Firmament. Palech painting, about 1700. Private collection

20 Nārasingha (Vishnu with lion's head). Relief from Kuldia. Asutosh Museum, Calcutta

19 Cherubim and Symbols of the Evangelists. Detail from a French Bible illustration of the ninth century. S. Paolo fuori le Mura, Rome

22 Two Demons carrying jugs.
Agate seal from Vaphio, Laconia

21 Winged Goddess. From Tamluk, Bengal.
About first century A.D.
Asutosh Museum, Calcutta

23 Winged Deity with animals. Louvre, Paris

24 Angel before a Ruler.
Miniature of the Mughal period.
Indian Museum, Calcutta

25 Aphrodite and Pan.
National Museum, Athens

27 The Sun-Eagle Garuda.
Indian Miniature, about 1780

26 Satyr with girl on a swing. Vase painting from Chiusi, about 440 B.C. Staatliche Museen, Berlin

29 Nike. Museo Nazionale delle Terme, Rome

28 God, the Devil, and Archangels. Detail from The Story of Job, by Francesco da Volterra. Camposanto, Pisa

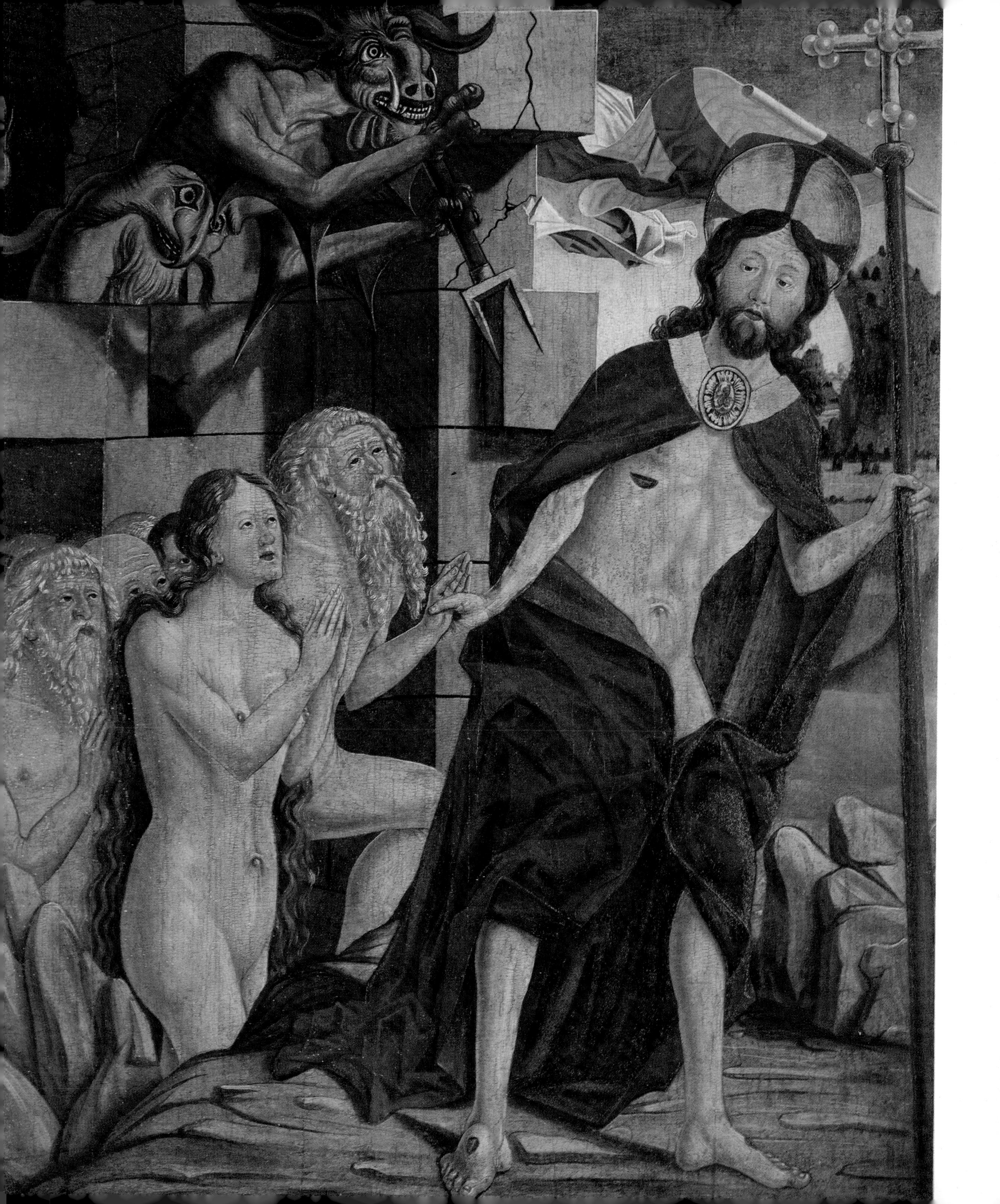

50 Devil. Detail from Christ in Limbo,
by Friedrich Pacher.
Museum of Fine Arts, Budapest

51 Animal-headed Deities. Mythological papyrus of
a priestess of Ammon. Egyptian Museum, Cairo

34 The god Sobek on a pillar from Kom Ombo, Egypt

32 Cretan seal

33 Lion-men and Bull-men.
Relief from Kargamis, about 1050–850 B.C.
Archaeological Museum, Ankara

In Egypt, on the other hand, numerous gods were depicted with animal heads. Among lion-headed goddesses may be mentioned Tefnut, Menhit, Sachmet, Shesemtet, Bastet (usually with a cat's head) and Mut, this last being really a vulture-goddess (23). Suchos, also referred to as Sobek, is portrayed either with a crocodile's head (Plate 34) or as a crocodile. The hippopotamus-goddess, often named as Toeris, but also found under the name Ipi during the time of the Old Kingdom, is a figure that frequently recurs. Selket, the scorpion, and Chepre, the scarab, are also represented as composite creatures. The god of Thebes, Amun, is shown as a ram, or with the head of a ram and most frequently it is Chnum, the Upper Egyptian god of the cataract region, and Herishef, who have ram's heads. Bird-headed divinities are also numerous; one of them is Mut, the war-goddess already mentioned, sometimes portrayed with a lion's head but also with a vulture's. The falcon-headed god Chentechtai sometimes has bull's horns as well. Chenti-irti also has a falcon's head and was, moreover, believed to be eyeless. The most important deity, the great Horus, also appears in the shape of a falcon; he is probably one of the oldest Egyptian gods with an animal shape. Another god of the empire is Re, a sun-god like Horus, but only occasionally depicted with a falcon's head. The goddess Hathor was worshipped as a cow, but is shown in illustrations simply as cow-headed and sometimes just with cow's ears. Lastly we mention the jackal-headed gods Anubis and Upuaut, the ibis-headed Thot, and Seth, whose animal form is not clearly defined.

It is not possible here to discuss more fully the Egyptian deities depicted as animal-men, nor even to enumerate them all. This selection will be enough to enable us to recognize and evaluate their significance as monsters. Some writers of the ancient world, for instance Plutarch, have pointed out, in order to justify the Egyptian animal-cult, that 'it was seemlier to portray the divine in beings possessed of a soul and endowed with perception and intelligence than in images consisting of perhaps costly but dead material'.

Genuine demon figures are wanting in early Egyptian art, but they are all the more prominent in the later period, for example Bes, who is sometimes shown with wings and a tail, but in general characterized merely by his wry face and dwarfish figure (Plate 124).

When we come to review the oldest monster-forms, especially those that represent gods and demons, the result is at first surprising and contradicts the theoretical speculations. In southern Mesopotamia, in Sumer, the earliest figures known have either a purely human or a purely animal form, except for a few animals in an upright posture. On the other hand, those forms that belong in our third category, that is combinations of different animals such as the snake-necked lion, the elephant bull – presumably taken over from India – and the lion-headed bird, occur somewhat more frequently. But during the same period, commonly known as pre-dynastic, animal-headed demon figures already appear in considerable numbers on seals from Susa in

35 Genies, Bird-men and Life-trees. From the Palace of Assurnasirpal II in Kalchu, ninth century B.C. Staatliche Museen, Berlin

neighbouring Elam, the Iranian territory bordering on Sumer in the east, and it seems that from here such types spread to Sumer itself, where they are increasingly to be found in early dynastic times.

We do not know whether Elam and Sumer shared a single civilization, or at least matured contemporaneously on parallel lines, or whether the two regions remained separate in their development, and in any case we know very little about Elam. There are thus two possible interpretations: either the representation of demons as animal-men only developed gradually, from original demon-animals to partial human shape, or it was influenced by the civilization of an outlying region, where it had first originated.

In early dynastic and especially in Akkadian times, that is in the second half of the third millennium B.C., the whole stock of demon types had become firmly established in Mesopotamia. In some instances the human-faced gods also assume some animal features, especially wings and horns, or their forms are combined with water and fire, with branches and mountain-shapes. The bull-men already discussed are most numerous, but lion-men and bird-men also appear quite frequently. Wings are still relatively rare. They are found, as already mentioned, on an Akkadian goddess, but not on the animal-men. An exception is a human-headed bird-man with outspread pinions, but he is more accurately classified as a man-animal. Winged demons appear later in large numbers in Assyria and in Syria in the second and first millennia, often in shapes which, in terms of later Christian iconography, we would simply describe as angels. In Egypt animal-men appear earlier and in greater number than in Mesopotamia but here they represent not demons, but gods. The images of the gods have here a completely different origin whereas the genuine demon-image seems to have developed only gradually under Mesopotamian influence. On the other hand demon-animals occur relatively early in Egypt: the griffin and also the sphinx should be mentioned here despite their connections with royal symbolism.

Satyr and woman

Different again is the situation in India, as we have learnt from the archaeological discoveries of the great cities of the Indus civilization, Mohenjo Daro, and Harappa, Kot Diji, Lothal and others, all of which flourished in the period from the third millennium B.C. to the first half of the second. So far no representation of a god in purely human form has here been found. Some figures, presumably to be regarded as gods, have heads with several faces and horns. Bull-men are rare. On the other hand there are numerous monster figures in which parts from different animals are combined, and human-headed animals as well as many-faced and many-bodied monsters may be regarded as the earliest Indian forms. Winged monsters are totally absent, and birds in general hardly play any part in the various combinations of shapes.

This brief historical summary suggests the following conclusion: the magical notions of pre-class societies first of all either give way to the creation of gods in human shape

– as in the developed civilization of ancient Mesopotamia – or in so far as they are based upon long-standing animal cults, they influence directly the representation of gods, as happened in Egypt and India. Then followed the formation of demons in combined animal and human shape, but on the other hand, demons in human-animal and mixed animal combinations occur in Egypt as well as in Mesopotamia and India already in the same period as the earliest representations of gods. The demons in the shape of animal-men, which are the subject of this chapter, may have originated in Elam, may then have been developed in large numbers in Mesopotamia, and from there spread soon to Egypt by way of Syria, and then across the Aegean islands to Greece. Winged figures, which are especially important for the later European development, do not occur in India, but appeared in large numbers during the second millennium in the Near East and Egypt. From there they spread to Greece, where they played such an important part that, together with the many Amoretti and Cupids found also in Italic art, they became, in fact, the predecessors of the winged figures of Christianity.

The cow-headed goddess Hathor. Egypt

Having gained some insight into the development of bull-man and satyr, angel and devil, we shall now turn to certain special shapes and special local developments.

In our definition of animal-men we have already pointed out that it is not so much the human body as the human posture that is distinctive. The oldest bull-men in Elam and Mesopotamia usually have bull-torsos but move in an upright, human way. This is one more argument for thinking that the animal body was given human characteristics and not vice versa. The only exceptions are the animal-headed Egyptian divinities, which have human bodies. But side by side with these monsters, the Egyptians, of course, had also images of animals in natural shapes.

Leaving aside their religious connotations, such animal bodies in human posture tend to look somewhat like caricatures, as if the animal shapes were a distorted reflection of the human world. Such animals in human posture still have this function in modern caricature and satirical illustration, where it is clearly not the animal world that is caricatured, but animal traits or similarities in man are exposed and held up to ridicule. There are some very early examples of this in which the connection with man is emphasized not by an actual mixing of shapes but by the human stance and by the man-made objects carried by these animals.

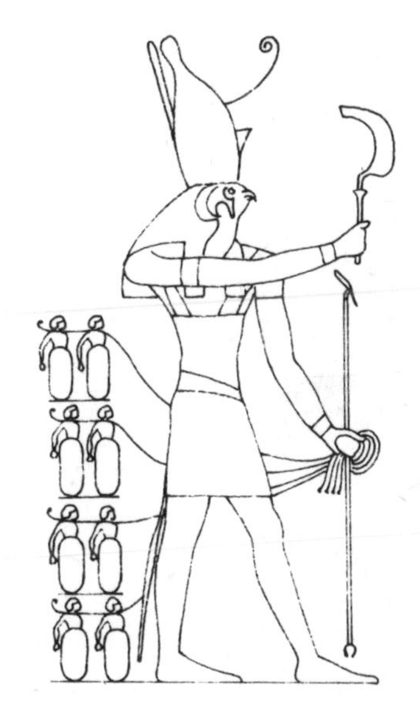

The falcon-headed god Horus. Egypt

The oldest examples of this type come from Elam, but such figures in a more intelligible context are found in the early dynastic period in Mesopotamia, especially on inlay work and seal-impressions from the royal tombs of Ur. Here animals which move like humans are shown drinking and making music. Sometimes social distinctions are clearly suggested: on one seal-impression various animals holding cups and musical instruments approach an enthroned lion, upon whom they are obviously waiting. Here we find for the first time, and in visual form, the basic idea of the fable of Reynard the Fox: King Noble the lion and his Court. A famous stone relief from Tell Halaf shows a very similar scene, but here the enthroned lion plays on a lyre in front of dancing and music-making animals, and the carousal itself seems to have reached an advanced stage. We find similar scenes depicted on Egyptian papyri: a lion and an antelope playing a chess-like game on a board, or an enthroned mouse waited on by other animals (24). This kind of subject-matter can be followed, via a few scenes from classical antiquity and the animal-grotesques of Romanesque capitals, down to the illustrations to *Reynard the Fox*, in which animals often act like humans.

On a papyrus fragment preserved in Cairo a rat is waited upon and has its hair dressed by cats and a baby rat is nursed by a cat (Plate 40). Here we catch for the first time the suggestion of a reversal of reality, a device which was to achieve great popularity, in the form of a 'Topsy-Turvy World', during the European Baroque period – especially in popular prints – and has remained alive to this day. Animals in human situations and the 'Topsy-Turvy World' have since been often used for a seemingly veiled but in fact widely understood criticism of contemporary life and social abuses. In the nineteenth century animal caricature achieved great popularity, especially in the prints of the Frenchman Grandville, who found many imitators in England and Germany. Here the accent lies upon the human characteristics cast into animal shape: individual figures and even particular personalities are assimilated to certain animal species and even individual animals in an attempt to caricature portrait-like features as animal physiognomies. The *Reineke Fuchs* (Reynard the Fox) illustrations by Hans Grundig and the political cartoons of our time still make use of these ancient pictorial types. The wealth of such material is so great that we cannot enter into details, especially since such figures, as has been repeatedly stressed, are not monsters in our sense of the word (25). In English book-illumination of the twelfth and thirteenth centuries the motif of animals in human posture, described as animal-grotesque, was particularly prized. We also find animal-grotesques, in the real sense of the term, in the Far East, where some of them even became popular heroes, especially in Japan. There is Tanuki the Badger, Kitsune the Fox, Usagi the Hare: animals of the forest which play all sorts of tricks on men and can also transform themselves into men and other animals and even into lifeless objects (26). Japanese goblins and sprites assume monstrous shapes to work their mischief, especially the Ten-gū, mountain-spirits (literally 'hounds of heaven'), thought to derive from the Indian Garuda, who carries the god Vishnu. Garuda is depicted either as a man or as a monster, half bird, half man (Plate 27). Instead of birds' beaks, the Ten-gū have excessively long noses, which are believed to show their connection with the Indian Garuda, and which, incidentally, count as a mark of beauty in Japan, though perhaps not in this outsize.

It is an interesting fact that bird-headed monsters are so prominent in the Far East. As we have already seen, their history is as old as that of the bull-men, though they are not found in the early civilization of India, either in Harappa or in Mohenjo Daro. But later on the Garuda described above appears in India, and numerous other

Left: King Lion waited on by animals. Mesopotamian seal, 3rd millennium B.C.
Right: Lion and donkey drinking together. Mesopotamian seal, 3rd millennium B.C.

Left: Mouse waited on by cats. Egyptian papyrus, British Museum
Right: Lion and donkey at a board-game. Egyptian papyrus, British Museum

Left: King Lion. From *Buch der Weisheit* Ulm, 1483
Right: Flight of Aeneas. Animal caricature, late antique period.

Left: Phallic bird of prey worshipped by birds. Mosaic from Herculaneum.
Right: Dance of the Animals. Illustration to *Reineke Fuchs*. By W. v. Kaulbach

winged monster-figures, including 'angels', are to be found from early Buddhist monuments onwards, probably a result of Persian influence. Bird-headed men also found a place in Christian iconography. They are often found in early book-illumination and even St John appears as a bird-man (27). The deacon, regarded as the sin-free soul of the just, was also represented in this form (28). Thus as well as the winged figures of the ancient world, these bird-headed figures, sometimes also provided with wings, may descend directly from the oriental bird-men and may in turn have influenced the form in which angels were represented.

The lion-headed demons of Mesopotamia and the lion-headed gods of Egypt did not prove so durable and have not contributed to the emergence of any similar type in more recent art. In later antiquity they are still found in the Mithras cult, and in India the Nārasingha, or man-lion, was a form in which the god Vishnu appears (Plate 20). But in Christian iconography they hardly played any part at all, except that the rare late Roman lion-headed figures with short ears and shaggy whiskers may possibly have influenced some of the gargoyles on medieval buildings. Elephant-headed monsters are of much greater interest. They seem to have been confined at first to India and from there to have spread further into East and South Asia. In European art, they are very rare, and perhaps directly inspired by Indian models (29). In early India an elephant's head or torso appears only with animal monsters in animal posture. Later, however, one figure becomes particularly popular: Shiva's son, the elephant-headed god Ganesha, who rides on a rat and usually has only a single tusk. He was the god of letters and learning and is still to be found on the title-pages of modern Indian books. His first appearance in European art may have been earlier than the evidence we now have suggests. In the *Arabian Nights* he is mentioned, in the story of Ali Baba and Zaker of Damascus, as the ferryman whom one dare not address without mortal danger (30).

A figure which has maintained a very vigorous existence in European tradition from classical times right up to our own day is the Minotaur, a fabulous creature in the Cretan labyrinth, which devoured children and was slain by the Greek hero Theseus. He is, as the name indicates, a bull-creature and is usually shown as a bull-man. He has become familiar again today through the numerous pictures and series of etchings by Picasso (Plate 45), who took up this ancient symbol and introduced it into our world of ideas as an archetype of unbridled strength and often terrifying savagery.

Midas, a legendary King of Phrygia, underwent only a partial transformation. In a musical contest between Apollo and Pan he supported the latter and was punished by Apollo, who gave him ass's ears. Though Midas strove to hide his long ears under a turban, his secret was revealed by the indiscretion of his barber. The story of Midas is one of those told by Ovid, the Roman poet, in the *Metamorphoses*. Though the poem deals with complete transformations, usually into animals, and not with composite creatures, some of the main figures, especially the hunter Actaeon and the nymph Daphne, are usually visualized and represented in composite shape. The reason is apparently that the transformation took place by stages and what is depicted is an intermediate stage between the original and the final shape. Similarly in fairy-tales, the victim of a spell, on being released by certain actions of the hero, loses a part of the bewitched shape in each succeeding night until finally restored to human shape. In such cases each composite shape is merely a temporary one and is succeeded by another.

Actaeon, a young and handsome hunter, had the misfortune to be discovered while watching the goddess Artemis bathing naked. He was punished by being turned into a stag, and his own dogs then tore him to pieces. He is depicted, mostly in illustrations to Ovid, as a man with a stag's head or just with antlers (Plate 37). 'And quickly, no longer threatening, she gives the head the antlers of a strong stag, stretches out the neck and points the tapering ears; and she transforms him, his hands to feet, his arms to out-stretched legs, and clothes his limbs with a speckled hide.' (31) Daphne, too, may be mentioned here although, as a tree-monster, she belongs to our fifth category. She spurned Apollo's wooing, and continuously pursued by him, she was transformed into a laurel tree by her father, a river god, in answer to her own prayer. Both myths have been very frequently illustrated, even in more recent times, often as single figures by sculptors (Plate 38). These temporary shapes seem to have held a special interest for artists.

'The Primadonna'.
Print by Grandville

36 Ganesha: Indian god
with elephant's head. Private collection

'Centaur-Gladiator'.
By Tono Zancanaro, 1944

38 Daphne. By Wenzel Jamnitzer.
Grünes Gewölbe, Dresden

37 Actaeon. By Jeremias Ritter. Seventeenth century. Grünes Gewölbe, Dresden

39 Reineke and Grimmbart steal a chicken. Illustration to 'Reineke Fuchs' by Wilhelm von Kaulbach, 1857

40 Satirical papyrus. Egyptian Museum, Cairo

41 Statue of Sechmet. Temple of Mut, Karnak, Egypt

42 The Minotaur, by G.F. Watts. Tate Gallery, London

43 Serpent-Dragon on the vase of Gudea of Lagash. Louvre, Paris

44 Female Deity with animal–head. From Ur, 4000–3500 B.C. Iraq Museum, Baghdad

45 Minotaur leaning over a girl. Etching by Picasso.
Print Room, Munich

46 Hanuman. Kalighat painting. From Calcutta. Nineteenth century. Archer collection, London

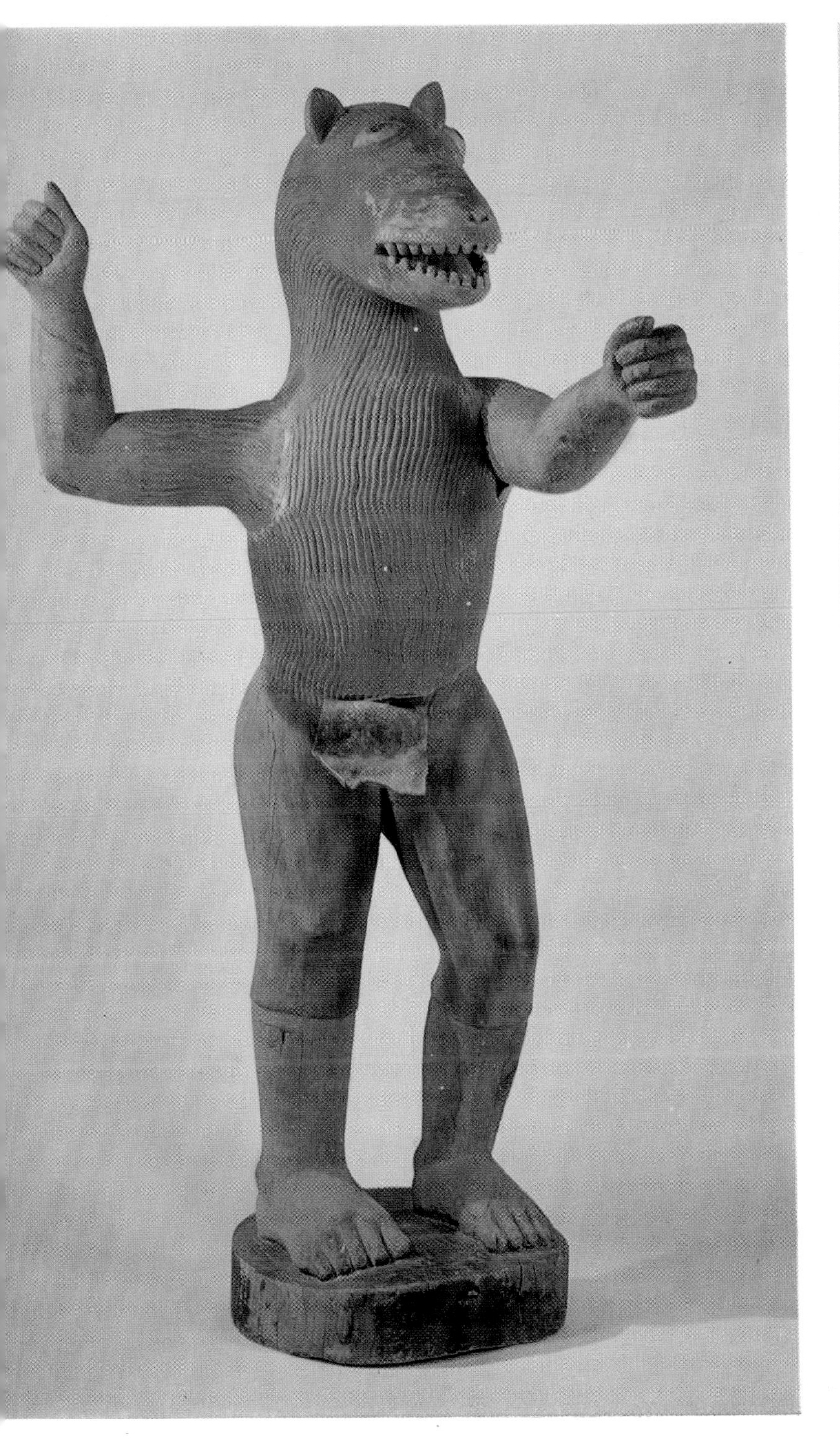

47 Glélé, king of Dahomey, as a lion. Wooden statue. Musée de l'Homme, Paris

48 Béhanzin, king of Dahomey, as a shark. Wooden statue. Musée de l'Homme, Paris

50 Cernunnos. From the Gundestrup cauldron, about second century B.C.
National Museum, Copenhagen

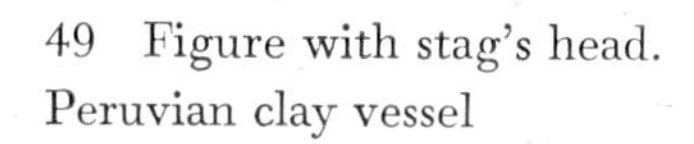

49 Figure with stag's head.
Peruvian clay vessel

51 Demon-King riding. Islamic miniature, fourteenth century.
Bibliothèque Nationale, Paris

The horns of the bull-men were later often transferred to other figures, and it is not always clear whether they are to be regarded as part of a head or only set upon it, for example, in connection with the so-called horn-shaped crown. A statue of Apollo found in Enkomi and dating from the thirteenth century B.C. (32) shows horns growing out of the head, a very remarkable feature for a god who was always portrayed in later Greek art as the prototype of masculine beauty. In Mesopotamia and the neighbouring civilizations the horn-shaped crown became a head-decoration for gods in human shape, but also for temporal rulers. It is, however, nothing more than a derivative attribute and thus is of little interest to us. Horns growing on a head have often been depicted: the Apollo of Enkomi is a good example. In heathen Europe the Celtic god Cernunnos was widely known as 'the Horned One'. In all other respects he was portrayed as human, but from his head sprouted a pair of massive stag's antlers. One of the most interesting portraits of this god is to be found on a silver cauldron from Gundestrup in Denmark (Plate 50) – interesting because he is shown seated in an Indian posture, with legs crossed under him, and is surrounded with other motifs which also point to the East and especially to India (33). The composition of a scene found on this bowl, which is believed to be Celtic, is similar to that on an Indus seal of the third millennium, on which a horned god is surrounded by four animals.

Der Bapſteſel zu Rom

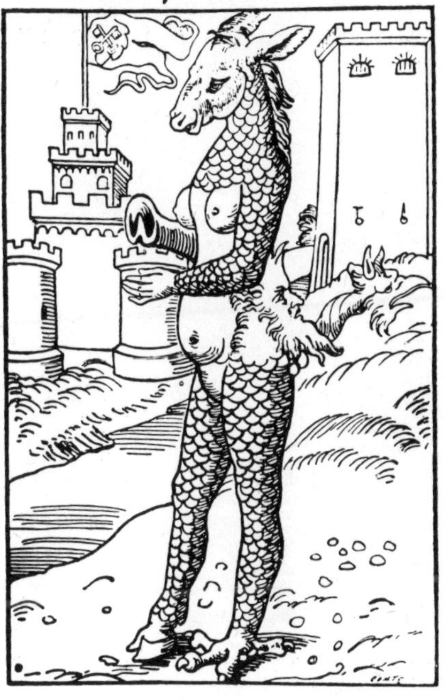

Pope-Ass. Woodcut by Lukas Cranach, Nuremberg, 1496

In India the goddess Durga was later occasionally portrayed with horns, but this attribute was in all probability borrowed from her adversary, the buffalo-headed demon *(asura)* Mahisha. In Buddhist iconography, especially in Tibetan and Mongolian art, horned gods occur frequently. They are often portrayed with buffalo or bull-heads, but sometimes with only the horns, which are set upon grimacing faces.

India had still other monsters of this type, and some of their old names are also known. The god Vishnu appears not only as the man-lion, Narasinha, but also in the shape of a boar-man, Varāha. Earlier incarnations, too – e.g. as tortoise and fish – are portrayed not only in purely animal form but also occasionally in mixed or 'monster' form. Sometimes there are female counterparts (the so-called Shakti forms) such as the Varāhī, a woman with a boar's head. The horse-headed Assa-mukhi, probably a female demon, is known from the Jatakas and from ancient Buddhist representations. A Cambodian divinity also has a horse's head (34). Pausanias, by the way, mentions the image of a Greek deity with a horse's head. Demeter, the 'goddess mother of horses' had turned into a mare, her pursuer, Poseidon, into a stallion. Particularly popular in India, and better known to us, are the figures from the Rāmāyana epic. Among them is Hanuman, a monkey, who behaves like a man and is portrayed in near human shape, clothed, but always with a tail and sometimes, in the usual manner of Indian divinities, with multiple arms as well.

Next we mention the hideous gorgon, Medusa, whose head was so terrifying to look upon that the beholder was turned to stone. In most illustrations there is just a distorted grimace with lolling tongue, but she has no composite shape. However in some early pictures she is given wings and in late antiquity she is sometimes depicted with snakes twisted around her head. Perseus severed Medusa's head from her body and later presented it to the goddess Athena, who carried it upon her shield as an unfailing means of protection. Hence the head of Medusa is often depicted in later art without the body, so that the snake-locks but not the wings are to be seen.

Gorgon. Drawing by R. Kannenberg

Snake-headed monsters are relatively rare. A demon with human torso and snake-head appears on an early dynastic Mesopotamian seal, and on Egyptian papyri of the New Empire we again find human bodies with snake-heads. But most snake-monsters, like the bird-monsters, have animal bodies and come under the category dealt with in the next chapter. In European folk-tales, e.g. in Croatian legends, there are also certain female demons who have a small stature, no nose or ear, little snake-eyes set deep in a pointed head, hands like cat's paws, and goat's feet (35). They are known as 'plague-women'.

Among the Slavonic peoples memories of ghost and demon figures have been preserved much longer and more vividly than in other parts of Europe. We have at least descriptions, though no portrayals, of some of these monsters. One of them, called Pszpolnica, is said to be covered all over with black hair, and has horse's hooves but a human face. Whoever is unable to talk to her for one hour about flax or millet has his head struck off by her with a sickle. She disappears after one o'clock (36). She is also known under the German name of 'Mittagsfrau' (Middaywoman). The Laskowice or Leschia are evil forest spirits, men with goat's feet and horns (37).

The description of the Gorgon brought us back to the winged monsters, and in this final section we mention some other important figures of ancient myth which belong to this group. Hardly less terrifying than the Gorgon are the Erinyes, the Furies dwelling in the underworld. They are frequently, though not always, given wings, and sometimes they also carry snakes in their outstretched hands. The French illustrator Doré, like Schadow in an Orestes illustration, has pictured them as a group of massive female bodies swooping down on gigantic wings through the air.

Beside these terror figures, the ancient Greeks had Nike (Plate 29), the goddess of victory, who is usually winged, and Iris, the messenger of the gods, originally the rainbow personified. The winged figures which eventually became most prominent in European art were the god Eros (or Cupid) with his numerous retinue, the Erotes (or Amoretti), and the Angels. A strong assimilation took place between these two groups. From the thirteenth century onwards the youthfully handsome, more supple angel-figure was favoured, rather than the hieratically severe types of early Christian and early medieval art. In the fourteenth and fifteenth centuries the child-like angels, the 'putti', came to the fore, and in Baroque and Rococo art they finally dominate the scene entirely. It should be mentioned that the wings, like the horns, were looked upon as detachable from the body or, alternatively, could be worn as garments. As far back as the Gilgamesh epic we read that the dead, like the birds, are clothed with feathers (38). The best examples in this group are, however, the swan-maidens who fly down from fairy-land to the earth, mostly to bathe or sport with their playmates; one of the beauties is then robbed of her gown by the hero. The most beautiful of these tales is to be found in the *Arabian Nights*, but they are so numerous and there are so many variations that they figure prominently in the modern analysis of the fairy-tale (39). The Nordic Valkyries, too, are such swan-maidens. Of course they are not composite in shape, but they touch upon and remind us of the winged monsters and other creatures which we have surveyed in this chapter.

Elephant-headed Demon and Djinn. French illustration to the *Arabian Nights*. Stuttgart, 1838

Sphinxes, Centaurs and Sirens

ITH sphinx, centaur and siren, and the comparable Nāga (less well known to us but very popular in Asia), we come to the group we call man-animals. Here the animal body determines the posture, while the human head is the distinctive feature and makes it clear that these are not to be considered real animals found in nature, but creatures gifted with special powers and obviously closely related to man. In part they may go back to notions of demons and spirits, but as there are relatively few of them they represent beings of a particular significance. The sphinx, male or female, and the bird-bodied or fish-bodied sirens have remained more stable, both in form and in significance, than most of the monsters considered so far; and this applies also to the Nāga of South and South-East Asia. The sphinx and presumably also the human-headed bird come from Egypt. In Mesopotamia, in addition to the bird-man, the original, bird-bodied siren slowly becomes more common, just like the fish-bodied siren in the art of the Middle Babylonian period; later it is very often represented.

The centaur, on the other hand, certainly originated in Mesopotamia – even if not in its classic horse-bodied shape – unless older centaur-like figures on Indus seals are considered evidence of its Indian origin. But it seems more probable that the shape of the centaur in the broadest sense was determined, by – among other things – the human-faced bulls, which are usually classified as animal-men because of their upright posture, and which we have already noted in the ancient Mesopotamian art of early dynastic times. The Nāga, too, can be derived from either India or Mesopotamia; the continuity of civilization speaks for India, whereas the earliest representations point to Mesopotamia and neighbouring Elam. In any event, it is clear that in the centuries decisive for the development of such types a comparatively close contact, not merely limited to commercial relations, must have existed between these widely separated regions, so that notions of that kind could easily and quickly pass from one to the other.

The Egyptian sphinxes, consisting of a lion's body and a man's head – though conceived almost exclusively as female both in Greek and in earlier Syrian and Cretan-Mycenaean art – have their prototype in the huge monument near the great pyramids of Gizeh from the period of the 4th dynasty of the Old Kingdom (Plate 54). But it has been established that there are a number of predecessors, especially a slightly older monument from Abu Roash, which in addition is described as having a female head (40). The question whether the Great Sphinx was the first representation is not of great moment to us. As it has exercised an enormous influence right down to our time it must be considered the most permanent and significant among all the monsters. In this instance it is not so much the type, but a particular ancient monument, that has been of decisive importance.

Regarded typologically the sphinx is but a special form of a wider group: centaur-like monsters, of which others, some older Mesopotamian ones but especially later Near Eastern ones, also have the characteristic lion's body as the basic torso. The Great

Crocodile-man. 'Demagogy'
by A. Kubin, 1939

Sphinx had its own cult under the name 'Horus on the Horizon' (in Greek, Harmachis), which, however, is only attested from the New Empire onwards (41).
In folk-literature the so-called riddle of the sphinx occupies a prominent place: 'What has a voice, goes on all fours in the morning, on two feet at noon, and on three in the evening?' The answer is man at the various stages of his life: childhood, maturity and old age (with stick). Greek myth connects the riddle with a monstrous sphinx at Thebes, who devoured any wayfarer who could not answer the question. Oedipus finally found the solution, whereupon the sphinx threw herself from her cliff (42). This Greek legend was widely known, but subsequently attention turned much more to the great Egyptian figure. The Greek sphinx was, as the word implies, a 'strangler' (43), whereas the ancient Egyptian sphinx, much less dangerous, represented the king and his power. Though the Greek concept may appear the older, it can hardly be doubted that it was influenced by the Egyptian. In ancient folklore the strangler had presumably a very different shape, vague and indistinct, before mythology gave it the shape of the Egyptian sphinx. The representation of the pharaoh as a lion with a king's head is regarded as a parallel to the figures of the Egyptian gods. Chronological and psychological equivalence here gains greater significance from the combination of human physical features with shapes borrowed from the animals worshipped in ancient cults (44). The relationship between the sphinx and the pharaoh is attested by a later inscription. When King Thutmose IV, tired from the hunt, fell asleep in the shadow of the sphinx, the latter appeared to him in a dream and commanded him to remove the sand that covered him. The inscription begins: 'O my son Thutmose, it is I, your father . . .' Thutmose was at the time still a prince. The sphinx promised him the throne as a reward.
In later ages, in Mycenaean and Syrian regions, in Greece, in Islamic and medieval European art, sphinxes differ radically from the prototype at Gizeh. They are still usually represented as human-headed lions, but many have wings, which sometimes end in human heads, and in addition the tail may be decorated (Plates 52, 53, 55). The genuine sphinx is rare, and it is almost always female. Only more recently has European art again taken up the sphinx without falsifying it, deriving it directly from Egypt. In the nineteenth century it was misused for all kinds of symbolic fantasies. Many genre painters and late romantics attempted to portray the eternal feminine, enigmatic, erotically dangerous, by a more or less deliberate distortion of the original work. Thus for example Franz von Stuck painted not only the sphinx in its animal-human shape but also, as a parallel, a female nude lying on its stomach with the upper part of the body raised up. Other artists – Kubin for instance – stressed the ghostly sense of a 'laughing sphinx'.
The generic name 'sphinx' also includes monsters in which the lion's body is replaced by that of some other animal. For example, there is an ancient Assyrian cow-sphinx, which has its parallel in India: the Kāmadhenu in the folk-art of Bengal. Other ani-

mal components such as bird's feet and the tail of a bird or a scorpion are also found as additions. As a generic name, the word 'sphinx' turns out to be inappropriate because, as we have already seen, we should have to include the centaur in the same group. It might seem more logical to make the idea of the centaur the general one and to leave to the sphinx its original limited significance just because it stems from a single monument. However, it is more convenient to regard all such monsters, including those that combine parts of the human body with those of lions, as man-animals and to use this as a basic general category in contrast to individual types with names of their own.

Especially in Islamic art the expression 'sphinx' is applied to a wide range of monsters, sometimes with a lion-body, but also with that of a tiger or a leopard (45). It has been pointed out that Muslim authors took their inspiration principally from Persepolis and that Achaemenid art had a greater influence on Islamic visual imagination than Egyptian. It follows that it was not the original sphinx but various Mesopotamian man-animals – from which the Achaemenid forms are derived – which were ancestors to the later sphinx-like monsters of Islam.

Sphinx. Mesopotamian, about 2000 B.C.

In the Far East man-animals like the sphinx or the centaur are unusual. But in the last two millennia monsters with bird-bodies have been popular in this region, especially in South and South-East Asia. From ancient China, however, the monster-figure of Wu Liang Tse must be mentioned (46): the body of a beast of prey combined with two human upper halves and heads. But man-animals do not seem to have taken root there; the majority of monsters seem to be based on animal combinations or on the demons already discussed. Even in India man-animal combinations are much rarer in early times than those of animals. But Indian art in the post-Achaemenid period was overtaken by a flood of such man-animals, which presumably – like the Islamic examples – were inspired by Achaemenid models, for we must remember that in pre-Alexandrian times Persian domination spread far into Indian – today Pakistani – territory. But this abundance of man-animals in the monuments of the Ghandāra, Shunga and Andhra periods was not destined to exercise its influence for very long. Only the monsters with bird and snake bodies proved long-lasting.

Sphinx. From Persepolis

Classical mythology and numerous excellent works of art have made the centaur such a well-known type that it is often felt to be no longer a monster at all. The centaur with its more recent popularity is as clearly attributable to Greece as the sphinx is to Egypt. Though there were predecessors and even very similar figures in pre-Hellenic times, the mythological background has had such an obvious and powerful effect on later cultural development, on literature and art, that we must consider the centaur, too, as a special type within the category of man-animals.

The original Greek representations of centaurs have six limbs, the front limbs of the animal being duplicated by a pair of human arms. Four limbs are used for locomotion and the arms for the other human activities, which in the case of the centaurs usually

'Lion-woman'. Italian broadsheet, 1585

means fighting. Most of the Near Eastern man-animals often called centaurs must thus be eliminated because they only have four animal legs but no human arms. They are, therefore, man-animals of another type even when, like the monumental Assyrian gate-guardians in man-animal shape, they have five legs; at least that is how it looks from an oblique front view. From a strict side view only four legs are visible; from a direct front view, two. Because of the monumental block-character of the sculpture, which has the effect of showing two bodies – the combination of two animal-halves parallel to each other but separated by a central block – altogether eight legs can be counted. In such a technical arrangement we cannot properly speak of an intention to change the natural form, and the monster-character of these guardians is accordingly limited to the combination of animal components with a human head.

The meaning of the Greek word 'centaur' is unknown, and hence there has always been a tendency to look for models in the Near East. As well as the many man-animals falsely designated as centaurs, there are in fact some which fulfil at least the minimum requirement of having six limbs. These are central Assyrian and central Babylonian monuments, including sculptures on the so-called 'kudurrus' (boundary-stones), and seals. They show centaur-like monsters with horse's bodies, and some with lion's bodies. Still older, however, is a 'centaur' with a tiger's body on an Indus seal, based on the same structural principle: a halved tiger's body has been added to a complete human body so that the former in horizontal posture, together with the human legs, forms the animal body. It seems that here a very early date is not only guaranteed by the place of discovery but is also indicated by the kind of combination of man with animal. At all events the aforementioned Mesopotamian examples stress the animal character more strongly in that a complete animal body is joined, without its neck and head, on to a human head and neck by means of the shoulders with the two arms.

Sphinx. From Egypt, XVIII dynasty

Both varieties are found in ancient art but the Mesopotamian form with four animal legs came to be adopted as the better solution. This is the centaur which was taken over in later Indian, post-Achaemenid art (Plate 62). The explanation for all this is not a simple one. An examination of the developments of form and meaning leads to the following hypothesis: in the early art of the Near East man-animals, as opposed to the animal-animal combinations, are few and far between and are restricted in the first place to creatures with a bull or lion body. These oldest man-animals do not yet have human arms. They can be interpreted as embodiments of demons, in which the animal traits are predominant, while human components are scarcely in evidence. However, when demons of human shape appeared during the second millennium and took ever stronger hold of the imagination at the side of the anthropomorphic gods, the animal-monsters, too, acquired some human features.

Sphinx. From the Taman peninsula, fifth century B.C.

In this process the peoples of Mesopotamia may have adopted certain images which had been elaborated elsewhere (the sphinx in Egypt, in India the tiger-centaur). But

52 Winged Sphinx with an additional lion's head and a snake's tail. Relief from Kargamis, about 1050–850 B.C. Archaeological Museum, Ankara

53 Greek Sphinx. Ivory from Sparta, Eastern Attica. National Museum, Athens

54 The Great Sphinx of Gizeh, Egypt. About 2600 B.C.

56 Sphinx and Man-bird.
Arabian miniature, dated 1237.
Bibliothèque Nationale, Paris

57 Centaur with bow and arrow.
Miniature from an Islamic
astrological treatise, about 1250.
Bibliothèque Nationale, Paris

55 Sphinx from Delphi. 570–560 B.C.
Archaeological Museum, Delphi

خادم قد علته كبرة وعرته عبرة وقال يا قوم لا توسعونا سبا ولا توجعونا

عتبا فانا في حزن شامل وشغل عن الحديث شاغل فقال له ابو زيد نفس خناق البث.

القول على الوجه الاول من نظر طالع البرج القوس والمشتري

قال الحكيم المولود بهذا الطالع يكون دري اللون يعلوه بياض وهو نهاري مضى حار يابس طبيعته مرة صفراء

58 Tiger-woman. Miniature of the Kangra School, eighteenth century. Prince of Wales Museum, Bombay

60 Fight between Centaur and Lapith. Relief from the Parthenon, Athens, about 445 B.C. British Museum, London

59 Mohammed on the magic horse Alborak. Miniature, fourteenth century. Topkapi Museum, Istanbul

the steps immediately preceding the last phase of the presumed spread to Greece cannot be traced. Minoan-Mycenaean art takes over the sphinx, but seems to show little interest in centaur-like or other man-animals. Thus we must, as we have already said, regard the centaur as an essentially indigenous Greek invention, and this is supported by the frequency of literary and visual references.

Many apologetic attempts have been made to explain away such figures in the classical art of the Greeks. Centaurs, satyrs, and sirens, however, as well as some other, less distinctive monsters, populate the Greek imagination to such an extent that they must be regarded as essential to it and not as foreign, more or less accidental, accretions. Here we may recall the treatise *De Incredibilibus*, in which an attempt is made to give a rationalistic explanation of the centaurs. It takes up the legend of the Thessalian king, Ixion, father of the centaurs, who tried to seduce Hera. She accused him before Zeus, who tricked him by substituting Nephele, a cloud, in the guise of Hera, with the result that he begot these misshapen children by Nephele. The author of the *Unbelievable Tales* suggests that in Ixion's time the land of Thessaly was overrun by herds of wild cattle. The king offered a reward for their extermination, and mounted archers from the village of Nephele rode out and shot the invaders down. Thus, it is said, the legend arose that Ixion became, through Nephele, the father of the *kentauroi* – the 'bull-piercers'. (47)

Centaur. Madrid, National Library, Codex 3307

Homer (48) does not mention any specific animal shape but refers to the centaurs as savages living on mountains and in forests. It is not clear whether their composite shape appeared first in literature (Pindar) or in art. In addition to the Ixion legend the most important one, often depicted, is the battle of the centaurs with the Lapiths at the wedding feast of Peirithous (Plate 60). (The Lapiths, or 'stone-men', were also originally composite creatures.) The most beautiful representation of this legend are the sculptures from the west pediment of the temple of Zeus at Olympia. But as well as these uncouth savages, there were such centaurs as Cheiron, the teacher of Achilles, according to Homer the justest of beings and an expert at healing. He, too, appears in visual art, for example on a famous fresco in Naples, as a man-animal, an affectionate teacher, expounding the art of the lyre to the young Achilles. Hans von Marées has taken over this type directly. There are also numerous representations of the centaurs in the Heracles legend. When Nessus was fatally shot by Heracles, he advised Deianeira, with his dying words, to take blood from his wound and, if Heracles should ever be unfaithful to her, to win him back by spreading it on his robe. The magic of this cunning centaur was later to prove fatally poisonous for the hero. In medieval illustrations the centaurs embody unrestrained savagery and paganism; females also now appear, and they are sometimes used for purely decorative purposes (49). From the Italian Renaissance onwards the centaur has pursued a career of unparalleled triumph in the history of European art; here we see once again that a hybrid creature of such a distinctive character can hold its own in the world of

Dancing centaur. After Picasso

Female centaur. West portal of San Michele in Lucca, thirteenth century A.D.

generally realistic imagery. From Pollaiuolo, Pisanello, Botticelli, Michelangelo, Giovanni da Bologna (Plate 61), from Baldung-Grien and Rubens to Böcklin and Menzel, to name but a few, many of Europe's most outstanding artists have preserved the centaur in its ancient form, and even Rodin and Picasso have portrayed it repeatedly and so made it an accepted feature in contemporary art.

In addition to hippocentaurs, the family of these man-animals comprises the onocentaurs, bucentaurs, leontocentaurs (with bodies of asses, bulls and lions), and others. Sometimes horse-fish creatures, like those on engravings by Andrea Mantegna (Plate 97), are described as sea-centaurs. If this description is incorrect for these latter, which have nothing human about them, the generalization of the centaur idea is equally misleading, as already mentioned. One exception is a sign of the zodiac, the constellation of the archer Sagittarius, which is frequently portrayed as a centaur.

At an early date mythological characters and their deeds had been located in the night sky (50) – or, as other scholars believe, had been derived from constellations – Equus as Pegasus, Capricorn as goat-fish, Cetus – the whale – as a dragon and the Archer himself, who might be either a bull-footed satyr or a horse-bodied centaur. In a Carolingian manuscript at Madrid the ancient visual traditions have been faithfully preserved and they show how many of these ideas and images came to be adopted in later European art. Islamic art, too, has monsters in astrological contexts: Sagittarius, Leo – a four-footed animal with the face of a bird of prey – and Gemini – a human-headed bird (51). The latter can be disregarded for the moment, but Sagittarius is shown as a centaur shooting at his own dragon-like tail (Plate 57).

The onocentaur, with an ass's body, has a literary tradition in the *Physiologus*: 'And the onocentaurs have human shape from the face to the loins, their backs are those of asses, unbroken are their hoofs and their whole body is tense.' (52) An extremely old form of man-animal has been found in ancient Spanish art: large zoomorphic stone sculptures, presumably carved under Greek influence. This type, called *bicha*, is, however, not so much akin to the true centaurs as to the Assyrian *lamassu*, and combines a bull's body with a human face (53).

In the inscription on the Hammurabi stele, the *lamassu* are referred to as gods or guardian spirits, for example of the city of Assur. The monumental figures of guardians of the gate in Assyrian palaces have accordingly been called *lamassu*. Orientalists have tried to generalize and to include not only these man-animals but also the winged and animal-headed demons already discussed, and indeed all ancient oriental monsters, under the heading 'cherub'; the sphinx, too, would then become a predecessor of the Christian angels (54). Even if the *lamassu* may have been demon-figures which only gradually turned into guardian divinities, the man-animal shape, which has nothing to do with angels, remains characteristic. The *lamassu* of later Assyrian times have winged bull or lion bodies with bearded human heads. The horn-shaped crown points to the divine character of these gate-keepers (Plate 63).

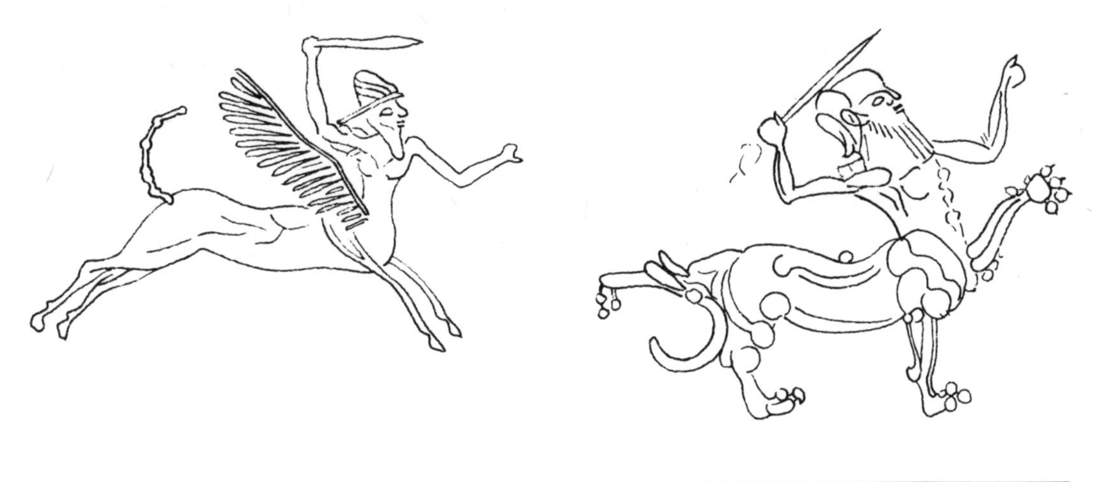

Left: Winged centaur. Kassite seal, 2nd millennium B.C.
Right: Lion-centaur. Early Assyrian seal, 2nd millennium B.C.

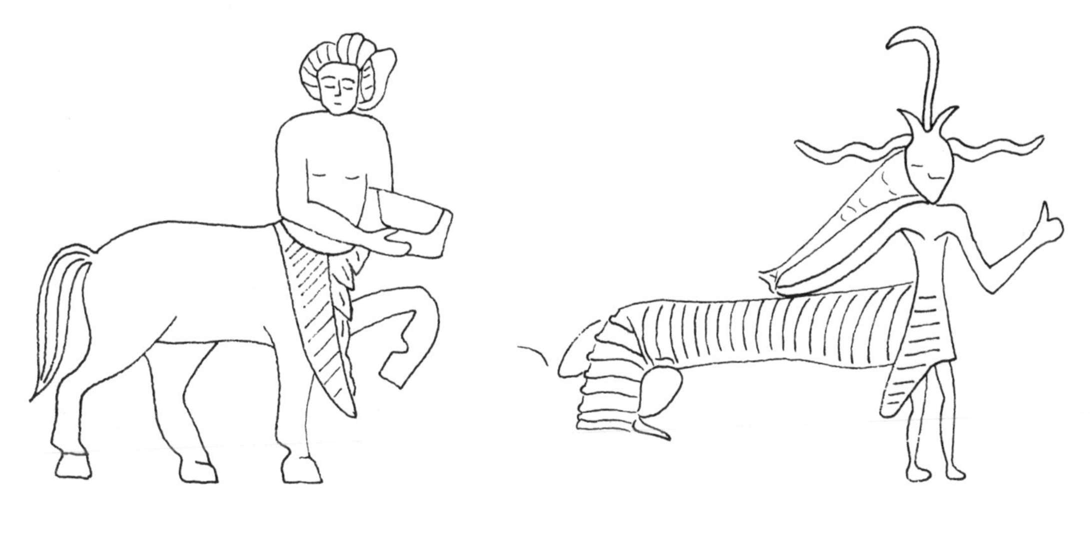

Left: Centaur. India, first century B.C.
Right: Female tiger-centaur. Seal. India, 3rd millennium B.C.

Left: Centaur
Right: Centaur. Greek vase painting, fifth century B.C.

A human-faced ram is found on Indus seals at the same time as the genuinely centaur-like man-tiger.

The man-animals of later Indian art have many variants. As well as true centaurs there is a sea-centaur, which deserves this name more than do those of Mantegna, since it combines a snake's body and fish-tail with a human thorax, human arms and horse (or bull) legs. The human-faced cow, Kāmadhenu, appears relatively late in Indian art; the examples known to me come from Bengali folk-art. But predecessors can be found on the Bhārhut reliefs: man-animals, sometimes described as sphinxes, with lion's bodies with or without wings. Finally we mention the animal-bodied Nārasingha, which – in contrast to the type with human body and animal face, one of the forms in which the god Vishnu appears – occurs frequently in the art of Ceylon as a genuine man-animal.

A monster of a special kind is the Manticora, a four-footed creature with a long neck and a woman's head. She wears a Phrygian cap, her body ends in a scorpion's tail, and she is supposed to be able to run faster than a bird can fly, and to hiss like a snake. She appears in medieval bestiaries as a symbol of the prophet Jeremiah. Réau lists a number of representations in French works of the thirteenth century (55).

Centaur couple. Woodcut. London, 1520

We now come to a third group of man-animals. These have been portrayed in ways differing considerably from one another and have also become familiar in more recent poetry and fairy-tales: the sirens, usually still known under their ancient name. Unfortunately the name is used, without sufficient distinction, for creatures often very different in substance and easily distinguishable in shape: female figures with bodies of birds or with bodies of snakes or fishes. 'There he saw Melusina. But not, as on the first occasion, seated upon the wood, and tightly wrapped in veils, but rising bright and naked to the waist out of the dark waters behind the yew-tree; from her soft bosom downwards she was covered with silver scales; and she stood and wriggled over the water with her fish body cracking like a whip, driven forward by the massive purple fin...' In this modern re-telling of the story (56) the well-known figure, which turns up often under various names, is described in a little detail.

Unfortunately, the old folk-book of Fair Melusina is hardly more explicit: 'Raymund saw his wife and helpmeet sitting naked in a bathtub. And from her navel upwards she was immeasurably and ineffably a model of female beauty, her body and face inexpressibly beautiful. But from the navel downwards she had the tail of a terrible monstrous serpent, of azure blue with a silvery white colour and underneath flecked with silvery spots, such as befits a serpent's shape.' (57)

Here we have the first two variants of our type, both characterized as water-creatures. In the text of the folk-book, Melusina flees from her spouse, but no further details are given about her body; in the illustration to the book she has wings as well as a snake's body (58). Thus a third variant is established, or rather added by the illustrator, and

61 Nessus carrying off Deianeira. Bronze by Giovanni da Bologna, about 1580. Staatliche Kunstsammlungen, Dresden

62 Indian Centaurs. Relief from Mathurā, about second century A.D. Museum, Lucknow

63 Lamassu. Late Assyrian colossal statue. From Dur Sharrukin, 721–705 B.C. Louvre, Paris

64 Gold seal from Mycenae

65 Seal from Kalibanga, North West India

66 Vyala-yaksha with snake-legs. Relief from Mathurā, about second century A.D. Archaeological Museum, Mathurā

67 Warrior with bird-body. Capital. Brandenburg Cathedral

68 Zeus and Typhon. Greek vase. Antikensammlung, Munich

69 Siren carrying a soul. Harpy from the 'Harpy Tomb' at Xanthus, about 500 B.C. British Museum, London

70 Soul-birds. Relief from the Tomb of Amen-em-inet at Memphis. Egyptian Museum, Munich

71 Harpy, by Thomas Häfner. 1967

72 Two-headed Hekabe.
Pergamon Altar, about 180 B.C.
Staatliche Museen, Berlin

73 Giant with snake-legs.
Pergamon Altar, about 180 B.C.
Staatliche Museen, Berlin

at the same time the oldest and commonest form of siren is adumbrated, in this example certainly unconsciously and unintentionally.

This oldest type of siren in the shape of a bird dominates Greek mythology especially (though Homer in telling Odysseus' adventure with these seductresses does not attribute bird-bodies to them), and seems to go back to the notion of the soul-bird, which was already well established in ancient Egypt (Plate 70). The expression 'ba', transcribed in Greek as 'bai' which we translate as 'soul', (though it is to be noted that the Egyptian notion of the soul was not the same as ours) is represented by the bird-shape with a female head. The typical beard of the gods is often added to the face (59). In ancient Mesopotamian art, too, there are shapes which unite human and bird forms in varying proportions. The early dynastic period had a bird-man and also a man-bird, but their significance cannot be defined with certainty. In the case of most bird-men of the Akkad period the posture is completely human, though where human shapes are present, bird and human postures are not so easy to distinguish as those of man and quadruped. We have decided to place in our second category not only the bird-bodied sirens, but also the fish and snake-bodied variants.

The bird-men of the Akkad period also have a bird's tail or else the lower part of the body is shaped like that of a bird. The older form, however, seems to be the man-bird, with the body and feet of a bird and the head and two arms of a man, and this form is closest to the Egyptian type. Frankfort connects the bird-man on the Akkad seals with representations of the Zu myth (60) and puts forward an interpretation such as he also develops, incidentally, for the parallel type of the snake-man (61). According to him, the pure animal figure, the man-animal mixture, and the pure human figure with some animal attribute or accompanied by an animal are to be considered equi-

Melusina. Woodcut.
Antwerp, 1491

Siren. From a Mesopotamian seal from Ur, 3rd millennium B.C.

Man-bird. From a Mesopotamian seal of the Akkad period

Soul-bird. Egypt, late period

valent. In the myth, Zu had stolen the 'Tablets of Fate', was vanquished by the god Ninurta and punished. In the older Sumerian myths the emblem of the god Ninurta-Ningirsu is the lion-headed bird Imdugud, perhaps also a precursor, in different form, of the man-monster Zu. According to our method, however, categories are determined by differences in shape and we shall therefore postpone consideration of Imdugud until our next chapter. Whether the shapes of the earliest men-birds were developed in Mesopotamia or in Egypt remains to be decided. The great number of variants in Mesopotamia speaks for this region. In content, however, the Greek myths are easier to connect with Egyptian notions of the soul-bird (62). In the Odyssey the sirens are described as seductive creatures whose songs lure men into danger. This legend has continued to exert its spell owing to the literary tradition inspired throughout the centuries by the great creative power of Homer. Today, however, when mention is made of a siren, we instinctively hear the fearsome wail of the alarm to which the word has been transferred – this first took place with ships' sirens – rather than the sweet alluring sounds imagined in antiquity.

The Greek siren-birds approximate very closely to the fish-shaped water creatures with a human bust, such as the Tritons, Naiads and Nereids. The sirens were sometimes named 'Acheloïds', after their father Acheloüs, a river god and son of Oceanus. In the literary imagination, the bird figure could easily be replaced by a fish figure. It is therefore not surprising that in times when literary tradition is predominant, as it was in medieval Europe, the texts describe the sirens in both forms. Thus for example in Guillaume Le Clerc de Normandie's bestiary the sirens are women from the waist up, while their lower halves are either fishes or birds (63).

A second man-bird figure of classical antiquity seems to confirm even more strongly the relationship to the Egyptian 'ba'. These are the harpies, goddesses of the storm in Homer, Iris' sisters of the splendid locks, who, according to Hesiod, 'fly away on speedy pinions, swift as the howling wind and the fleeting birds.' In the Argonaut myths they become furies in the combined shape of young women and birds of prey (Plate 69), and in Vergil's *Aeneid* they are placed at the entrance to the underworld. Typologically, however, it is difficult to distinguish between harpies and sirens. In the Old Testament, too, the bird-soul image occurs, for example in Psalm 11,1: 'How say you to my soul, Flee as a bird to your mountain?' or in Psalm 124,7: 'Our soul is escaped as a bird out of the snare of the fowlers: the snare is broken, and we are escaped.'

Human-headed birds also play an important part in Islamic literature and art and in the civilizations of India and South-East Asia. Here, in contrast to the European development, the fish shape of the sirens is rare and only the bird-figure is widespread, though with a different meaning. The meanings of these figures seem to vary greatly, especially in Islamic regions (64). There was the male, human-faced bird Anqā, which is identified with the Persian Simurgh and even before Adam's time sat upon a throne on the mountains of Kaf. The Cetus and Gemini constellations have already been mentioned as having man-bird shapes. The bird, Zāghsār – similar to the crow – perhaps goes back to Indian legends. It can speak, and some texts say that it was brought from India as a present for the Caliph (65). In illustrated manuscripts this Zāgh is represented with a human head (66).

Murgh-i-ādami are two peacock-like birds, which are endowed with the gift of human speech and whose faces are similar to those of men. They sit on trees and speak to one another. People who listen to them hear important things which they had not known (67). The appearance of man-birds in pairs and their informative speech point to a type widespread in Indian tales (68). This type entered later European lore by way of the ancient Alexander literature, in the Pseudo-Callisthenes.

'We journeyed sixty-five days on this road and came to a place called Obarcia. And on the seventh day we saw two birds, very strong in body, with faces like those of men. And immediately one of them spoke in the Greek tongue: "Alexander, you enter the land of the Gods" and it spoke again in the same tongue to me: "Alexander, let your victory over Darius and your subjection of King Poros be enough for you." And when we had heard these voices, we turned away from the land of the Obarcenes and set out for home.' (69) It is by way of such travellers' tales, tricked out with much imagination but also with traditions adopted from foreign countries, that many monster-figures have passed, especially, into medieval literature and art. We shall speak about them presently.

Siren. By C. Corvinus. Frankfurt, 1579

In India an independent man-bird figure appears, the Kinnara. The Kinnari are demigods, who together with the Gandharvas, Apsaras, and others, are regarded as attendants of the gods and especially as divine musicians. They are very widespread in visual art, and are found often, from Bhārhut onwards, in India itself, in Burmese, Thai (Plate 75) and Cambodian art, and also on Java and in Turkestan and as far away as China. In Malayan folklore there is the Malimana, a bird with human head; it is depicted on ancient Javanese vessels (70) and probably is connected with the Kinnari.

In later European art sirens in man-bird shape are to be found as stands on liturgical wash-basins, on the town-crest of Nuremberg, in the work of Hans Thoma and Marc Chagall, as well as in the art of caricature, to mention only a few instances. The so-called 'Lichtelweibel', winged women with bird-bodies and tails, such as the well-known sculptures by Peter Vischer, on the four corner pillars of the Sebaldus tomb in Nuremberg, also belong in this category (71).

If the bird-bodied siren is rooted in classical mythology, the fish-bodied and the rarer snake-bodied forms are a product of local folklore. In Germany they are known under many names and are usually held to be very beautiful. A particular feature is the full breasts, which, it is said, mothers can throw over their shoulders and thus suckle the children they carry on their backs. They are mostly shown naked and festooned with

The 'Siren of Ravenna'. Paris, 1573

moss and reeds (72). In many medieval representations these fish-shaped sirens have two tails (73). Sometimes they also have a male head (74). A clue about their sex is found in the description of the Undines, who played a part in occult science: 'Remember', said the Count von Gabalis, 'that the sea and the rivers as well as the air are peopled by elemental spirits. The ancients called these water-people Undines and nymphs. Male creatures are not numerous among them. The females exist in greater number; their beauty is uncommon and the daughters of men cannot compare with them.' (75)

From more recent times we have the numerous versions of the Melusina story, the Lorelei of the Rhine and Heine's poem, and Andersen's beautiful tale of the little mermaid – subjects which have been illustrated time and again. Many water-nymphs people fairy-tales and legends; indeed, fish-men go back as far as ancient Mesopotamia, where they appear as Abgal or Apkallu. They are the subjects of Enki, according to Akkadian tradition seven in number, but only some of them are monsters, including the fish-man. Very probably, the Oannes mentioned in Assyrian texts (the Hellenized form of the name Berossos) is also a descendant of this Abgal. But even in representations of the fish-man Oannes, it is not the animal shape that is characteristic but the upright human posture, the human head and the human feet (76).

Of all the many representations of fish-bodied monsters we mention only the paintings from Pjandjikent, south of Samarkand (77), which must be seen in association with the Gandhāra style. In the zoological section of his *Nuzhatū-I-Qulūb* (78), Hamdullah Al-Mustaufī Al-Qazwīnī mentions Insan, the water-man, who is similar to the land-man in all respects except that he has a tail and is less tall. In the story of Abdullah the fisherman and Abdullah the water-man from the *Arabian Nights* the hero himself is a denizen of the sea, though nothing further is said of his shape except that he is an Adamite, who obeys Allah's commandment and shows brotherly love to all God's creatures. He emphatically refuses to be referred to as a genie.

We now turn to another man-animal, which has both Near Eastern and Egyptian prototypes and has gone through a later development in Europe: the Nāga. Furthermore, he was one of the most important monsters in India, rooted deeply in its folklore, and it is in all probability from here that he spread to almost all the countries of South-East Asia. In Indian art the Nāga is depicted as an animal, in the shape of a snake, sometimes with several heads; as a snake-man (Plate 81); or in purely human form, except that out of his shoulders, from behind his human head, one or more snakes' heads sprout; and finally in completely human form, accompanied by a snake.

Frankfort has noted a similar interchangeability between various forms of bird-men on Mesopotamian seals, and also for the snake-men of the Akkad period (79).

The Indian Nāgas – there are male and female forms (Nāgis) and the ruler in the Nāga kingdom, the Nāgarāja – are distinguished in literature from human beings, but in

74 Bestiary on enamelled casket. Early thirteenth century. British Museum, London

75 Kinnara, in the Wat Phra Keo Temple, Bangkok. Thailand, early nineteenth century

76 Fish-Goddess. Near Eastern, eighteenth or seventeenth century B.C.
British Museum, London

79 Nereids and Tritons on ornamental daggers. Italian, early seventeenth century. Bayrisches Nationalmuseum, Munich

80 Two-tailed Melusina. Mounting on a rock-crystal bottle. Workshop of Annibale Fontana, Milan, sixteenth century, Grünes Gewölbe, Dresden

78 The Fall of Man. Painting by Hugo van der Goes, about 1470. Kunsthistorisches Museum, Vienna

77 Frolic in the Waves. Painting by Arnold Böcklin, 1883. Neue Pinakothek, Munich

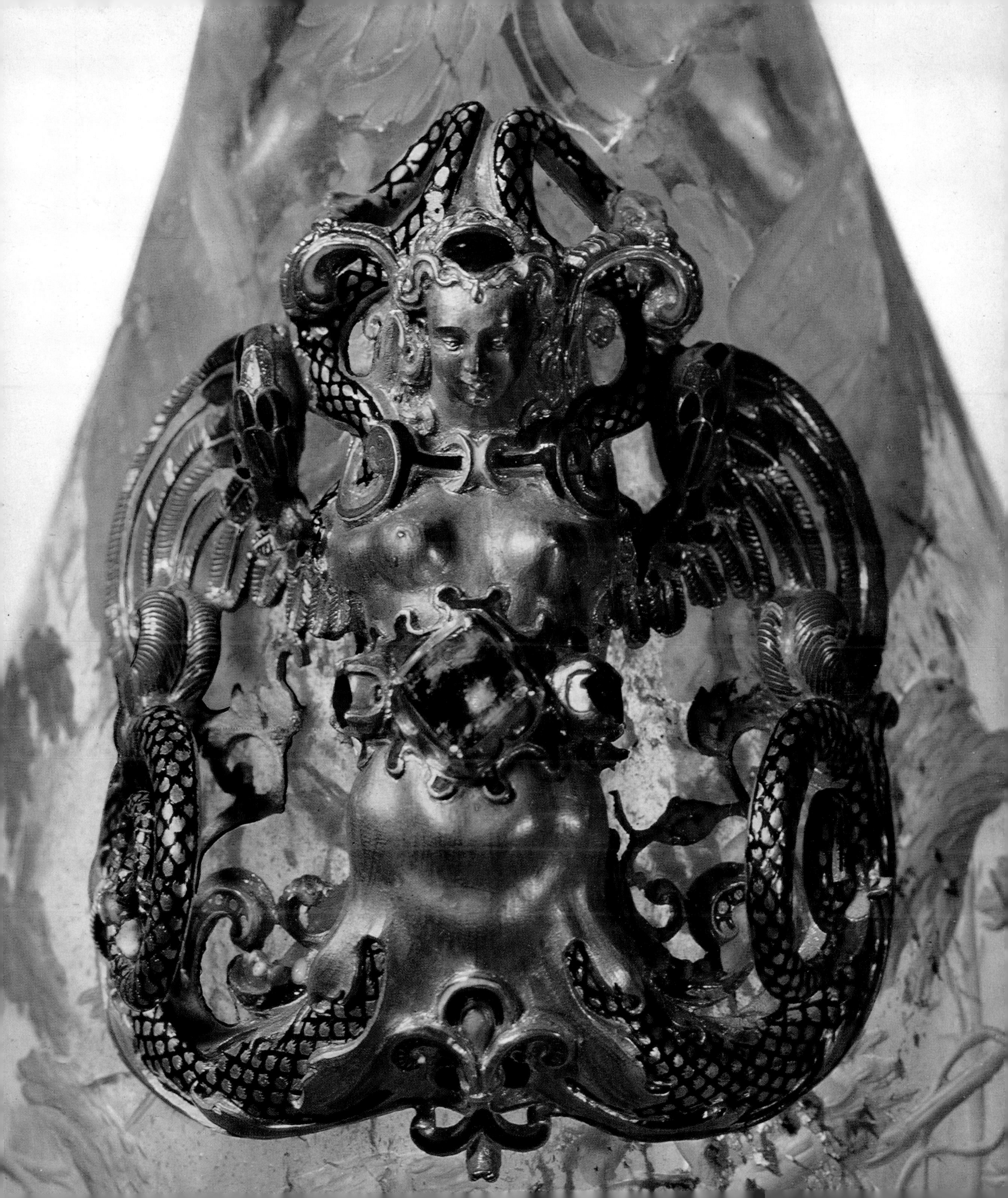

social respects are described as very similar. Repeated attempts have therefore been made to connect them with some aboriginal inhabitants. These aborigines are said to have worshipped the snake as a totem animal, to have received the name of the snake as a tribal designation, but later to have been identified with the animals and so to have entered Indian mythology as snake-like creatures. It is particularly in Buddhist legend and in the Jataka, the rebirth stories, that the Nāgas play an important part. They bring the Buddha gifts, lend him their protection and adopt his teaching, and therefore on Buddhist architectural monuments they often serve as guardians warding off evil like the *lamassu* at the gates of Assyrian palaces. This is exactly the function of the often abstruse, fabulous creatures on the portals and façades of Romanesque churches and Gothic cathedrals.

81 Nāga pair. Stone relief from Gondwana. Indian Museum, Calcutta

In the Vishnu legend, too, the snake plays a significant role. The god Vishnu rests upon the World-Snake in the Ocean, a creature of massive proportions, usually pictured with many heads. As the god Krishna he combats and defeats the many-headed serpent Kāliya, but then releases him in answer to the entreaties of the lovely snake-women, usually depicted as human with a female bust and a snake torso. This is the type of snake-monster which is most frequently met in Indian art. Examples of consummate artistry may be seen on the great rock relief of Mahābalipuram.

The Burmese chronicle of the town Tagaung tells of a Queen Hlasandi, who consorted with a Nāga and was later executed. When her womb was cut open, an embryo consisting of a human upper half and the lower half a snake was found in it (80). In Burma, too, snake cults are of great significance, reaching back to pre-Buddhist times. The same is true of most other South-East Asian countries, where snakes, Nāgas, appear as followers of the demon Rāvana in scenes from the picture-cycle of the Rāmāyana; one of them is the snake-bodied demon Taksaka. Somā, a princess from Campa (Vietnam), is referred to as Nāgini and seems to have been depicted as a snake-monster (81).

Siren. Arabic

Male snake-bodied monsters can be seen on a Chinese relief from Shantung. For instance the figure of the mythical emperor, Fu-hsi, who is said to have reigned from 2852–2738 B.C., and to have taught men to fish and domesticate the six animals. He is also credited with the introduction of family names and of writing. He is described and depicted as snake-bodied, sometimes with the head of an ox instead of that of a man. His sister, Nu-kwa, is similarly shaped and, like her brother, appears on the relief from the earlier Han period (82).

Snake-monsters seem to have been represented also in the New World. The Mexican god Quetzalcoatl, the green-feathered snake, a god of the air, is perhaps shown as a monster, though the parallel shaping of human and animal features points to an attributive kind of characterization, a kind of mask. While man-snakes occur mainly in Asia, some ancient Near Eastern, Egyptian and Greek notions are important enough to be mentioned here. In Egypt the goddess Uto, called by the Greeks Buto, after her

Kinnara. Thailand, modern

Lilith. Woodcut.
Augsburg, 1470

town, was worshipped in the shape of a Uraeus snake. Sometimes she had wings, was crowned and at times bore the features of a woman. As guardian of the young Horus, she approximates to the goddess Isis, who on occasions, in her form of Isis Thermuthis, merged with the snake-shaped harvest goddess of that name and was also depicted as having the body of a snake. These images, however, may have been influenced by Greek models (83).

Meresger (sometimes read as Merit-seger), goddess of the Theban necropolis (84), was also represented as a human-headed snake, sometimes with three heads – of a man, a snake and a vulture (85). As far back as the Akkad seals in Mesopotamia we come across a creature formed half as a man, half as a snake, which in one case is characterized as divine by the signs 'God and Snake' (86). Here we may recall the famous description, in Genesis 3, of the temptation in Paradise, which hints at the involvement of the serpent in the earliest human history and thus at its significance. The Old Testament does not expressly refer to the snake as a composite creature, but as endowed with human speech, a feature which, translated into visual terms, could clearly lead to the man-snake type. Lilith, in all probability a Babylonian storm-demon originally, became 'Adam's first wife' in later Jewish tradition and in Goethe's *Walpurgisnacht*. She, too, has the shape of a snake with the head of a woman. The serpent of Paradise, in her role as deceiver, has been portrayed innumerable times in modern art with a human head or with a female bust and the lower body of a snake.

Cecrops, the first king of Attica, is represented as a snake from the waist downwards, just like Erechtheus, another autochthonous king. Both were probably pre-Attic divinities and their snake-form points to their origin as earth-gods. Chrysaor, like Pegasus an offspring of the Gorgon Medusa, begot the hideous monster Echidna: 'And she (Chrysaor's mate, Callirrhoe) bore yet another birth, huge, monstrous, no wise like to mortal men or to the deathless gods, within a hollow cave, even the divine

Echidna stubborn-hearted: half a fair-cheeked nymph of glancing eyes, and half a monstrous serpent, terrible and great, spotted, ravenous beneath the coverts of the holy earth,' as Hesiod tells us (87). She in her turn is the mother of the many-headed dog, Orthus, of Cerberus, of the Lernaean Hydra, of Chimaera and also of the Sphinx, here termed Phix, all creatures of the monster-type. Finally Hecate must be mentioned, reigning over the kingdom of the black arts and herself of monstrous shape, described among other things as a giantess with snake-locks and feet. On the Pergamon Altar we find snake-legged giants fighting the gods (Plates 72 and 73). Late antique works show us Glycon, a Gnostic-Mithraic demon, with a human head and a snake-body (88). The later European tradition of these snake-monsters has already been mentioned in connection with our discussion of the Melusina figure, where it was emphasized how deeply rooted such notions became in the popular imagination.

Finally, a comparatively rare type may be referred to, the so-called scorpion-man, only traceable in Mesopotamia and adjacent regions. Named in Sumerian and Akkadian texts as Girtablulu, the scorpion-men were said to have been created by Tiamat and to be of gigantic proportions. They guard both sides of the great gate at the entrance of the mythical mountain range of Mashu. They were portrayed as far back as early dynastic times, with scorpion-bodies, human arms and head, sometimes also with legs. The scorpion's sting was attached to many other creatures, above all in Assyrian art, where it is found on human-faced, winged and bird-footed demons.

Mermaid. Illustration by
W. Heath Robinson to Andersen,
Little Mermaid

Dragons, Griffins and Other Winged Animals

WE now enter the dense jungle of creatures whose components are taken from two or more species of animal, but which have retained a pure animal character without any suggestion of human traits. The real grotesques are reserved for a final chapter; even so the monsters in the present chapter are so manifold that classification is almost impossible, unless we keep to the few names, which themselves unfortunately do not always convey precise concepts of form. There is hardly one dragon like any other. Griffins were originally lions, with or without wings, with bird's heads; but lion-headed winged creatures with lion-bodies are called lion-griffins, if they have at least two bird's feet. However, even this last name has never been consistently applied. Winged animals, winged lions and winged horses are relatively clear, if not very old terms. But there is also a large number of creatures with fish and bird-bodies, only a few of which can find room within this book.

In Jakob Grimm's *Deutsche Mythologie* (German Mythology) there is a simple definition: 'The snake creeps or coils itself on the ground, but when it has wings, it is called a dragon.' Other authors, for instance C. Elliot Smith (89), tell us that the dragon is a snake or crocodile, covered with fish-scales, its legs and wings and sometimes its head are those of an eagle, falcon or hawk, and that it has the forefeet, and sometimes the head, of a lion. The Chinese dragon is described quite differently (90) as having the ears of an ox, the feet of a tiger, the claws of an eagle, the horns of a deer, the head of a camel, the eyes of a devil, the neck of a snake, the body of a cock and the scales of a carp. Such descriptions could be continued at length and they even vary within one country. Thus a Chinese dragon may have rabbit's eyes, a frog's underbelly and a cow's ears, and can hear through its horns (91).

Here, the term 'dragon' will be used simply as the collective name for a mainly popular notion derived from tales which usually deal with the struggle of a god or hero against a monster. The most frequent type may be a snake, but there are also others. The Greek hero Perseus, in order to free Andromeda, fought against a sea-monster described as a dragon, whose shape, however, is not clearly defined. The components taken from birds and beasts of prey are sometimes characteristic but by no means universal.

The word 'dragon' comes from Greek *drakon* (via Latin *draco*) and means snake. Simple etymological derivation, however, will not suffice to explain a monster. Nor can we find this word in the descriptions of Mesopotamian, Egyptian, Indian or Chinese monsters, since it did not exist in pre-Hellenic times. The term 'dragon' (or 'wyvern') turns up so often in our literature on the subject, because translators use the word freely – neither in its original meaning nor in its later, originally Christian-European, pictorial application, but as a general term which means roughly 'monster' or 'fabulous creature'.

The Babylonian Mushussu, translated as 'fire-red dragon' and, according to the written sources created by Tiāmat, is a snake, but appears in illustrations as a monster

Dragon-initial. By the Master E.S.

with a snake's head (Plate 82). On the head there are horns, the body is scaly, the forefeet are those of a lion, the hind legs those of an eagle, and the long tail terminates in a scorpion's sting. Originally an animal of Enlil, in Babylonian times it becomes an animal of Marduk. The same monster, with wings added, became the animal of the god Ningizzida in late Sumerian times, but the exact name of this form has not come down to us (92). In the opinion of many experts, Tiāmat himself, whose shape is not described in written sources, is to be recognized in one of the dragon-like monsters which are illustrated as being defeated by a god.

On the basis of yet other texts, and of illustrations believed to refer to them, the Lahamu, the water-demons belonging to Enki, are assumed to be a further snake-dragon type (93). They are snakes with two short forelegs and a horned snake's head. According to another text they can also be partially fish-shaped. Thus these few ancient Mesopotamian examples already exhibit some of the basic components of later dragons. Snake, lion, eagle and scorpion contribute the shapes, and some unidentified animal the horns.

Unger records as a further type the lion-dragon, an animal of Assur and Adad: a lion with a horned lion's head, lion's forelegs, eagle's hind legs, scorpion's tail, and wings. The animal of Ninlil is similar except that instead of horns it has pointed ears, and a bird's tail instead of a scorpion's. The remarkable thing about all the Mesopotamian monsters so far considered is the complete absence of components which might have served as models for our dragons, such as parts from giant lizards or crocodiles. On the other hand, however, the monsters which appear as dragons in translations are not limited to the category of animal-animal compounds. We have already quoted the example of the Lahamu demon-figures, but multiple-headed monsters certainly also played a part. Tiāmat, for example, might also have been represented as a seven-headed hydra, just like the snake-demon Illuyanka from Asia Minor.

In Egypt we find the giant serpent Apophis, which was fought by Osiris and which has been considered a dragon, mainly on the basis of the mythological implications of such struggles waged by the gods. Though worship of the crocodile was widespread in Egypt, and there were also divinities with crocodile heads, there was no development of a crocodilian dragon type. On the other hand the Leviathan of the Old Testament is described as a serpent and dragon of the sea (94), and in the Book of Job (41.5–25) we read a very long but very imprecise description of such a mythical monster. The body of the Leviathan is thus described:

Who can open the doors of his
face? his teeth are terrible round
about.
His scales are his pride, shut
up together as with a close seal.
One is so near to another, that
no air can come between them.
They are joined one to another,
they stick together, that they cannot be sundered.
By his sneezings a light doth
shine, and his eyes are like the eye-
lids of the morning.
Out of his mouth go burning
lamps, and sparks of fire leap out.
Out of his nostrils goeth smoke,
as out of a seething pot or cauldron.
His breath kindleth coals, and
a flame goeth out of his mouth.
In his neck remaineth strength,
and sorrow is turned into joy before him.
The flakes of his flesh are joined
together: they are firm in themselves; they cannot be moved.
His heart is as firm as a stone;
yea, as hard as a piece of the nether
millstone.
When he raiseth up himself,
the mighty are afraid; by reason of
breakings they purify themselves.
The sword of him that layeth
at him cannot hold: the spear, the
dart, nor the habergeon.
He esteemeth iron as straw,
and brass as rotten wood.
The arrow cannot make him
flee: slingstones are turned with
him into stubble.
Darts are counted as stubble:
he laugheth at the shaking of a
spear.
Sharp stones are under him:
he spreadeth sharp pointed things
upon the mire.
He maketh the deep to boil
like a pot: he maketh the sea like a
pot of ointment.
He maketh a path to shine after
him; one would think the deep to
be hoary.
Upon earth there is not his
like, who is made without fear.
He beholdeth all high things:
he is a king over all the children of
pride.

Griffin. West portal of San Michele in Lucca, thirteenth century

Griffin. India, first century B.C.

Griffin. Egypt, XVII dynasty

It is in the Greek version of this text that the word *drakon* occurs and if there is any authority on which we may base our conception of the dragon this is it. Unfortunately, the description is very imprecise.
It certainly makes no mention of human features or of several heads. These, however, are mentioned in Psalm 74:13, where it is said that God crushed the heads of the dragons in the waters. But the interpretation of this passage is not so clear as is maintained by those scholars who try to connect the biblical Leviathan with the mythical seven-headed snake of Syrian texts (95).
Greek notions of the dragon are different again. Ladon, who guards the apples of the Hesperides, is described as a dangerous snake who watches over the apples deep within the dark earth and at its furthermost edge (96). Python, too, the dragon of Delphi, overcome by the god Apollo, was originally a snake. But there are also creatures which must be taken to be demons but which nevertheless are peculiar animal-compounds similar to the biblical dragon. One of them is Typhon, the child of Earth, who fought against the gods and was only conquered by Zeus himself.
'His hands are busy with the works of strength, and unwearied are the mighty God's feet: and from his shoulders grew a hundred serpent heads, heads of a dread dragon that licked with dusky tongues, and from the eyes of his wondrous heads fire flashed beneath his brows, and from all his heads fire burned as he glared. And in all his terrible heads were voices that uttered all manner of cries unspeakable. Sometimes they uttered such sounds as the gods might understand: anon the roar of a bellowing bull, proud and untamable of spirit: sometimes, again, the roaring of a lion of dauntless heart: sometimes noises as of whelps, wondrous to hear: and anon he would hiss, and the high hills echoed to the sound.' (97)
Here we not only have the multiple-headed creature, but all the allusions to animals exemplified by the various voices lent themselves readily to visual representation; indeed, the general conception has an entirely oriental character (98). In a Sumerian hymn (99) a god, Ninurta, is described as 'a dragon with the forefeet of a lion and the hind feet of an eagle'. Here, too, the basically human shape is, as it were, revoked by the description.
This limited selection of dragons and related shapes from antiquity makes it obvious that there is no clearly defined dragon-type. All attempts to discover such a thing are doomed to failure just because the most varied notions and the most divergent names merged to produce a general idea characterized by variety, not uniformity.
No less manifold are the types of dragon that appeared outside the Near East, Greece, and Europe. We leave aside the Iranian myths, which tell at length of a dragon fight in primeval times, the monster being described as having three maws, three heads and six eyes and as capable of a thousand tricks (100). But the dragon country *par excellence* is in the Far East. A standard description of the Chinese dragon was given earlier in this chapter. The dragon-horse Lung is said to have emerged from the

82 The Dragon Mušhuššu.
Relief from the Ishtar Gate in Babylon. About 580 B.C.
Staatliche Museen, Berlin

83 Griffin, on a seal of the Cretan-Mycenean period

84 Dragon on the west portal of Notre-Dame, Paris. Thirteenth century

86 Liturgical basin in the form of a griffin. From Lorraine, twelfth century. Victoria and Albert Museum, London

85 Dragons on the tympanum of the Convent Church at Hamersleben. Twelfth century

depths at the beginning of time, together with the first emperor Fu-hsi, whose snake-shape has already been referred to. It is asserted by older Chinese authors that dragons can, at will, make themselves the size of a silkworm, or puff themselves up to such an extent that they fill up all the space of heaven and earth, and moreover that they can change their shape and make themselves invisible.

An emperor of the Northern Sung dynasty once undertook the task of classifying the dragons, declaring them to be dragon-spirits and raising them to the rank of kings. There were the blue dragon-spirits, mild rulers; the red ones, kings who bless the waters; the yellow ones, kings who listen benignly to all requests; the white ones, virtuous and pure kings; the black ones, kings living in the watery depths. The various colourings obviously form the basis of the classification, but significant for the type is the name itself, Kiu-lung, or hornless dragon. Other attempts at classification have resulted in four groups: the heaven-dragon; the spirit-dragon, which sends wind and rain; the earth-dragon, which causes the flow of the rivers but cannot fly; and the dragon of buried treasure, who guards the riches in the depths of the earth and protects them from men (101).

Anyone who supposes that criticism of such monsters of the imagination was only possible in what we call the West should read a few sentences on this subject from a Chinese disquisition written by an author of the Han period: 'It is either characteristic of the dragon that it lives in the clouds, gives birth to its young there and never comes down to earth; or it rises up and sinks down, and then it brings its young into the world down here and when these grow up, they rise up to the clouds. To say that the dragon ascends into the air, implies that it is a spirit; if it were not a spirit, it could not reach the clouds, since it is characteristic of spirits that they ascend so high. But man is nobler than the dragon; how then does it come about that the nobler creature cannot ascend so high, while the baser and lesser can? ... Moreover, the dragon possesses an outward appearance and hence moves in a visible manner; if it moves thus, it can also eat; but a being which has an outward appearance, moves visibly and eats, cannot be termed a spirit. Further, is it not commonly said that the dragon is king of the three hundred species of animal? As king of the animal world it must also have a body, since what is a king without a body?' (102)

Griffin. Greek vase from Rhodes

Griffin. Carpet from Pazyryk

Sometimes the Ch'i-lin, actually the unicorn, is described in literature as a dragon, no doubt because of the scales covering its whole body. We shall return to this monster in the chapter on the unicorn. Under Chinese influence dragons, which appear in Chinese art of all periods, have entered the literature and art of neighbouring peoples. Thus, for instance, the Vietnamese have their Long-mã, the horse-dragon, which however, unlike Chinese illustrations, is represented with a horn (103). But there are considerable differences in other respects. Thus the Vietnamese believed that dragon and fish had a common origin but different destinies (104). The fish must dwell in the water but the dragon can ascend into the air. This points to the Vietnamese dragon's fish-character, which is quite foreign to the mainly snake-bodied Chinese dragon.

In Islamic culture we encounter the dragon Thu'bān, called by the Arabs *tinnīn*, by the Turks *lu* and by the Mongols *Moghur*. He is described as very large, terrifying, with many teeth and flaming eyes, and was at first a snake but in the course of time developed into a dragon (105). Here we find a parallel, not to the seven-headed Syrian monster, but to the description given in the Book of Job, quite apart from any etymological relationship of the Tun or Tannīn of the Old Testament with Arabic Tinnīn.

In European art we have not only many representations of the Christian dragon-slayers George and Michael, but dragons are also found from an early date, as single figures or in groups, on the portals or capitals of architectural monuments (Plates 84 and 85). The multiple-headed dragon, too, reminiscent of Mesopotamian and classical hydra-forms, appears as the apocalyptic monster (Plate 88): 'And there appeared another wonder in heaven; and behold a great red dragon, having seven heads and ten horns, and seven crowns upon his heads. And his tail drew the third part of the stars of heaven and did cast them to the earth.' (106) In secular art there are illustrations from classical mythology, and the dragons of earliest Nordic lore and of the Germanic heroic sagas, the Midgard snake and Fafner, are frequently reproduced.

All the shapes which we have met in the ancient Near East are there: the winged snake, the two-legged snake with horned cat's head, sometimes with a crocodile's jaws as well, dragons in lizard-shape, four-legged monsters with a snake's body, others like a crocodile or with a fantastic head – here oriental models are hardly recognizable – and finally, four-legged animals with the body of a beast of prey, sometimes a long snake-like tail, wings and a horned head. Some, such as those in the work of Hans Thoma, may have been directly inspired by oriental monuments. Decades ago large sections of a processional way in Babylon were reconstructed in original size in the Berlin Pergamon Museum and so one of the most important illustrations of dragons of the ancient Orient can now be seen every day by thousands in the heart of Europe.

Lion-headed griffin. Assyrian

Brief mention may be made of a smaller type of dragon, known as the 'asp' which played a modest part in the medieval bestiary. It was represented in a number of dif-

Four-headed dragon. Russian woodcut

ferent ways: sometimes it has a lion's, or even a human face, and more than two pairs of legs. It was said to be so sensitive to music that, in order to avoid its charms, it pressed one ear against the ground and plugged the other with the end of its tail (107).

In classical tradition the griffin is a combination of bird and lion. Unlike the dragon, its shape has been faithfully preserved in Mesopotamian-Egyptian, classical, and later European pictorial tradition. Its earliest visual form was previously traced back to Egypt, but a few Near Eastern illustrations, especially a seal-impression from Byblos, have proved to be even earlier, though measured by the number of illustrations, griffins were most popular in Egypt and later in the Minoan-Mycenaean empires and in Syria (108).

Unlike the Byblos griffin and early Egyptian representations on cosmetic palettes, the oldest illustration from Susa (Elam) shows a griffin with the forelegs of an eagle. In Egypt they were shown at first with or sometimes without wings, as for example in Beni Hassan; others were shown crowned, as in the New Empire, or with ringlets hanging down their necks – presumably under the influence of Syrian illustrations. A gradual experimentation can often be seen in the oldest representations, for example in the way the wings are sometimes attached horizontally and parallel to the body. Later representations are consistent and always clearly recognizable, especially on seals and ivories in Syrian art of the second and first millennia B.C.

Greek representations of griffins tend to have a head similar to that of a beast of prey and thus approximate to dragon forms, and the same is true of older Italic representations, but in later Roman art the traditional griffins reassert themselves. Scythian griffins, or rather what are so described in Scythian art, sometimes exhibit completely new features, such as fin-like wings, or a neck covered with strange spikes, perhaps deriving from the ringlets of older forms. In Byzantine art, and especially on textile materials, the griffin is still included in scenes of fights with animals, while in the Christian art of the Middle Ages it becomes more and more a decorative element, probably a borrowing from Roman illustrations of this type. The griffin-flight of Alexander, a scene derived from the Alexander romance, may be mentioned as an important narrative motif. The text, however, does not speak clearly of a griffin, but tells of birds which Alexander trained for a flight to heaven (Plate 91). It needs hardly to be added that nowadays, when we speak of a gryphon or griffin, we think of it as having the shape of a normal bird.

Perhaps under the influence of certain types of dragon or even inspired by oriental images, the griffin later suddenly has once again the forelegs of a bird, which it had had on the Susa representation of about 3000 B.C. An engraving by Martin Schongauer may be quoted as an example. This type, mostly shown rampant, became more and more popular as a heraldic symbol on crests and flags and has continued in this function right up to the present day. It may be recalled that in many popular festivals in southern Europe, but especially in the Basle carnival, the bird-griffin is still very prominent in masked parades. Thus the griffin and the sphinx, both of them essentially Egyptian forms, have been among the most enduring types of monster in the history of art.

In a lengthy essay on the griffin in oriental art (109), H. Prinz has drawn up a terminology, according to which he distinguished the following types: the bird-griffin, a combination of a lion's body and a bird's head, with or without wings; the snake-griffin with a lion's body often covered with scales, with a snake's head, a lion's forefeet, and a bird's hind legs, with or without wings, and often with a scorpion's tail; and the lion-griffin, a combination of a lion's body, often scaly, a lion's head, a lion's forefeet, a bird's hind feet and a bird's tail, with or without wings. Here we have a complete muddle – the snake-dragon and the bird-griffin have been merged into one group, and a creature which some hold to be a dragon and others a griffin has been

Griffin. Egyptian cosmetic palette. Ashmolean Museum, Oxford, early 3rd millennium B.C.

Griffin. Seal-impression from Susa, early 3rd millennium B.C.

Griffin. Scythian

named a lion-griffin, in spite of the fact that it had already been interpreted as a lion-dragon. We have already made clear our opinion on this subject. If confusion reigns, and this is inevitable with this particular subject, at least the few monster-types which can be defined with some accuracy ought not to be dragged into it. This applies especially to the bird-griffin, which we designated simply as a griffin. For the same reason, i.e. to preserve the definition of the genuine griffin, we would describe Prinz's other two types as dragons, especially if we recall the oriental snake-dragon and realize that the lion variant agrees with it in most details apart from the head.

We can now summarize everything concerning the so-called lion-griffin, more accurately called a dragon. It is not found in Egyptian art but can be clearly made out on an Akkad seal. In Assyrian art it is more prominent than the snake-dragon and then becomes the sole dragon-monster in Achaemenid art. On its way eastwards it reaches the art of the steppe-civilizations, where it has been found, for example, in Pazyryk, though without the characteristic hind legs of a bird. It is illustrated on a Sassanid silk material from Taq-i-Bustan in a halved form, that is with only two forefeet and a kind of bird-body. The bird-body variant, as well as the genuine bird-griffin variant, seems to have reached Europe on textiles and to have influenced Islamic art at the same time. Here this halved lion-dragon appears as the famous Persian Simurgh, to which is attached a fish-body with fin-tail (110), as a constellation.

In later European art this type of dragon was simply added to the many forms already mentioned, and only the bird-griffin, that is the griffin proper, has survived as an independent type. We shall now turn to some monsters which are first found in the Middle Ages and which are derived more from literary than from visual sources. The type just mentioned and characterized by us as a halved lion-griffin can perhaps be explained in this way and may have given rise to illustrations of the Roc-bird and also to the shape of the basilisk.

Arising from a mixture of bird and snake, the image of the basilisk (or cockatrice) changes and is only rarely found with the head of a lion (111). It usually has a cock's head with a crown, cock's feet (up to eight) and a snake's tail, and is reputed to kill with its look. In the *Wunderbarliche Geheimnisse* (Wondrous Secrets) by Jakob Horst the basilisk is 'a poisonous beast, one and a half feet tall, with three points on its forehead, triangular, crowned as it were with a royal crown, straight of body, quite

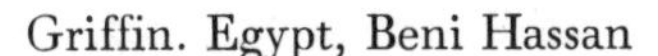

Griffin. Egypt, Beni Hassan

Griffin. Mycenae

Griffin. Megiddo, 2nd millennium B.C.

hideous and with glowing eyes, with which it poisons and kills all life. In Saxony there was once a savage type of basilisk, with a pointed head, yellow in colour, three feet long, very fat, with a speckled belly with many white spots, with a blue back, a bent tail, and a large maw compared with the proportions of its body.' (112)

The basilisk is often illustrated but seems to have been a later creation, based only partly on older dragon or griffin forms, and mainly on its literary reputation as 'regulus' (little king), that is, king of snakes. Possibly, as has already been suggested, it has also been influenced by the marvellous birds of the Orient, the Roc and the Simurgh (113).

Simplified dragon and griffin forms are seen in winged animals, that is, those which are distinguished from real animals solely by the addition of wings. The most famous of them is Pegasus, frequently hymned and illustrated as a winged horse and as an allegory of inspired poetry. This idea was, however, a late development; in the Greek myth Pegasus is the horse which Bellerophon rides when he attacks the Chimaera.

Many winged animals are found already in Syrian-Palestinian, Assyrian and Hittite art; most of them are lions and bulls, stags and bucks, while the horse is rare. The winged lion is perhaps the oldest and is attested in early dynastic and Akkadian times; in Mesopotamia it was depicted frequently at the time when the griffin, which differs from it only by its bird's head, was popular in Egypt. The winged horse eventually became more frequent than the other forms about the middle of the second millennium B.C., when the horse attained greater significance, especially in warfare as the drawer of the chariot, but also as a mount. In folk-literature, especially in fairy-tales, winged horses, or flying horses not always described as having wings, were to displace even the birds as the aerial vehicles *par excellence* (114). An example of this is the magic ebony horse in a story from the *Arabian Nights*.

Another is the silver horse of the Archangel Gabriel, on which Mohammed rode from Mecca to Jerusalem, then through the Seven Heavens, and back to Mecca. The journey was accomplished so swiftly that, on his return, he still had time to catch up a water pitcher upset by his hasty departure and prevent it from falling over. The Gorgon Medusa, already mentioned, was perhaps originally imagined as a winged horse. In Indian myth the 'pakshirāja', upon which Vishnu rides, is a combination of bird (vulture) and man, and in Indian fairy-stories this becomes a winged horse, or a normal horse with supernatural powers (115).

Horse-griffin. Italian, seventeenth century

We have already mentioned that in the ancient Near East winged lions and winged bulls play a much more prominent role. Their importance has continued in Christian art, where they became attributes of two evangelists and have been portrayed countless times as the lion of St Mark and the bull of St Luke. These winged animals are also found not only in Achaemenid art (which also took over the lion-dragon, classified by H. Prinz as the lion-griffin), but earlier on also in Luristan and later in the post-Achaemenid monuments of India. The mixed Persian-Greek style produced winged

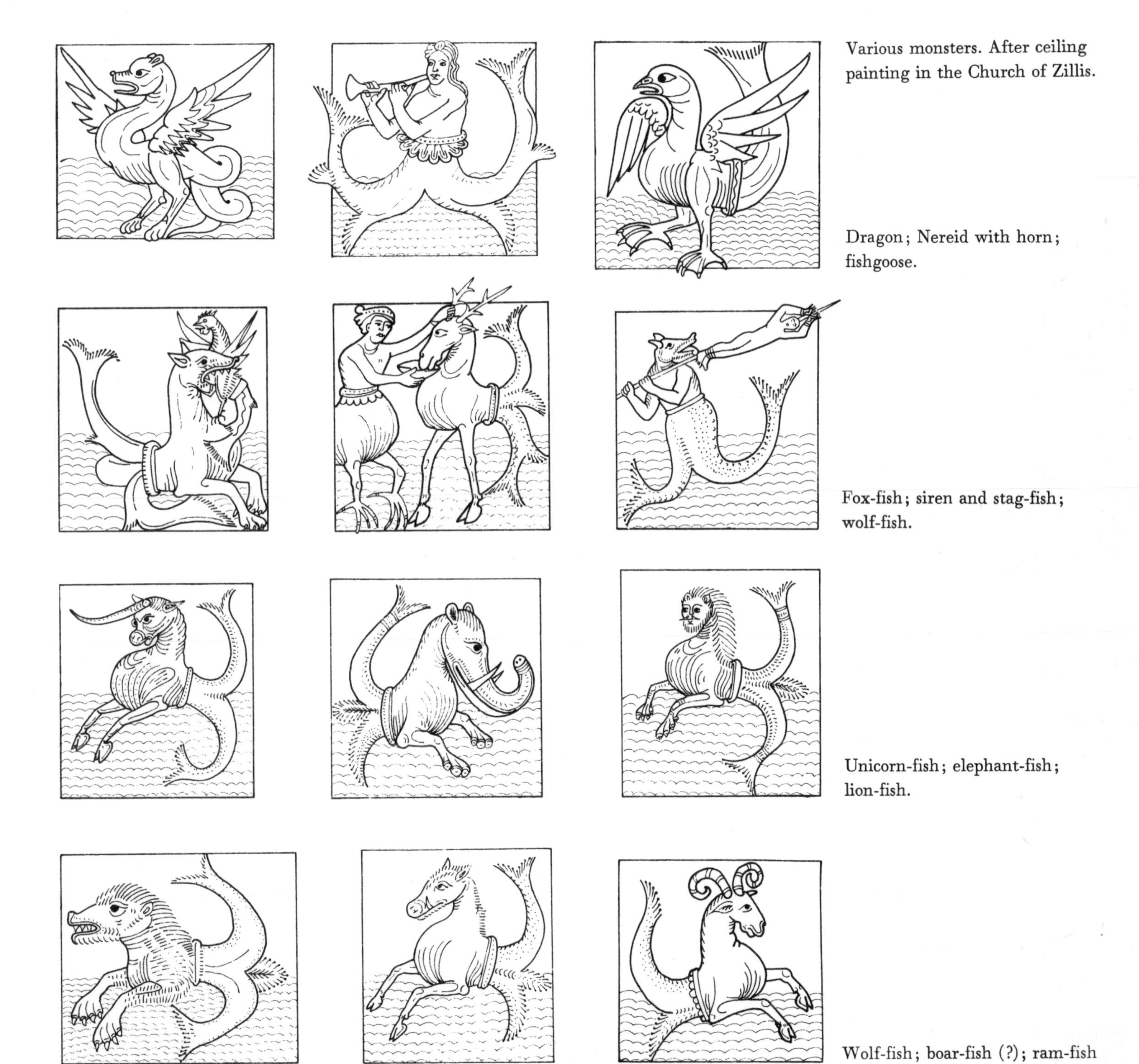

Various monsters. After ceiling painting in the Church of Zillis.

Dragon; Nereid with horn; fishgoose.

Fox-fish; siren and stag-fish; wolf-fish.

Unicorn-fish; elephant-fish; lion-fish.

Wolf-fish; boar-fish (?); ram-fish

animals, such as the famous winged goat in the Louvre, which are among the finest works of that epoch. On the wonderful gold vessels from Marlik the winged animals, like the later griffins, are shown rampant. Typologically these two forms are closely connected and are later often represented together in groups and in series, for example on Byzantine ivory horns.

Dragons and griffins also lead to the consideration of some fish- or snake-bodied monsters, which are variously described as sea-monsters, sea-centaurs, sea-horses, horse-dragons, and so on. They have a few antecedents in the Orient, but they are most common in Iranian-Hellenistic, Iranian-Indian and Scythian art, in fanciful decorative shapes, often as hippocamps with the front part of a horse.

The goat-fish, of early Mesopotamian origin and persisting right on into later European art, is a special form in this group. In Sumerian called 'Suhur-maš', roughly meaning 'carp-goat', it is the animal of the water-god, Enki. On Middle Babylonian Cassite boundary stones the goat-fish is an emblem of Nabu (116). It is shown with straight or outward-curving horns on a goat's head, with the front body of a goat and the rear body of a fish and a tail fin, sometimes also with wings. In this shape the goat-fish appears also as a sign of the zodiac, for example in Denderah, as Capricorn in medieval European art (117). It is not unlike the above-mentioned dragon with two forefeet, which differs mainly in its head and front legs. An eastern variant, with different animal components, is known as the Makara and combines, in its most important though by no means only form, the front part of a crocodile with the tail of a snake.

Basilisk. Nuremberg, 1510

Older perhaps are those variants which have the head and forelegs of an elephant. But nearly all are water-monsters, which occasionally develop into dragon-like four-footed creatures. This type spread from India to Kashmir, Nepal, Tibet, Indonesia and Indo-China (118). Here we cannot go into details but it should be pointed out that the Makara figures of South Asia can compete in number and in richness of imagination with the dragons and griffins of the western world. They are connected with the ancient god Varuna, but are in particular vehicles of the river-goddess Gangā, or sometimes simply decorative elements in architectural ornamentation.

In ancient Mesopotamia and Egypt there were also monster-forms which were of very great local significance, but which apparently failed to survive beyond a limited period. The lion-headed bird Imdugud was relatively seldom copied. According to Frankfort it was one of the symbols of the god Tammuz, who embodied the productive forces of nature. The lion-bird is, as it were, his warlike aspect, which spreads terror and death (119). It occurs as far back as pre-dynastic times, and even in the period preceding literary tradition. On seals it hovers above animals with outspread pinions or attacks them. It is the emblem of the god Ningirsu of Lagash. In Akkadian myth its powers are transferred to Ningirsu's defeated adversary Zu. In later tradition it becomes the storm-petrel. As has been said, this strange monster itself was short-lived, but we must remember that numerous compounds of beasts and birds of prey,

87 Dragon attacking a lion.
Engraving by Zoan Andrea.
Bibliothèque Nationale, Paris

89 Moses and Aaron exorcizing a Dragon. Persian manuscript illumination. Bibliothèque Nationale, Paris

88 Seven-headed Dragon from the Revelation of St John. From the Cranach Bible. Bibliothek, Zerbst

گفت قوله تعالی قلنا لا تخف انک انت الاعلی فرمان آمد که یا موسی مترس که دست تو بر
از دست ایشان باشد هر کجا حق آمد باطل روا نبود وجاء الحق وزهق الباطل ندا آمد که بیفکن آنچه

در دست داری موسی عصا بیفکند بر زمین فرو شد گرد میدان بر آمد اژدهایی عظیم گشت و دم حلقه کرد

92 Dragon, on a Chinese New Year card. Private collection

93 Foot of the snake-staircase to the pilgrimage temple at Wat Suthep Chienmai, Thailand

91 Alexander seated on two griffins. Mosaic from Otranto. Twelfth century

90 Griffin on an Iranian patera. Third or fourth century. Staatliche Museen, Preussischer Kulturbesitz, West Berlin

ALEXANDER REX

迎龍
靜肅
迴避
清河

94 Griffin and Symbols of the Evangelists. Illustration to Dante's Divine Comedy by Sandro Botticelli. Staatliche Museen, Berlin

that is many dragons and griffins, exhibit a very close correspondence at least in their basic parts, though not in their combinations.

Winged goat. Persian silver vase, fifth century B.C.

A remarkable compound is the so-called snake-necked lion, which is found, almost simultaneously, in the earliest periods of both Mesopotamia and Egypt. Strictly speaking it is only a mixture in so far as the lion's neck was so unnaturally extended that it resembles a snake's body, even in the way it coils, though the head at the end of it is again that of a lion. It is highly unlikely that this creature was quite independently and almost simultaneously invented in Mesopotamia and in Egypt. The Mesopotamian representations seem to be older and it is thus probable that the snake-necked lion spread from Mesopotamia to Egypt, where it appears together with other motifs of a similar provenance. On early Egyptian monuments there is also another snake-lion, whose neck is not so extended but which is clearly distinguished by a snake-head. Perhaps both shapes express the same ideas – ideas not unlike those expressed in the Mesopotamian snake-dragon already described.

Winged horse. Assyrian seal, 1st millennium B.C.

There are some snakes which have retained their shapes, but which have horns or wings. The horned snake is found on Akkadian, Elamite, Middle Babylonian and Assyrian monuments, whereas the winged snake seems only to be attested for the late Egyptian period. We find it again among the dragon-forms. According to the Theban mythology of Graeco-Roman times the god Amun was regarded as a snake-god and called Kematef. This notion seems to have been taken over by later Greek writers (120), who described him as the primeval snake-god, Kneph, and called him, in Greek, Agathos daimon, no doubt also conceived in the form of a winged snake.

A type of formation which we noticed in discussing the griffins was also employed in other monsters: the curtailing or halving of the complete animal. Such halved figures are found in the case of the Makara, for example, of the lion-dragon and also of the four-footed mixed type, which, when halved, appears as a kind of biped and is so called.

These bipeds can have a human face or a double face. Here we deal with those forms in which purely animal monsters are halved. They are found on early Anglo-Saxon coins (121) and in book-illuminations of the thirteenth and fourteenth centuries. Many such figures were created by the inventive Hieronymus Bosch; they are not to be confused with those animals which move like men. Often they are original creations of the imagination, owing nothing to tradition, as for example on the pews of Bamberg Cathedral.

Winged animal. Egypt

Whether a composite creature is represented is not always clear, even where the relevant texts contain references to demon-like formation. Here belong the Chinese lion-dogs, the hounds of Fo, which are mostly shown as strangely shaped lions but occasionally have wings, too, and even a single horn (122). Another example are the demonic locusts, mentioned earlier, from the Revelation of St John. Various passages from the copious mythology and fairy-tales of the African, Amerindian and Polynesian peoples provide such descriptions. Thus in the fairy-tales of the Cabyles mention is made of the Luachsh, wild animals clearly regarded as monsters (123). On Madagascar there is the Songomby, a kind of wild horse with monster-features, the one-legged Tokan-dia, and Kinoly, the demonic corpse (124). But since there are no illustrations of these creatures it is pointless to speculate about how they were visualized. We can only repeat what we said in the introduction: the ideas underlying the development of composite monsters were apparently present in the human mind, but before the rise of differentiated societies visual representation does not seem to have been attempted. In the popular lore of Europe, too, there were many notions of this kind. Mention may be made of the Icelandic Skoffin, which perhaps most resembles the basilisk. It is described as the cross-bred offspring of a tomcat and a vixen, and its look is said to be fatal (125).

Leaving aside numerous individual formations, there remain some groups within our present category which differ not in the way they are made up but in the species from which their components are selected. They are mostly found in the art of South-East Asia, where the tiger and the elephant, together with the snake, appear as the most prominent animals. Thus we have in India, as early as the Harappa period, the horned tiger, which clearly plays the same part here as the lion does in Mesopotamia and Egypt. We must, however, remember that later, when Near Eastern cultural forms spread into India in the Achaemenid and post-Persian era, the lion here succeeded the larger and stronger indigenous predator, the tiger, which had pervaded ancient Indian civilization, and from then on played a predominant part, particularly in Buddhist literature and art.

Imdugud. Silver vase of Entemena. Lagash, Mesopotamia, 3rd millennium B.C.

The elephant, unlike the tiger, always retained its importance in the formation of Indian monsters. We have pointed this out in our discussion of the elephant-headed god Ganesha. Sometimes the elephant is even combined with the tiger, but this elephant-headed tiger is known only from relatively late works of folk-art. For instance, it appears on playing cards in the Museum of Baroda, probably from eighteenth-century Rajastan, and also, in the form of a winged elephant-tiger, on wood sculpture from Udaipur. Such features in folk art always point to an earlier type, which has been dislodged from more formal art but survives in popular beliefs and crafts. Models for it are also to be seen in the elephant-bull, which is well attested for the Harappa period, and which once seems to have reached even Mesopotamia (126): it appears on one seal of the proto-literary period, at a very early date and unique in the Mesopotamian visual repertory. Such elephant-monsters are also known in literature. In the story of Zeyn Alasman, in the *Arabian Nights*, a ferryman appears in the shape of an elephant-tiger. 'Within the boat was no one but a ferryman, whose head was like an elephant's whereas his body was a tiger's.' As has already been said, a kind of sea-elephant was also depicted in early forms of the Makara. In Burma the planet-god Kate rides a monster which is described as the 'animal of the five beauties', and has a

Winged lion. Scythian

Left: Elephant-headed bird.
Atkanda-lihiniya. Sri Lanka,
Sinhalese motif, modern
Right: Elephant-bird. Nepal temple,
seventeenth century

Left: Elephant-tiger. Udaipur, India
Right: Elephant-fish. Indian,
1st millennium B.C.

Left: Ganesha
Centre: Elephant-headed man.
Right: Elephant-headed genie.
French illustration to the *Arabian Nights*. Stuttgart, 1838

stag's antlers, an elephant's tusks and trunk, the mane of a lion, the body of a Nāga and a fish-tail. Burmese folk-poetry has also the remarkable figure of a water-elephant, which is as small as a mouse but shaped like a normal elephant and of enormous strength. The other elephants live in mortal fear of it, since elephant's brains are its favourite food (127).

When we turn our attention to some Indian lion-monsters, we must bear in mind what has been said above: as all the sources are relatively late, it is quite possible that the lion forms had been substituted for original tiger forms. In Indian writings on art theory there is mention of Kautūhalas, probably a name applied to such monsters (128). According to Alice Boner they have the head of an elephant and the body of a lion. Monsters of this type denoted as Gajaviralī or Gajasimha have been preserved on ivory thrones presumably from Orissa (129). The Gajasimha is popular in the late medieval art of Ceylon as an animal figure on balustrades. Alice Boner describes the same figure as Gajavirāla (130) and in earlier descriptions names like Yali or Sarabha are favoured (131). The last-mentioned monster is, however, interpreted by Ettinghausen as a kind of unicorn, an eight-footed deer said to live on snow-covered mountains and called Sharav in Arabic (132).

In India there are also lion-monsters and fantastically shaped lions which have no elephant components, for instance the Makarākrti hari, that is the lion-headed Makara figure (133), the Sardula (134), a horned lion portrayed in Ellora and on the Kesava temple of Somnathpur, and the Vyālaka (135). Unfortunately, typological demarcations in Indian art have not been sufficiently worked out to allow more than a bare listing of names.

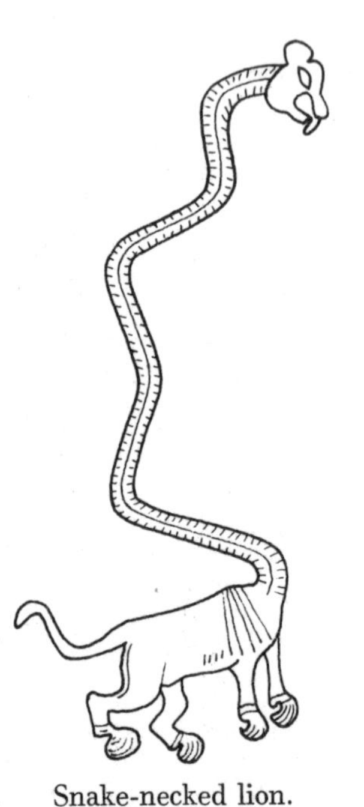

95 Hippocamp. Workshop of Elias Geyer. Leipzig, about 1600. Grünes Gewölbe, Dresden

Snake-necked lion. Cosmetic palette. Egypt, 3rd millennium B.C.

Snake-necked lion. Mesopotamian seal, 3rd millennium B.C.

Snake-necked lion. Egypt, Beni Hassan (Middle Kingdom)

96 Back of a throne carved from a tree trunk, from Kubbitol. Seventeenth century. Historical Museum, Stockholm

97 Hippocamps. Engraving by Andrea Mantegna.
Print Room, Amsterdam

98 Griffin and nautilus goblet. Grünes Gewölbe, Dresden

99 Hippocamp made of Baroque pearl. Eighteenth century. Grünes Gewölbe, Dresden

100 Griffin on a gold seal ring.
From Mycenae

101 Winged Monsters. Breast plate from Ziwiyeh, Iranian Kurdistan. Late eighth century B.C. Private collection

102 Magic horse. Ceramic tile from the Gobineau House, Teheran

103 Bone-eater. From the Ani papyrus.
British Museum, London

Behemoth and Leviathan.
William Blake. London, 1825

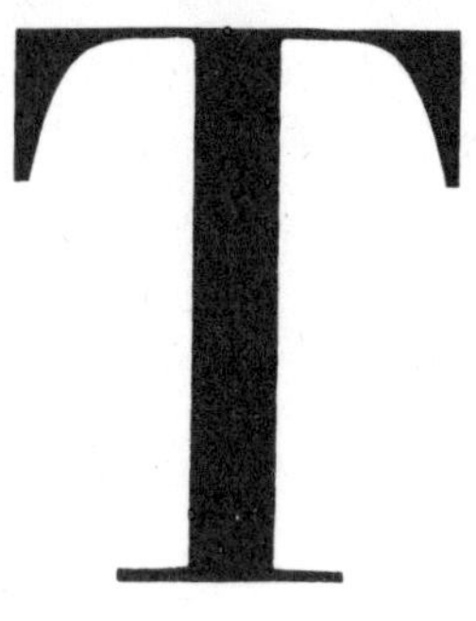

HE heading of this chapter gives just two examples of a much wider range of creatures to be discussed, all of them characterized by simplified or multiplied bodily features. Not all of them are monsters with an individuality of their own, but even the more decorative combinations of animal and human components into multiple-headed or multiple-bodied figures are intended, at any rate in visual representations, to constitute new, independent forms, although they share many individual characteristics with creatures dealt with in the previous chapters. Here, too, much is controversial, especially the 'unicorn', which we shall discuss first. Of no other fabulous creature has it been asserted so repeatedly that nature itself produced it, and the existence of 'unicorns' has been inferred not only from the fossilized remains of prehistoric animals, but also from living animals such as the rhinoceros. In the reports of ancient writers about the marvels of the Orient the 'unicorn' plays a very prominent role and many such a writer was at pains to give an account so true to nature that he actually pointed to the rhinoceros. But illustrations on ancient Near Eastern monuments tell a different story, for here, and even much earlier on Indian seals of the Harappa period, the genuine rhinoceros, faithfully reproduced, and the mythical one-horned creature appear together. Another, more recent interpretation of the one-horned creature as an entirely natural being is equally unconvincing: its supporters maintain that the one-horned animals with obvious bull's bodies are nothing more than illustrations in strict profile. In these cases, it is said, the artist knew that the animal really had two horns but he only showed one of them and this, in profile, completely hid the second horn. Such an explanation is completely at variance with what we know of the laws of ancient oriental art. Indeed, the greatest effort was always made to achieve complete clarity in the representation of shapes, and perspectives were neglected in order to show the most comprehensive view of a man, animal, plant, or object, without regard to the possible distortion of natural proportions. It is thus only logical to assume that, when a Mesopotamian artist wanted to show a two-horned animal, he would have made both horns visible. If he depicted only one horn he must have intended to represent a one-horned animal, no matter whether such an animal really existed in nature or was merely the product of his imagination.

Unicorns and Divinities with Multiple heads

It therefore seems that we are justified in speaking of a 'unicorn' wherever there is only one horn, except where one-horned rhinoceroses are clearly and faithfully delineated. The 'unicorn' is one of the oldest types in our present category; although it is not, strictly speaking, a composite creature, but rather a simplified form, in which the horn, theoretically speaking, may have been taken over from another species.

The literary history of the 'unicorn' goes back to the Gilgamesh epic, that is to the earliest written traditions of ancient Mesopotamia. In addition it has a visual history which takes one back by tortuous paths to the earliest pictorial works of Mesopotamia that have come down to us. However, both in the literary and in the visual traditions India looms large. The 'unicorn' occupies a prominent and numerically predominant position on the prehistoric seals of the Harappa period. In early Indian literature, in the Mahābhārata and in other texts, the Rishi Ekaśringa (the 'unicorn') is the figure that enables us to trace the origins of the legend in the Mesopotamian Gilgamesh-Enkidu poetry as well as the further variants recorded in ancient accounts of India. We have here unusually complete reports, which enable us to understand the evaluation and representation of the unicorn in Christian art, prompted by the interpretations in the *Physiologus*.

From the *Physiologus,* which represents but a late stage in the development of this subject, and gives a somewhat forced account biased on the side of Christianity, we can expect clues but not an accurate reflection of earlier tradition. Nevertheless, it is worth quoting it literally since it unmistakably confirms the fabulous character of the animal. 'And', said the psalmist, 'it shall be raised up, my horn, like that of the unicorn.' The *Physiologus* said that the unicorn had the following attributes: 'It is a small animal, like a little buck, but it is very cunning and the hunter cannot approach it because it is endowed with great strength. It has one horn in the middle of its head. Now I will relate how it is trapped. They send a pure virgin, clothed, to meet it. And the animal springs on to the bosom of the virgin. And she takes hold of it and it obeys her, and she carries it to the king's palace.

It is now taken for a representation of our Saviour because the horn has been raised up from the house of our father David, for our salvation. The angelic powers could not take possession of it, for it lived in the body of the truly immortal Virgin Mary: 'And the Word was made flesh, and dwelt among us.'

Von der Natur / art vnnd eygen-
schafft der Thier / welcher namen anfahet inn
frembden sprachen / darmit sie vonn den alten genant worden am Buchstaben V.

Unicornis ein Einhorn.

Vnicornis ein Einhorn / ist bei vns ein frembd vnbekandt thier / zim-
licher grösse / doch gegē seiner treflichen stercke zu rechnen / nit groß von leib /
von farben gelbfarb wie buxbaumen holtz / hat gespalten kloen / wonet im
gebirg vñ hohen wildtnussen / hat vornen an der stirn ein sehr lang scharpff
horn / welches es an den felsen vnd steinen scherpffet / durchsticht darmit die
D iij grossen

Unicorn. Woodcut.
From Gesner,
Historia animalium.
Zurich, 1551

Second attribute: there is an animal called a unicorn. In those places there is a large lake, and the animals gather to drink. But before they gather, the snake comes and casts its poison into the water. The animals notice the poison and do not dare to drink, but wait for the unicorn. It comes and goes straight into the lake and, making the sign of the cross with its horn, it renders the poison harmless. And all the other animals drink.' (136)

The taming of the unicorn by a woman and the rendering harmless of the poisoned water are motifs which point unmistakably to India, the former being also the basis of an episode in the Gilgamesh epic. Enkidu, living among the animals, could not be brought into the town to King Gilgamesh unless he was lured by a harlot (and not by a 'pure virgin') especially despatched for the purpose. She wins him away from his companions the animals, and leads him to human dwellings. In Indian epic and in ancient Buddhist sources this incident is transferred to a hermit living with the animals in a wood. He is Rishyaśringa or Ekaśringa, meaning the horned hermit or unicorn. Ekaśringa is described as the son of a hermit who has unwittingly begotten him by emptying his seed into a lake where a gazelle was bathing and was thus impregnated. Thus Ekaśringa is the offspring of a human father and an animal-mother, a fact which explains his name ('unicorn') and also his hybrid shape. Mesopotamian writings, however, include no references to the hybrid shape of Enkidu. On the other hand a single-horned animal is traceable in Mesopotamian art from the proto-literary period onwards, and in neighbouring Elam, too, unicorns are to be found from the time of the Susa seals onwards. In this region the lion-headed bird, the snake-necked lion and this unicorn are the earliest known mythical creatures.

The second incident related in the *Physiologus,* the cleansing of the water, is also clearly connected with Indian mythology. Here the god Shiva drinks the poison out of the ocean in order to cleanse it. There seems to be no parallel or precedent for this in Mesopotamia. In the Ekaśringa episode, however, the water is the intermediate agent in the procreative process, it is through bathing in the lake that the animal-mother becomes impregnated with the seed. In the later tradition animal-mother and monster-son, seed-bearing water and poison-bearing water, seem to have been fused together in order to underscore the purifying effect in the Christian interpretation, where the parallel between immaculate conception and the involuntarily impregnated animal-mother is especially striking. The ability of the unicorn to render poison harmless has also given rise to the belief that its horn is an important medicament. In powdered form it passed for an effective antidote to poison.

Throughout the development of the unicorn legend the basic features have been very clearly preserved and the ancient progress of Enkidu from savagery to culture, from the animal world to friendship with mankind, is typified in the shape of the creature. In Mesopotamia and later in Europe it has the shape of an animal but in India it has a basic human shape with indications of its animal origin.

It should also be remembered that the unicorn occurs in China, too, though here the traces of the ancient legend have been almost totally obliterated. But even here its horn is credited with healing powers and this confirms the connection.

Representations of unicorns vary greatly both in the shape of the body and in the type of horn. In Mesopotamia the original shape is clearly that of a bull with a more or less crumpled horn, which sprouts from the brow and generally points forward. This type is also found on early Indian seals of the Harappa period. In the early dynastic period in Mesopotamia there are already bulls with an upright stance and one horn, and on the seal impressions from Ur there appears even a deity in human form with a single horn on the brow. In the Middle Babylonian period we find slimmer, horse-like figures, followed in Assyrian and Achaemenid art by goat-like bodies and also by single-horned dragons.

The unicorn apparently makes no appearance in ancient Egyptian art; nor in Greek and Roman art, though the literary tradition mentioned above sets in with the tales of travel in India by Greek authors. In East Asian and in Islamic art, however, unicorns are all the more frequent. Before we comment briefly on these illustrations, it should be once more emphasized that there was no continuity of visual representation down to classical antiquity and that, for this reason, later European unicorns either derive from literary sources or are based on Eastern pictorial models.

According to a statement in the Chinese *Bamboo Chronicle* (137), the Ch'i-lin, sometimes mistakenly described as a dragon, appeared for the first time in the reign of Huang-ti (2697—2597 B.C.). Like the dragon and the phoenix, this creature brings peace and prosperity. The male animal is called Ch'i, the female Lin, but only the combination of both names designates what was regarded as the noblest creature in the animal kingdom. The species has the body of a deer, the hooves of a horse, the tail of an ox, and a single horn. It never eats living things, does not even tread on growing grass. It only appears when wise and virtuous rulers reign.

Things are extremely complicated in the field of Islamic art, which has not only various names for unicorns but also two different visual traditions, one going back to real rhinoceros models and the other to earlier representations of the true unicorn. In a fundamental study (138), R. Ettinghausen has investigated this problem. He bases his interpretation on an enamelled Syrian glass jar with griffins, sphinxes and winged lions as well as unicorns. These cannot be confused with the genuine rhinoceros in this context, and Ettinghausen emphasizes the fact that here there can be no question of two horns, one hiding the other. This unicorn has the body of a wild beast with tail and wings and is thus in all probability derived from Achaemenid representations of dragons, griffins and winged lions. Ettinghausen has tried to prove that the animal represented was identified with the Karkaddann or rhinoceros, irrespective of whether its body was that of a lion, a horse, an antelope or some other quadruped. Among other Islamic unicorns is Harish, whose anatomical description is similar to that given by the *Physiologus*; according to some sources, it is tamed by a virgin or else by a beautiful woman from a brothel (139). The Shādhahvār or Āras is an antelope-like animal with a massive horn, from which fourteen short branches sprout off alternately in different directions (140). A smaller unicorn, Al-mi'raj, looks like a yellow hare with a black horn.

The unicorn is very popular in Christian iconography and has often been illustrated even at a time when, as at the end of the fifteenth century, the Church forbade the depiction of the unicorn legend. The context in which it was represented, however, went through a basic transformation. From the beginning of the fifteenth century onwards the most frequent motif is the unicorn hunt, during which the animal seeks refuge in the bosom of the Virgin. In almost every case it has the body of a horse with a large straight horn, twisted like a drill, on its forehead. One of the exceptions is the gigantic single-horned buck in Böcklin's picture *Das Schweigen im Walde* (Silence in the Forest). The unicorn has become popular as a heraldic device, especially in Britain, and in some caricatures stands as a symbol for the country. Mention should also be made of the German folk-tale about the valiant tailor; in it the unicorn is captured when the fleeing tailor jumps behind a tree and the animal impales itself on the trunk, an episode illustrated again and again. Thus one of the earliest animals of fable has retained its popularity, even though its form has changed somewhat, from the time of ancient Sumer right down to the present day.

Multiple-headed, multiple-limbed and multiple-bodied creatures have one characteristic in common, but comprise very different kinds of ideas and visual images. Multiple heads have been given to humans, to animals, and to monsters but can also serve to join halved animal bodies in a kind of symbolic heraldry. Multiple limbs have remained almost exclusively restricted to human figures, whereas multiple bodies, like heads, have been given to man, animal, and monster. They have also been used for symbolic or for purely decorative purposes, and that to an even greater degree than multiple heads. At all events, it is among the multiple-headed figures that we find most of those leading an independent literary or pictorial existence, usually under a specific name known to us. In the forefront are the gods of the Indian pantheon, and those of the East and South-East Asian pantheons, which developed under Indian influence. Since these are depicted not only with more than one head but usually also with multiple arms, it seems best to deal with both phenomena together.

Goethe has commented on these Indian sculptures in a hardly flattering manner: 'the weird cave excavations, / the sombre throng of troglodytes, / with snout and trunk, an absurd rout; / a crazy pile of ornaments – / it's a fine way of building. / Let no one take them as an example, / these elephants and gargoyle temples. / They are a mockery of holy fantasies – / one feels neither nature nor God.' And he added: 'I would myself like to live in India, / if only there had been no sculptors.'

Today we can judge such ideas in their historical perspective; we know they were determined by a taste which, in the early nineteenth century, respected only the visual arts of classical antiquity. These aesthetic prejudices can be excused by the complete absence of good and suitable material illustrative of Indian art, the originals of which were known only to a few. Today we recognize even in the multiple-limbed figures of Indian gods (given that they are of good quality) a particular expressive impulse, which need not be any the less artistic than, say, a Greek centaur or an Egyptian sphinx.

Agni may be represented with two heads, Shiva with three, Brahma with four, and some deities, such as the war-god Kartikkeyya (Plate 113), have even more. But only the illustrations of Brahma adhere to the canons laid down in manuals of art-theory, while Shiva and the other gods are usually represented with only one head. Multiple arms, however, are found much more often; all divinities had at least two pairs, but there are examples with three, four, six, and more pairs of arms, especially in representations of the gods dancing or partaking in some warlike activity. Thus if there were rules in India, then the sculptures exhibit just as many exceptions. These gods have four or more hands, in which they hold their various attributes, and it was these that the artist was concerned to emphasize.

On the other hand it is significant that multiple legs seldom occur. There is a three-legged Shiva, expressive simultaneously of both dancing and standing. In contrast with Greek at,, Indian art has no winged gods, with the exception of some minor works of the early period. This should make us realize – if we have not done so before – how unjust it would be to blame Indian sculptors who, instead of adding wings to arms, merely multiplied the arms, when we condone unnatural forms in Greek sculptures.

In the exquisite sculpture of India the artistic arrangement of the four arms is so beautifully done that a casual observer is either hardly aware of their number or gets the impression of a movement conveyed by static visual means. The extra heads or arms are so organically combined with the rest of the figure that it seems as if several independent but quite normally shaped human figures could be abstracted from one and the same visual representation.

An archetype of the multiple-headed Indian figures has been recognized on a seal engraving from Mohenjo Daro (Plate 105), and multiple-faced or multiple-headed divinities are also to be found, though not frequently, in Mesopotamian art. Thus on seals of the Akkad period Usmu, a companion or servant of Ea (Enki), is represented with two faces, in a similar way to the ancient Roman god Janus, who, with eyes in front and behind, could see beginning and end at the same time. A standing goddess on an ancient Babylonian relief has two extra heads growing out of her shoulders (141). This plurality of heads and sometimes of other parts of the body becomes a stylistic principle with numerous variations in the art of Luristan, a principle which offers convincing new artistic creations in the best pieces, but only formal arabesques in the less successful. In Gallo-Roman and Celtic art three-headed gods are no rarity (142).

Multiple-headed and multiple-limbed figures are most frequent in the late Buddhist Lama art of Tibet (Plate 116), Mongolia and China. Here the arms often spread out like rays to surround the head or the bodies of embracing lovers. Kwannon sometimes has as many as eleven heads. A whole crowd of multiple-headed demons can be seen on Syrian seals and late Hittite reliefs.

Three-legged man. South Indian

Little need be said about multiple-headed human figures in later European art. There are only a few specimens and these have nothing like the conviction that the Indian artist commonly achieved (143). It suffices to mention the attempts made to depict the Christian concept of the Trinity as a figure with three faces or three heads.

Corresponding formations of animal or composite figures are frequent in Greek mythology. There is the multiple-headed hydra, the three-headed guardian of the underworld, Cerberus, and the two-headed or more often three-headed chimaera. The hydra, the nine-headed Lernaean snake, which it was Heracles' task to kill, has models in Mesopotamian and Hittite art. On an Akkadian seal two-horned gods or heroes attack a seven-headed snake-monster, out of whose four-footed dragon-body six snakes coil vertically upwards, while the heads are arranged in a row on the stretched snake-like neck, four of them already drooping, three still extended forwards to engage the enemy. The same monster appears on an engraved sea-shell from a somewhat earlier period, but here even more snake-bodies grow like rays out of its back, while the snake-heads, also seven in number, sit directly on the shoulders. A similar animal, this time with a coiled snake-body, but again with many erect subsidiary bodies, with heads partly destroyed, is to be seen on a relief from the Hittite period found in Asia Minor. It is likewise engaged in battle with a god and, presumably, is the snake-dragon Illuyanka. A monster which appears on a large gold plaque from Hasanlu has only three heads on a snake-body and shows, besides, a human head, shoulders and arms stretched forwards.

A seven-headed snake twining itself around a club-head and a five-headed snake on an impression from Tell Asmar, only fragments of which have been preserved, are both from the early dynastic period.

There are thus sufficient examples of snake-dragons from the ancient Near East which could have served as models for the Greek hydra. Another seven-headed beast is the dragon of the Apocalypse, a monster belonging to literary tradition and, on that account, depicted with a great variety of bodies and various kinds of heads. From manuscript illuminations of the ninth century, showing winged snakes with additional heads or dragon-like bipeds, to the use of this visual type to caricature the Papacy in the guise of the Babylonian whore riding on the monster, and to caricatures of a still later period, in which the multiple-headed monster embodies temporal and spiritual abuses, a whole host of hydra forms can be found which, despite all variations, exhibit

104 The Lady with the unicorn. Wedding carpet, about 1500. Musée Cluny, Paris

105 Three-headed Deity. Seal from Mohenjo Daro, India

106 Chimaera. Etruscan bronze, fifth century B.C.
Museo Archeologico, Florence

107 Unicorn. Seal from Mohenjo Daro, India

108 Unicorn-bull. Seal from Mohenjo Daro, India

109 Two-bodied lion. Seal from Phaistos, Crete

110 Many-headed Deity. Shōga Takuma, Japan, 1150–1200

111 Double-headed man with wings. Augsburg miniature from the alchemy manuscript 'Splendor Solis', about 1600. Germanisches Nationalmuseum, Nuremberg

112 Elk with antlers ending in bird's heads. Decorative plaque from the Altai. Hermitage, Leningrad

113 Three-headed, many-armed Indian deity: The war-god Kartikkeya seated on a peacock. From Subrahmanya Chola, Southern India, about eleventh century

114 Diana of Ephesus. Ancient copy of an original of the fourth century B.C. Museo Pio Clementino, Vatican

115 Triple-bodied demon, from the ancient temple of Athena on the Acropolis. About 570 B.C.
Acropolis Museum, Athens

an astonishing vitality throughout the centuries. Here, as so often, the ancient Near East, and above all Mesopotamia, proves to have been a source of long-lived visual types.

As well as the hydra, whose shape is not more precisely defined, Hesiod describes Geryoneus 'of the triple head'; Cerberus, who 'has fifty heads and is shameless and strong'; and also Chimaera:

'But Echidna bore Chimaera, whose breath was raging fire, terrible and mighty, swift of foot and strong. And she had three heads: one the head of a fierce-eyed lion, the other of a goat, the third of a snake, even a mighty dragon. In front she was a lion, behind a dragon, in the midst a goat, breathing the terrible might of blazing fire.' (144)

The number of Cerberus' heads is variously given in literature. Hesiod speaks of fifty, Pindar and Horace of a hundred, Vergil and others of three (145). When illustrated he usually has three heads. The shape of the Chimaera, however, is precisely defined. In Greek and Italic art she usually has a goat-like head, which grows out of the back of her lion body. In a few cases it is a human head, and frequently, but not always, the tail ends in a snake's head. The Chimaera, conquered by Bellerophon in the Greek myth, has in more recent times become the embodiment of all fanciful visions and notions. Idle day-dreams, removed from reality, are described as 'chimaeras'. To 'chase a chimaera' is to occupy oneself in a fruitless pursuit.

The Chimaera has numerous predecessors in oriental and Creto-Mycenaean art. Most of them, however, have only two heads: on late Minoan seals a goat's head grows out of the back, whereas a monster from Sendjirli has a human head superimposed, sphinx-like, on a lion's head. The Luristan illustrations already mentioned should also be referred to in this connection: they show winged sphinxes or winged lions, upon the ends of whose wings additional heads appear; a type which is later also found in Etruscan art. In some few cases, for instance in the famous Etruscan bronze in Florence, two of the heads seem to be fighting one another, since the snake's head at the tail-end, twisted back, is biting a horn on the goat's head (Plate 106). Other representations might be defined as chimaeras, not so much because of their mythical predecessor, but because they have a number of heads attacking one another. For example, in a Georgian manuscript a centaur-like archer is twisting his human upper body round and training his bow and arrow on the snake's head hissing at him out of the end of his own tail. Two-headed and three-headed animals are found on Iranian and Indian seals, mostly with horns. In India one of the three horned heads is commonly that of the unicorn; the whole composition, with the head turning back, is reminiscent of the Greek Chimaera (Plate 108). Multiple-headed figures also occur occasionally in the Han period in China, such as the double-headed centaur already mentioned and a two-headed bird; but they are so few in number that they probably owe their origin to foreign influence. Multiplication of snake's heads is a special preserve of In-

Seven-headed dragon.
Woodcut by Hans Burgkmair.
Augsburg, 1523

dian art. The Buddhist Nāga is portrayed as a multiple-headed snake or as a human figure with three, five, or more snake's heads. The world-serpent Śesa or Ananta, resting in the ocean, carries Vishnu and protects him with its numerous heads. In the texts it is described as having a thousand, i.e. many, heads. Multiple-headed snakes protect Buddha, Jina and others by fanning out their heads behind and above the heads of their charges. The type represented by the Buddha-protecting Muchilinda can be found all over South-East Asia.

Widespread and of early provenance is the double-headed bird, usually an eagle. The earliest known representations, on neo-Sumerian and early Babylonian seals, show the bird in full front view with wings outstretched, feet apart, and tail fanned out. The two heads, one turned to the left and the other to the right, are reproduced in simple profile. On the earliest Mesopotamian seals, however, they are not bird's but lion's heads and so we must assume that a new visual type was created to replace the older, lion-headed bird, Imdugud. In analogy to Usmu with the human figure and the Janus face, the lion's head, previously shown face on, was doubled and enabled to look in opposite directions, but the old heraldic pattern of Imdugud was otherwise retained unaltered. In large-scale works of art the two-headed bird from now on clearly appears in the form of an eagle, first of all, it seems, on rock-carvings in Yazilikaya and Chatal Hüyük in Asia Minor. There it is shown carrying two goddesses or a royal personage: thus it has changed its function without essentially altering its form. Its further development can be followed in both westerly and easterly directions. We come across the double-headed eagle in India, first of all in Taxila, in Turkestan, and in China, and also in Islamic and in Christian art, always in the same heraldic form and therefore isolated from any narrative context.

It is remarkable that no heraldic bird with two heads appears in the art of ancient Egypt and of classical antiquity. This very ancient oriental image did not reach Europe via Greek and Roman art but came westwards by way of Central Asia and Eastern Europe. Asia Minor and Byzantium played here the most important role as intermediaries and sources of tradition (146).

Images such as the heraldic double-headed bird must be distinguished from creatures which double certain parts of the body as well as the head. These occur early in Iran and India, Mesopotamia and Egypt, and particularly in ancient Aegean civilization, sometimes also in the form of a bird. Thus an early Minoan seal has a handle or clasp shaped like a double-bird, the two bodies still recognizable, though joined together into one (147). Usually, however, the image is a combination of two split animals or even of animals reduced to head and neck, for example the double bull in Egypt, the boar and ram in Susa, Tepe Hissar and Tepe Gawra, and the double bulls in Sumer. These combinations occurred not only in two-dimensional art, such as on seals and, in Egypt, on cosmetic palettes, but also in small sculptures (148).

Sometimes the parts are so fitted together that a change in direction results; the forefeet of one animal-half point one way while those of the other half point the other way, as can be seen on an early Minoan seal from Mallia or on ancient Iranian examples. These are the predecessors of a type known in later art as inversion, i.e. the rotation of the body on its own axis, usually, of course, a body of normal shape. This motif is particularly well attested in the art of steppe peoples, in the Scythian region, in Siberia and the Altai. Parallel to this rare stylistic feature there is also, in these areas, the so-called coiled animal, its body not turning on its axis but coiling itself up. It, too, has sometimes two heads, which meet at the ends of the coiled-up snake-body.

Symbolic doublings, as has been pointed out, are also well attested in the art of ancient Egypt (149).

Back-to-back combinations were also very popular in Syria and in Phoenician art, as were Janus-like figures in general (150). These, however, are not so much real monsters as artificial composite forms of symbolic, pictographic or purely decorative significance.

Double-headed bird. Mesopotamian seal, 2nd millennium B.C.

The converse type of combination, too, the meeting of several bodies in one head, may either represent viable beings or it may be merely symbolic or decorative. The double-bodied creature is a frequent form as far back as the seal-engravings of ancient Mesopotamia. It occurs as a bull-man with human torso and head but with two bulls' diverging hindquarters, for instance on early dynastic and Akkadian seals.

Double-headed bird
Double-headed bird. Alaca Hüyük.

Here he sometimes holds his erect tails in hands stretched out on either side. A variant of this form has both legs shaped like independent animal bodies with heads hanging down.

Occasionally the outstretched tails end in additional animal heads. Almost an abbreviation of this type, though more clearly in monster shape, is suggested by the figure with a single body, whose arms end in animal heads, which is also found on an early dynastic seal. On a vessel from Melos of the seventh century B.C. there is a figure similarly formed, headless and with snake heads instead of hands (151). In Greece the giants were generally represented with snakes instead of legs (152). In late classical times this type survived in the shape of an anguipede and appears on Roman-Jewish seals as the divinity Abraxas-Iao.

All these figures, the bull-man with double hindquarters, the lion-legged man (153), and those with snake or fish legs, were probably intended to represent particular monsters. This can also be presumed in the case of some corresponding animal forms, though here two-dimensional decoration and fantasy, the sheer delight in visual inventiveness is increasingly evident. This spread later to the ornamentation of medieval capitals.

An early Mesopotamian seal (Plate 109) shows two confronted lions, joined at the shoulders to form one head, which is shown face on. This double-bodied lion is equipped with wings and may be regarded as a variation of the lion-headed bird, made at a time when the visual form of this type was at an experimental stage. Later, but still in the early dynastic period, a steatite dish – now in the British Museum – shows a bird and a lion placed together in such a way that the two heads are conjoined and in effect become one head seen face on. This may also have been one of the experimental forms of the lion-headed bird, in this case, however, with a double body made up from different animals. An almost identical composition on a capital in the church of Notre-Dame-du-Pré in Le Mans is in all probability the result of coincidence and not to be explained as the product of a tradition. Here, too, the frontal view of the lion's face is the central feature between a lion with a lion's body moving to the left and a complete bird's body turned the other way. Usually, however, we find two lion bodies meeting in one head. Examples are found on early dynastic seals in Mesopo-

116 Deity with three eyes and six arms. From Tibet. Private collection

117 Cretan seal

119 Winged two-bodied lion. Gold plaque from Ziwiyeh. Metropolitan Museum, New York

118 Many-bodied lion. Mosaic from Otranto. Twelfth century

121 Demon of hell and prisoner. Chinese painting of the Huan period from Lu Hsien Chung. Mode collection

120 The Whore of Babylon on a Limoges enamel plate. Grünes Gewölbe, Dresden

122 Many-headed Centaurs.
Mosaic from Otranto.
Twelfth century

123 Long-armed demon,
puppet from a shadow-play.
From Szechuan.
Marionette Theatre, Munich

tamia, on Mycenaean seals, on Ionian vase painting, on a Chinese relief of the Han period, and also in Central and West European architectural sculpture and even on the pediment of the church at Malmötrakten in Sweden (154). Medieval art also shows additional quirks, with the head facing forwards but turned upside down, or the bodies placed upright against one another, which had occasionally occurred also in the ancient Near East.

On Corinthian vases there are two bird-bodied creatures with a common head, either like Medusa or leonine. In India the motif of two elephants standing opposite one another is popular; their heads merge into one, which, however, is not shown full face but in profile, and formed in such a way that it can belong quite naturally to either body. There are examples of this in Badami, Hampi and Ceylon (155). In Islamic art we encounter the double sphinx (156). But more than two bodies can also merge into one head, for example three fishes (157). In India the motif of four deer bodies with a single head is frequently encountered, the same motif occurs on a vessel from Chalcis and a very similar combination of lion bodies is found in Sassanid art. Seven bodies of dogs, arranged radially, merge into one central head in the cathedral at Bayeux (158). Tricks of this kind are by no means confined to the type of monsters dealt with here. In ancient oriental art animal and human wheels, animals and men intertwined and chasing one another in a circle are well attested, but these usually keep their natural shapes. The fusing of the heads of various bodies can also be seen in modern art. Pablo Picasso, for example, has used the same method as that which we have noted on the steatite dish in the British Museum: the full face and profile halves of two heads are united into one face. The fanciful combination of animal and human parts, usually grouped round a central vertical staff which terminates in a human body and head, is particularly common in the art of Luristan; extra heads could even be added on top or at the sides. Here, as in the case of the coiled animals mentioned above and of the inverted figures of Scythian art, it was hardly intended to represent particular composite creatures, but the single parts were capable of any number of detailed variations.

From the wealth of material available we select a few further special figures. The Egyptian god Asch, Lord of Libya, who usually has the head of a falcon, but in a few cases a human head, later became a demon with three heads – lion, vulture and snake (159). In Sebastian Münster's *Cosmographia* there is a drawing of a triple-headed monster which may well illustrate this demonic god. A special combination is the so-called woman of the seven vices (160). She has the bust of a woman with bat's wings; from the middle of the body two animal heads jut out, one leg is that of a bird, the other a snake ending in a head, which is biting the bird-leg. An illustration in the manuscript *Buch von der Heiligen Dreifaltigkeit* (Book of the Holy Trinity) in the Berlin Print Room can also be interpreted as a symbolic combination. Here a man and a woman, each represented by half a body, are joined into one body with two heads

Double-headed bird. Church of Moulier-Saint Jean, twelfth century

Double-headed bird. Konin Museum

124 The god Bes from Karnak, Egypt

and the whole figure is equipped with massive wings. A brood of human and satyr heads on snake's bodies twines round the legs, terminating underneath the mixed human figure in a devil-headed bird, upon whose back the whole figure stands. The whole is a man-woman double being: Lucifer and his mother.

Awe-inspiring monsters of this kind may even be headless, like the Medusa in Max Klinger's cycle *Time*. In one outstretched hand she holds her own terrifying head, in the other a bundle of snakes ready to attack. In India there is the headless Cinnamastakā holding in one hand a sword, with which she has cut off her own head, and in the other hand the head; blood spurts from the head and the open neck, and flows into the mouths of two other figures and into that of her own head. Another headless figure is Baubo of Priene (161), who carries her face on her stomach, a type which we shall meet again in our final chapter.

Mention must also be made of the Greek Scylla, who, together with Charybdis, keeps fearsome guard over the straits. She has twelve misshapen feet and six extremely long necks, on each of them a hideous head with three rows of death-dealing teeth. She is stuck in a cave up to her middle, but her heads rear up out of the chasm (162). Far less dangerous is a three-legged donkey of Iranian mythology, which is blessed with six eyes (163).

Cinnamastakā. Modern Indian print

Some creatures apparently closely associated with our subject, such as giants, dwarfs and witches, are hard to characterize pictorially as monsters, because of their unnatural size. They are usually only illustrated when they also have certain other monstrous characteristics such as multiple heads, like Nordic and Irish giants, or a single eye, like the Greek Polyphemus. In Egyptian-Syrian art there is Bes (Plate 124), who has animal features such as round ears, a large mouth, an outsize head planted direct without neck on his shoulders, but he is only recognizable as a monster when, as occasionally happens, he is given a tail or wings. That he is a dwarf is indicated by the short limbs and the stocky body. Some familiar figures in Indian art, followers of the gods and distinguished from them by their stocky, dwarfish stature, usually lack distinctive monster characteristics. In literary works the features of a giant could be described very expressively and aptly: thus the *Arabian Nights* tells of a giant who stands with his feet on the earth but head high in the clouds: 'Head like the mouth of a well – front teeth like iron pickaxes – mouth like a cave – teeth like boulders – nostrils like trumpets – ears like targes – a gullet like a highway – eyes like lanterns' (164). Other giants are described as having long ears and split eyes, with elephant's tusks growing out of their mouths, and so on. However much such figures might stir the imagination, they seldom developed into consistent monster-types.

As a special type mention may be made of the Diana of Ephesus (Plate 114), who was shown with many breasts, a picture of fertility become flesh (165). The gynaecologist mentioned in the introduction says of her: 'Diana (Artemis) of Ephesus with her numerous breasts has a parallel in human polymastia, which is not at all infrequent.

In all probability the Greeks had taken over this image of the goddess from the Orientals. They were able to do this because this shape, if not exactly beautiful, was nevertheless human and seemingly useful.' (166)

In the Indian fairy-tale book, *Pantjatantra*, there is a two-headed bird, Bhāranda, which had a quarrel with itself. According to a fable by Th. Etzel (167), the one head grudged the other the pleasure of a rare fruit and took a poisoned nut to punish it.

> 'On the fruitful shore of the Indian Ocean
> Was a bird called Bhāranda. Like other birds
> It only had one stomach in its body, but alas!
> It had two heads!'

– and so, when the tale ends:

> 'The raging poison burned its stomach,
> Its heart soon beat its last,
> And groaning died in bitterest torment
> The two hostile heads.'

Scylla

Boat-man, Winged Sun and Marching Drum

HIS title is intended to cover all those composite creatures which incorporate other components besides animal and human ones: objects from nature such as flowers and trees, sun and stars, and the four elements themselves – earth, air, fire and water; as well as man-made artefacts – ships, gates, weapons, and the like. This group is not large and many of the examples given here date from the very beginnings of visual representation. It also includes many a creature which is almost impossible to illustrate and is found only in literature, usually in fairy-tales, where plants and objects are sometimes anthropomorphized. It is only modern book illustrators who have attempted to make this visually clear – the great world of art has virtually ignored such insignificant figures.

A good example is Grimm's fairy-tale of the wisp of straw, the piece of coal, and the bean. These three not only speak but also walk; the wisp of straw and the piece of coal drown in a stream while the bean bursts for laughing over them and is only saved by a travelling tailor, who finds it and sews it together again: since then all beans have had a black seam. This is only one example of many. There are speaking bed-legs, speaking bones of murder victims, speaking flesh, speaking rivers, mountains, statues, and so on. But little of this appears in pictorial tradition. As was said in the introduction, notions like this go back to older forms of thought characteristic of social systems not yet divided into classes. They are thus not reflected in the visual sources to which we have access.

The winged sun is perhaps the most common surviving pictorial type among the creatures in this category. For many the sun is inconceivable as a composite being, but we are concerned with a winged sun, that is, one thought of as mobile and endowed with animal life.

Traceable first of all, it seems, in Egypt at the time of the unification of the 'two lands', about 3000 B.C., the winged sun continued to be depicted down to Sassanid times in Iran and, as O. Eissfeldt has shown, is still found as a national symbol (168). This, of course, does not indicate continuous existence but a deliberate revival. From the second millennium onwards we find representations of the winged sun also in the Near East, in Asia Minor and Syria, among Babylonians and Assyrians, Persians and Parthians. As this motif developed throughout thousands of years, it is only natural that considerable differences should have arisen in its appearance and in its meaning. The Egyptian shapes, symbolic of the king, also exhibit a certain continuity in the association of two Uraeus snakes with the sun's disc (169). Similarly shaped, with wings stretched wide, is the Horus-falcon, or the Mut-vulture, and sometimes, too, the human-headed soul-bird Ba. The god Horus, worshipped in the shape of a winged sun's disc, was called Behetdi. In Assyrian and Persian art a human form is almost always connected with the disc, or takes its place: the god Assur in Assyria and Ahuramazda in Persia (170). The snakes often become bands ending in volutes. On a relief from Karatepe a winged, bird-headed demon supports the winged disc with head and uplifted hands. From the fact that even in early Near Eastern portrayals the sun is given a support such as a pillar – on the Mitanni seal of Shaushattar – or later a human figure, Frankfort concludes that here it probably signifies the heavens as a whole, which would mean a shift of meaning as compared with Egyptian notions (171). But the various meanings hardly affect the manner of representation. The decisive fact is that something lifeless is depicted as possessing life, and it is of no importance whether or not a god is concealed behind it, as for example in the hands rising out of a sun's disc on an Assyrian obelisk, one of them holding a bow.

Here we may recall the Egyptian liking for visual animation of symbols and written characters, which sometimes take on clearly the pictorial functions of composite beings. An example is the 'healing eye', portrayed in a wall painting on a Theban tomb of the twentieth dynasty – an eye with arms holding a vessel (172).

Among ancient Mesopotamian pictorial types there was a whole group in which the human figure was physically connected with water (wavy lines), with fire (rays), with mountains (scales), with spherical or spiky shapes (plants, branches). Here the decisive point is that in each case the characteristic is not co-ordinated to the main figure by way of an attribute but is a part of the body, organically connected with it. This fits the criteria we have put forward for a composite being, even if the same characteristic is used attributively in some earlier or later representation. Thus a purely human form holding a vase filled with water or twigs is to be looked upon as a water-god or god of fertility. The meaning is the same, but the manner of portrayal is different, in accordance with the law of exchangeability, which we have found in the case of snake-monsters and bird-monsters. What is important for our purpose – and this must be stressed again and again – is the visual appearance; only in reference to this can the meaning be interpreted. We have already referred to the fact that animals or men represented in a completely natural manner might have had a very special meaning for the contemporary beholder in prehistoric times, a meaning which he drew directly from the pictorial context or from the general notions of his time, whereas we lack this particular insight. Within the scope of the present work,

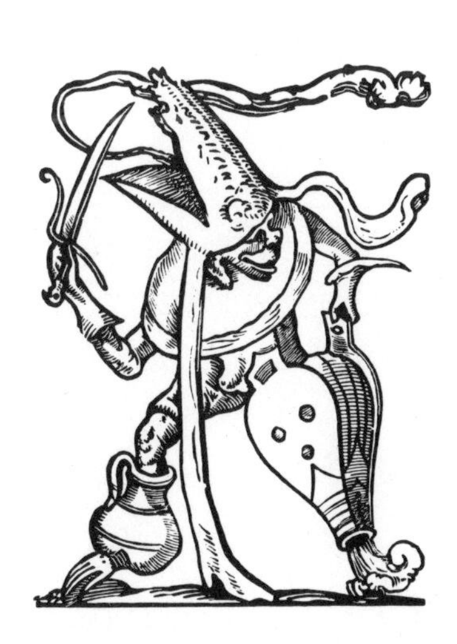

Grotesque figures. Illustrations to Rabelais, sixteenth century

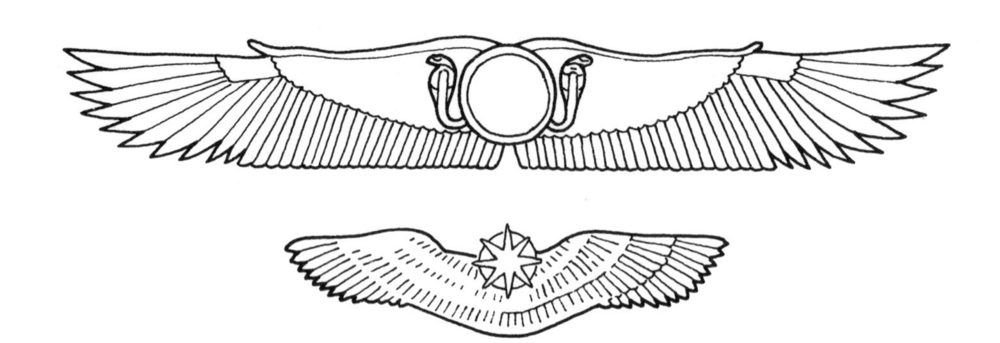

Winged sun-disc between two snakes: 'Horus of Edfu', Egypt

Winged sun-disc. Middle Assyrian seal, 2nd millennium B.C.

God Assur in winged disc. Assyrian, ninth century B.C.

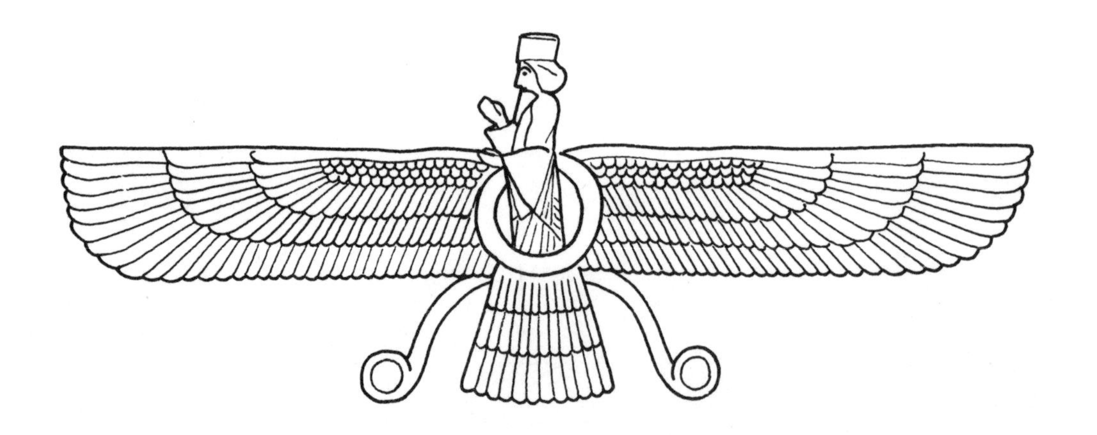

Ahuramazda in winged circle. Persepolis

however, it is the opposite process which is of interest, namely how it comes about that the artist – and here we are dealing with later periods of social development – by depicting a body of composite shape brings to light notions that would otherwise remain concealed. This is of course a question which can only rarely be answered. The fact that composite beings have been depicted can however be stated with certainty. The element of mystery – which at the same time creates a feeling of uncertainty – resides for the observer of past ages in everything possessed of life.

Let us first of all consider the figure of a man or a woman, so often found on seals of the Akkad period, with branches growing out of its shoulders and sometimes out of all parts of its body. There were already fertility gods in ancient Sumerian art. Thus on a beautiful seal of the Uruk period a man holds massive branches, upon whose blossoms two rampant rams seem to be feeding. On the Akkadian seals the plants are directly joined on to the human body and there only remains the question whether the plant-motif could be a garment, perhaps the 'ears-of-corn robe' in which the god Marduk was dressed in the ritual of the new year festival (173), or was intended to indicate an organic growth out of the body, as Frankfort insists in his descriptions of individual seals. In Christian iconography there is a type known as the 'Madonna in the ears-of-corn robe': Mary wears a long robe made of a material decorated with ears of corn. No stalks grow out of her body and none cover those parts of her body which are not hidden by the robe. Here we have a purely attributive characterization without any modification of the body. As far as the meaning is concerned the Virgin Mary in this type of picture is clearly portrayed as a 'vegetation deity', that is as an embodiment of the ancient fertility notions originally represented by a mother-goddess.

Assur as tree-god

In contrast with this – and we have made this digression for the sake of clarity – the ears-of-corn gods on the Akkad seals are not shown wearing such a garment; whereas this is not always very clear on some pictures, it is quite unmistakable on others. On

Tree-man. Bharhut. India, second century B.C.

Corn-god. After a Babylonian seal, 1st millennium B.C.

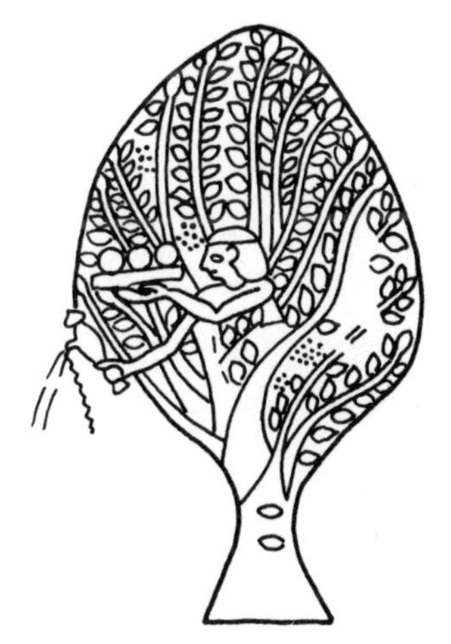

Tree-deity. Egypt, XVIII dynasty

these the ears of corn grow through the robe as well as on the unclothed parts of the body. In addition some of these figures hold ears of corn as attributes in their hands (174). On the seal of Naram Sin of Akkad a goddess of this type sits upon a throne holding in her hand a vessel overflowing with water, while behind her a statue stands on a plinth, showing the same type of vegetation goddess as a cult-picture. The attribute is not always a vase full of water, but sometimes a plough or a weapon. As far back as the Fara period we find a Sumerian corn divinity with date-panicles growing out of her shoulders (175).

In later times portrayal of such vegetation divinities in the form of composite creatures is rare but has not been given up completely. Thus we meet the god Assur as a tree-god, characterized not by ears of corn but by branches growing out of his body (176). But already in Akkad times there was another image, in which the constituents were transposed: a divine figure, recognizable by a crown of horns, growing out of a tree (177). Frankfort relates this type to the lament of the goddess Inanna for her son, Tammuz, who remains in the underworld, the creator of all life. 'This lament is a lament for the hemp – for he has created it. This lament is a lament for the barley – for he has created the seed-furrows', and so on, as the song goes (178). In our illustration, Tammuz is in his mountain-tomb; the goddess seeks, finds, and frees him. Only the upper part of his body is shown. He grows out of the trunk of a tree, which bows around both figures and forms the sort of cave which is described by Frankfort as a mountain-tomb. But it is clearly branches and not trees which grow outwards and hence it is more probable that they represent the hollow tree-trunk, which like a cave in earth or mountain can signify the depths of seclusion. Another verse of the song runs: 'This lament is the lament of the steppe – for he created the tamarisks'. In another song (179) is the verse: 'Lamenting goes my heart to the steppe, to the place where the youth is bound, to the place where Dumuzi [Tammuz] is fettered'. The references to vegetation are so clear that an intention to represent the god in the form of a tree-creature is entirely possible.

Water-man. Stele from Susa, thirteenth century B.C.

Some tree-creatures of this type are found in Egyptian art. Hands or a head and a human body grow out of a tree, but as an organic whole (180). And on an Indian relief, from Bharhut, illustrating a rebirth of the Buddha, we find a tree from which hands dispense food and drink. From the same Jatakas we learn much about the divinities, mostly of a lower order, living in trees. Thus the visual amalgamation of several notions is here quite unmistakable and the result is a creature completely analogous to the composite human and animal beings dealt with already, which combine certain forces and qualities into one whole. Both types, human elements growing out of trees on the one hand and branches or ears of corn sprouting out of human bodies on the other, can be traced again both in Western and in Eastern art. Thus there is a late Egyptian image of the goddess of the heavens, Nut, as a vegetation goddess, with branches growing out of all parts of her body from top to toe (181). In

Water-man. Early Iranian vase painting, 3rd millennium B.C.

125 The god Agni with rays of fire. Indian. State Archaeological Gallery of West Bengal

126 Demonic plant-monster: Human figure by Max Ernst, 1931. Museum of Modern Art, Stockholm

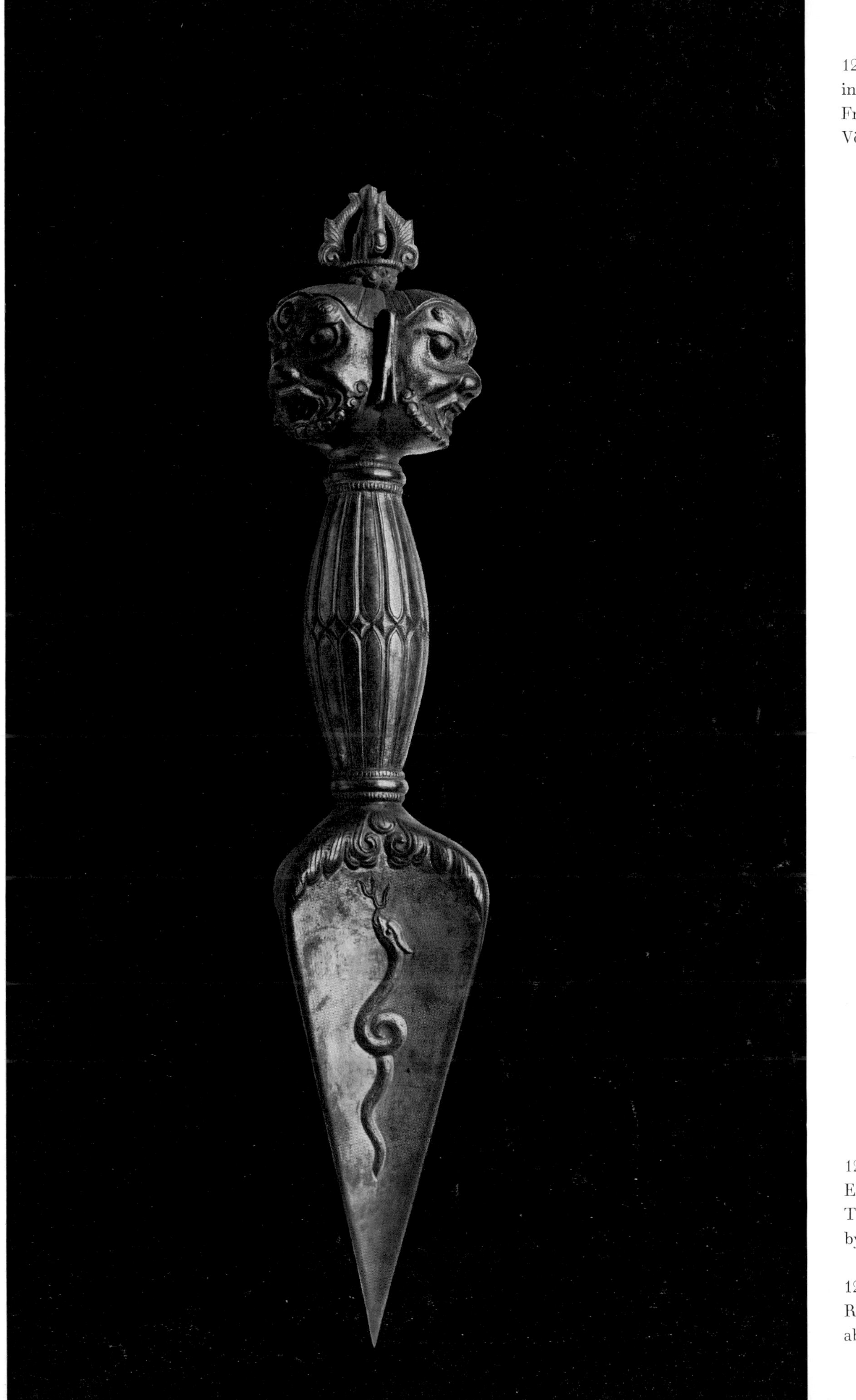

127 Magic dagger with hilt in the shape of human heads. From Tibet. Museum für Völkerkunde, Dresden

128 Cannon Monster. Engraving. Detail from The Temptation of St Anthony, by Jacques Callot

129 Sword-god from Yasilikaya. Relief on a rock face, about 1350–1250 B.C.

ac. Callot Inuen et fe

130 Boat-man, on a seal from Akkad

131–136 Late Cretan-Mycenean seals

138 Sun in human shape. Mexican relief

137 Fight with a sun-headed deity. From Khafaje, Mesopotamia. Beginning of 2nd millennium B.C. Oriental Institute, Chicago

139 The Drum. From 'Animals and Men'
by Hans Grundig, 1938–39

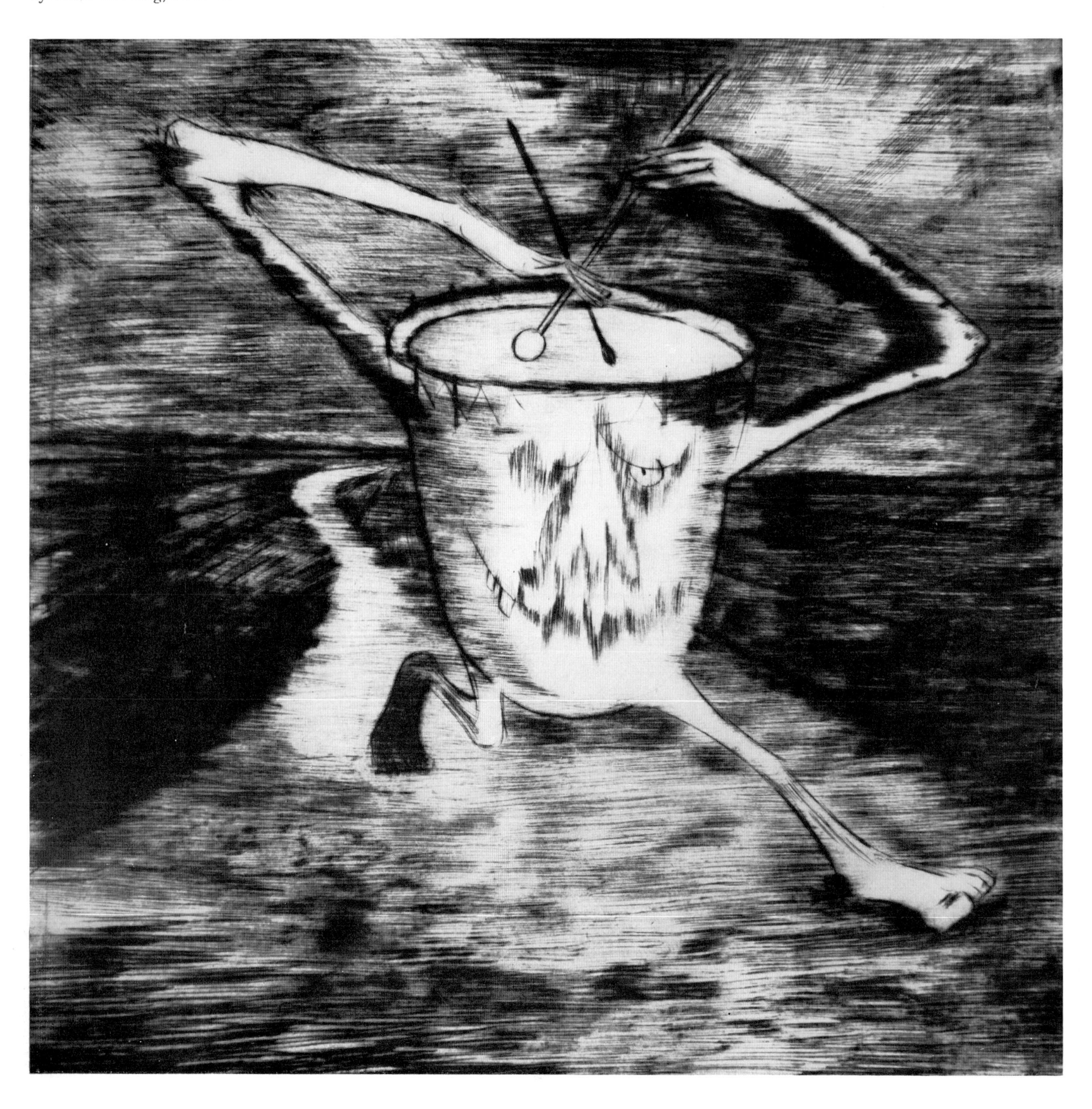

South Asian art, in India and Sri Lanka, the Purneghata, the vessel of abundance, is a common fertility symbol similar to the brimming water-vase of ancient Mesopotamian art. On a stele of Dalada Maligawa in Candy, Sri Lanka, the topmost female figure in a pyramid of figures is a kind of personification of this symbol, since she herself becomes the trunk of a tree, whose branches spread out from her head. In European folk-art human figures sometimes have leaves instead of hands and in certain styles in modern art, especially in Surrealism, this motif also appears. In a picture by Paul Delvaux, *Dawn*, four young women are seen naked to the waist, the lower halves of their bodies consisting of tree-stumps, with roots anchored in the earth like so many feet.

Sun-god in mountains. Akkad seal. Mesopotamia, 3rd millennium B.C.

Perhaps reference should also be made here to a Christian notion: the Jesse tree, which can be traced in art as far back as the tenth century. Here a tree is growing out of the body of the sleeping Jesse, a kind of family tree, based on the text of Isaiah 11:1: 'And there shall come forth a rod out of the stem of Jesse and a branch shall grow out of his roots.' (182) Islam has Zakkum, the tree of hell, whose fruits are the heads of devils. From the *Arabian Nights* the trees on the island Wakwak have become famous, trees with human or animal heads (183). In the Alexander legend, too, and in the *Shah Namah* we meet with speaking trees, which are accordingly illustrated as having human heads (184). Trees giving birth to animals can be found in travellers' tales such as those of John Mandeville (185). But we shall reserve discussion of such marvels for our last chapter.

Ea as water-god. Seal of Gudea of Lagash, end of 3rd millennium B.C.

Finally mention may be made of a figure from Greek myth which appears, at any rate in pictures, as a tree creature. The beautiful nymph Daphne was turned into a laurel tree. Here, as in the case of the hunter Actaeon, a genuine metamorphosis is intended, but some of the greatest artists such as Pollaiuolo, Tiepolo, Bernini and Poussin, and numerous modern painters and sculptors like Renée Sintenis, have portrayed Daphne in a transitional state, in other words as a composite creature (Plate 38).

The sun-god is also represented, in analogy with the Akkadian vegetation god, as having rays of fire shooting out of his shoulders and sometimes out of his whole body. Frankfort considers it possible that figures of the latter type represent not the sun-god Shamash but a fire-god or rather Marduk, the 'lord of the burning fire', as he is described in literature (186). Portrayals of this kind are extraordinarily frequent on seals of the Akkad period and the fire-god, no matter how he is identified, is yet another very characteristic, composite creature of the period. Though the nimbus, the circular sun-disc-like attribute of sun-figures, appears only much later, we should not forget that it sometimes occurs in the form of a bundle of rays arranged in a circle and is thereby quite clearly able to signify a fire. As a symbol the nimbus or halo was later very much generalized but the fact that it has its roots in the earliest known representations of fire can hardly escape notice.

Mountain-god. Hittite

A remarkable monster-figure, described as a Cyclops or a forerunner of Polyphemus, is attested on a small relief found in Khafaje (187). Here a god with a crown of horns kills a monster, whose human body is crowned with a shape like a star or rather a twelve-leaved blossom surrounding a one-eyed face. Should this be intended to denote the sun, then this shape represents its flames. It is also conceivable that it is a fire-demon appearing in a different form but one in which a combination of the human body with fire is suggested. In either case the emphasis on the one-eyed face remains unexplained. Reference to the Greek giant Polyphemus does not explain much. All it shows is that Greek notions of one-eyed demons go back to ancient Near Eastern models.

The personification of water, or the representation of a water-man, occurs on a piece of later Susa ceramic ware, where streams of water flow from a man's middle in wavy lines on both sides (188). But this type, too, is only found in relatively clear illustrations after the Akkad mythology had become fully developed, and even then it varies in shape and meaning. The original water-god Enki, later called Ea, is identifiable by two streams of water emerging from his body. Sometimes, to help the beholder to understand the picture better, fishes swim in the water. The god may also hold an identifying attribute, a water vessel, in addition to the water-waves connected to his body, and finally the branches characteristic of a vegetation god may grow out of his shoulders.

Of particular interest is the Akkadian personification of water in the shape of parallel bands of waves with, at either end, a human torso complete with a head. Since this water-monster is portrayed in a horizontal position underneath a ship carrying divinities, it shows itself to be fully possessed of life, not only supporting the ship but moving it forward, its outstretched hands clasping bow and stern (189).

A further water-figure is the rain-god, shown as a man with outstretched arms surrounded by vertically falling water, his figure and the wet accessories contrasting clearly with the drier parts of the seal picture. Here we have either a figure with its attribute or a composite creature, though the latter seems to me more plausible (190).

Of later date are water creatures of another basic type from neighbouring Elam and from the Middle Babylonian and Assyrian periods. Here the lower part of the body is made of waves of water clustered together in the form of columns, the upper part is human, and the hands hold vessels with or without water. The relief from Susa transforms the lower part of the body into scale-like streams of water and the feet into fin-like streams, which flow like twisting ribbons through vessels and on their way are grasped by the creature's hands and pressed against its body. Unfortunately the relief is damaged so that the total structure of this personified irrigation-plant is difficult to make out. This may sound somewhat frivolous, but in fact there were hardly any limits to creative fantasy in Mesopotamian and Elamite art. On an Assyrian seal we find the personification of a whole landscape (191): a figure which has a human torso and a lower body made of water is directly joined with a mountain-symbol and with trees growing out of it.

A similar combination of the most diverse elements to form a composite creature is recognizable on the relief from Assur whose minor figures have already been noted as water-men. The central figure is distinguished by branches growing out of its body, which also has scales, a feature which according to the conventions of Mesopotamian art should denote a mountain-body. Mountain-beings of this kind are frequently attested in the Akkad period, figures rising up as it were out of a mountain but, in visual terms, clearly composite creatures, like Tammuz growing out of a tree.

Boat-man. Early dynastic. Mesopotamia, 3rd millennium B.C.
Boat-god. Akkad seal, 3rd millennium B.C.
Double-bodied boat. Babylon. Seal, 2nd millennium B.C.

The mountain-man type continues in Middle Babylonian times and is also found in Hittite art, for instance in Yazilikaya. The connection with a mountain may be achieved by other means, similar to those used in the case of the rain-man described above: a god or an animal-man of fully human shape is placed in the middle of a mountain (192), is attacked by another god with lightning flashes or a bundle of fire-rays, and, as is shown by the flames blazing out of the mountain, has been set on fire and is about to be destroyed. On an early dynastic seal-impression from Ur a further mountain-monster is recognizable, this time in the shape of an animal: a recumbent, human-faced bull is joined with a mountain, which forms his hindquarters.

An especially remarkable figure on early dynastic and Akkad seals is the boat-man or man-boat (Plate 130), the living ship of the sun-god Shamash, as Frankfort explains (193). In early dynastic times the torso from the waist up is connected with the hull of the boat, which in turn ends in an animal-head. The forepart of the boat has the shape of a man, the arms holding an oar and the horned head looking forward. This type remains remarkably constant on the known specimens. In Akkad times a further development can be discerned. The boat-man now has a second leg, which seems to stride over the water, whereas the hind leg forms the stern of the boat. In the previous chapter we have already noted how a similar transformation in the figure of the two-bodied man expresses itself 'in terms of anatomy', as Frankfort puts it. In each case it is an attempt to emphasize the organic unity of the composite body. In the Akkad period the horns have become a horned crown. On a seal of later times, now in the British Museum, the boat-man, like the water in human shape, has become a double human being, the hull of the boat connecting two human torsos and heads.

With this type we reach an interesting phenomenon often to be observed in the Orient. At widely differing periods, in the Orient as in the West, there have been a number of types of ship which have an animal connection not only in illustrations but in actual specimens still in use. Animal heads or animal extremities are united with the hull, a formation generally termed theriomorph: it represents an attempt to enrich man-made objects, tools, vehicles, with animal force, and, with regard to visual effect, thereby to depict them as alive. In our example, the water vehicle, this is particularly conspicuous. Often ships are given the general shape of a bird united with a bird's head in such a way that the identity of ship with bird is quite clear. This is true, for instance, of the Indian animal-ships often mentioned in literature, classical and popular, such as the Mayurpankhi, the Bengali peacock-boat. The Burmese Glass Palace Chronicle mentions a ship covered with Nāga scales and equipped with a snake's head as the gift of a Nāga king to the Burmese king Duttabaung (194). In the West, too, a similar form occurs, e.g. in the representation of a Roman ship on the Moselle with animal heads at bow and stern, in other words, in the zoomorphic shape already met with in Mesopotamia with the doubling of a composite ship's hull. On Hieronymus Bosch's *Temptation of St Anthony* in Lisbon the hindquarters of a water-bird are transformed into the stern of a ship sailing through the air, with superstructure and mast. The galleon-figures, which adorned European ships in immense variety from the seventeenth to the nineteenth century, are allegories whose original, mythological significance has been lost; idols of an earlier age became purely decorative forms, to which only the ship's crews still attributed magical powers.

The first attempts to animate objects, mostly tools and vessels, and especially weapons, by decorating them with human or animal parts were made already in primitive society. They are often judged from a purely aesthetic point of view, as being merely a way of decorating objects, but they also represent an effort to invest the objects with magical powers by means of such decorative enrichment, to enhance their effectiveness – especially if they are weapons – by endowing them with human or animal qualities. Such tendencies do not, as we have said in our introduction, really involve the idea of composite creatures, since there was no conscious shaping or creation of a body. Still, they do represent early forms, which in some cases were later re-shaped to become particular composite beings.

From the abundance of archaeological finds mention may be made of animal handles from Natufien in Palestine (195), a snake-handled knife from Chatal Hüyük (196) and the bone handle in the shape of a human body from Tepe Syalk. It is perhaps not without significance that these archaeological proofs of the increasing theriomorphization of objects have been found so close to the regions in which the developed Mesopotamian and Egyptian civilizations were to arise and that they date from the immediately preceding periods. Objects of a later period adorned with animal or human parts are too numerous to be listed. But special reference must be made to the so-called animal style, represented by objects of daily use mostly decorated with animals or even shaped completely like them. This style is seen in the art of Luristan and Scythia, and also in some earlier forms, such as the famous rein-holders, adorned with animals, from Ur. In every case it is difficult to decide whether it was intended as an attributive, purely decorative, addition of animal parts, or as a transformation of an object into an animal body. We have no space here to investigate this question in detail, and so this subject will be briefly treated as a marginal, if very important, aspect of our subject.

In this connection it may be of interest to note that in the eighteenth century a Portuguese priest invented a flying machine in the shape of a bird and then scooped out its body and covered it as accommodation for aerial passengers. Flying bedsteads and carpets, familiar from fairy-tales, are not infrequently equipped by illustrators with parts of birds, such as wings, but also with heads and limbs. We also find notions of this kind in antiquity. Thus Triptolemus, the Eleusinian bringer of corn, sits upon a chariot consisting of winged snakes, and Dionysus rides on a winged car (197). It is just when Greek artists are reluctant to represent the chief gods in other than normal human shape that they have recourse to animated objects in the place of composite beings such as winged figures. Thus instead of wings we usually find the winged helmet or sandals of Hermes. The same tendency also existed in Mesopotamian art, where a horned crown takes the place of horns sprouting from the head. Cult-columns, divine symbols and divine attributes are given animal or human heads in Mesopotamian illustrations, especially on boundary stones but also on Syrian seals, so that one speaks of a lion-cudgel or a bull-column (198). Famous also are the nail-men, with a human torso terminating in a pointed nail (199).

In Egypt the personification of objects was no less frequent. A clearly recognizable example is the goddess Meschenet, a personification of the childbirth-brick (200). The seat for the women in labour consisted of bricks, which were believed to possess influence over parturition. The representation of Meschenet shows the brick with a woman's head on it. In the case of Egypt, we must point particularly to the popularity of thrones and other pieces of furniture with animal parts, especially lion's feet; arm-rests and seat-backs were often also formed from parts of an animal, heads or even whole bodies. Individual instances need not be mentioned here since every illustrated book of Egyptian art contains numerous examples.

Similar furniture is also found in Mesopotamian and Iranian art, but less frequently. Here it is mostly the lion and the bull which provide the models, undoubtedly because of their strength and power; they were the animals of gods and demons, whose qualities thus pass into the seat and especially the royal throne. As one example of many we may take the relief from Susa in the Louvre, on which both footstool and table have lion's feet (201). From Akkad times onwards royal and divine thrones had animal-headed backs, and are sometimes made in the shape of complete animals. On furniture of Assyrian times animal-headed legs are very common. Here, as in Achaemenid art, Egyptian influence would have been felt in addition to local Mesopotamian traditions; it can also, of course, be clearly traced in Palestine and Phoenicia.

This ancient Near Eastern tradition continues also further east, for example in the Buddha's lion-throne, representations of which do not occur before post-Achaemenid times. Here oriental and Egyptian influences merge with those of classical antiquity, while intermediate stages are shown, for instance, in Parthian-Sassanid art.
The animal thrones of Asiatic rulers were famous until much later times, for example the peacock-throne of the Mughal emperor, which was later carried off to Iran. Lion-footed furniture and even dragon supports were also made in China, though mostly in modern times. One old Chinese form, however, may be mentioned: on a relief from the Han period we find cloud-ribbons terminating in birds' heads, very like the representation of water on an Akkad seal by wavy lines, which end on either side in human torsos with heads (202).
The main line of development, however, runs by way of Greek and Roman art. The animal thrones on the Harpy monument from Xanthos are well known, as is also the throne on the copies of the Zeus of Olympia, or the lion-throne of Cybele. An example from the Roman era is the Vienna cameo portraying Augustus and Roma, on which splendid sphinxes form the supports of the imperial throne. Such animal thrones entered medieval European art from Rome by way of Byzantium. Thus Christ and Mary, and also abbots and temporal rulers, are shown seated upon throne-stools which, hidden by the sitter, allow only the heads of animals, mostly lions, to be seen jutting out at the sides, thus giving the impression that the whole throne is made in the shape of an animal. From the beginning of the fourteenth century down to the present day a throne supported by four lions, in Westminster Abbey, has been the seat on which English monarchs have sat at their coronation.
From the later Middle Ages and the Renaissance (the sphinxes on the throne of Donatello's *Madonna* are an instance) down to the time of our grandfathers and even our fathers, furniture of this type has been produced again and again, but basically it still corresponds to the old models. Sometimes the antique or oriental features are stressed, but the original apotropaeic purpose has long been lost.
In folk literature there are a number of motifs specifically characteristic of furniture. Thus there are food-dispensing tables such as the one in Grimms' famous fairy-tale, or chairs which warn of danger, or bed-legs which crush dangerous animals trying to approach the sleeper. Almost all household utensils were believed to possess such magic properties (203). Often the objects mentioned in the fairy-tales existed also as objects of everyday use. Thus the horse-headed fiddle of the Mongolian fairy-tale was a favourite accompaniment of Mongolian singers: usually it had one string and a horse's head topping its shaft (204).
Here only two further motifs will be dealt with which are often represented: the winged gate and magic weapons. The winged gate appears on the Akkad seals and was often depicted. Frankfort, however, seems not to accept this and conjectures that the intention was to depict the gate of heaven and that it is the sun that makes its

light stream out visibly behind the gate on both sides (205). But he admits that his interpretation is very hypothetical. For us the fact remains that the seals in question clearly show a gate with wings jutting out of its sides – certainly a bizarre notion, which may be difficult to interpret, but which is clearly conveyed by the image. In this case the thought behind the picture must be closely connected with specific ideas existing in Akkad times, since we know neither of survivors of this particular type in later art nor of predecessors in earlier Mesopotamian tradition.

Matters are different with the sword or dagger, a weapon first found illustrated in personified form on the rock of Yazilikaya (Plate 129). The Sumerian god Ningirsu owned, like Ninurta, the divine weapon Sar'ur, regarded by many as a personified weapon (206). Modern scholars interpret the sword-god of Yazilikaya as a chthonic divinity (207). He is formed from a divine head in a pointed cap and a hilt made up of animal bodies, a motif which only the human head distinguishes from the well-known forms of weapons with animal-hilts. If instead of being part of a large rock relief, a small dagger of this shape had been found somewhere, no one would ever have imagined that this was a god or a personified weapon. As it is, it confirms the implications mentioned above. This example shows that it is better to interpret a possible personification in the broadest way than to overlook it because of the small size of the object or of the representation.

There was also sword-worship in India, and even the incarnation of a deity in the shape of a sword, probably connected with Yazilikaya (208). In folk literature, too, the magic sword plays an extremely important role, being the chief weapon of heroes

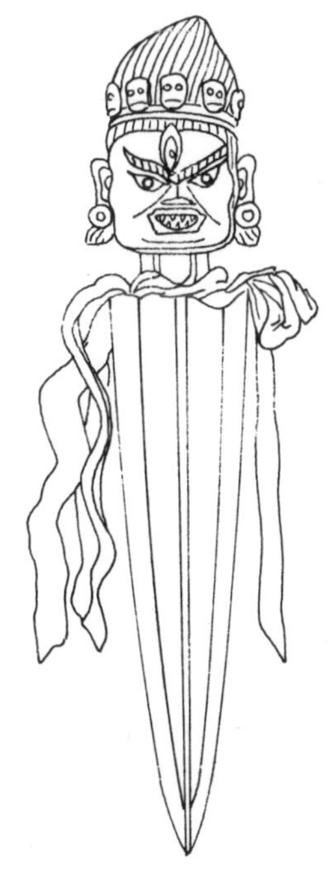

Dagger-man P'ur-bu. Magic dagger. Tibet

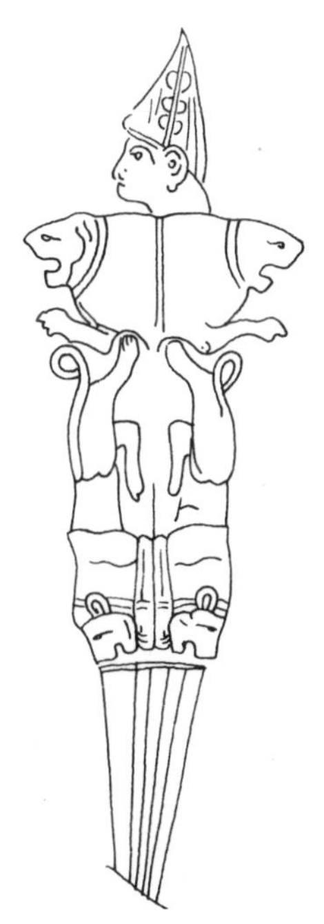

Dagger-god. Hittite. Yazilikaya, 2nd millennium B.C.

Many-headed dagger-man P'ur-bu. Tibet

in myth and epic, fairy-tales and legends, of many peoples. It is often a divine gift and lends its possessor the prowess of the god who has given it (209). There is nothing that magic swords cannot do. Other weapons, such as the javelin or bow and arrow, are far less powerful. There is a singular monster of this type in Lamaism, the magic or personified dagger, P'ur-bu. The head is that of a demon, a three-eyed being with one or more faces – something not unusual in the Tibetan world of demons – and is covered with a skull-shaped crown and set upon a blade. The dagger hilt itself can also be covered with ornamentation (Plate 127) (210).

When in Jacques Callot's *Temptation of St Anthony* a cannon in the form of a fire- and dart-spewing armoured dragon appears as a satirical symbol of war (Plate 128), or the big guns of modern times are given proper names to identify them as individuals, we can recognize rudimentary survivals of those magical notions.

We have covered a lot of ground so far and, with the aid of examples which are far from representing every type, have noted the essential characteristics of the categories which we have chosen and arranged according to their components. But even this systematic arrangement has left such a large residue that a final chapter will be devoted to at least some which still remain. Since, however, we would like to avoid the title 'Miscellaneous' and have anyway been unable to tap the rich sources of literature, we shall try to kill two birds with one stone by taking a trip into the land of fable.

Some readers may have wondered why the title of the present chapter includes a 'marching drum'. This question can now be answered. We have already pointed out that many modern artists are still eager to keep alive ancient artistic endeavours: to personify pictorially something which is not always so clearly conveyed by written description. It seems to us that the picture *Marching Drum* by the Dresden painter, Hans Grundig, is an excellent example of this (Plate 139). It does not march forth like the heroic swords of this chapter to spread death and misery, however much this may be justified as imperative revenge or heroic task: this drum marches out to proclaim the horror of war and to win the people for peace.

Tree-men and root-men.
Moritz v. Schwind,
woodcut, 1847/48

UCIAN, with whose biting comments on some previous writers we began our introduction, goes on to name Ctesias of Cnidos, who, he says, is capable of writing about the Indians and their country without either having seen them or heard of them from someone else. Here Lucian was doing the man an injustice, since Greek knowledge of India derives from Ctesias and from an older writer, Scylax; after these two came a long series of adventure tales and travelogues: Scylax, Menander and Megasthenes were followed by the so-called Pseudo-Callisthenes, who wrote in the same vein on the life and journeyings of Alexander the Great, and by such important figures as Pastor Lamprecht (c. 1140), Rudolf von Ems (c. 1230) and Ulrich von Eschenbach (c. 1280). The passages about the marvels of India were always the most fascinating; they were constantly adapted, adorned and enriched so that India became the wonderland *par excellence*. Such ideas survived down to the eighteenth and nineteenth centuries. Lucian, however, did not appreciate Ctesias fully, for the latter's account contained much that was true. The great Homer himself did not escape Lucian's censure, because he had created the arch-boaster and past master of all tall stories in the person of Odysseus, and made him romance about one-eyed cannibals, creatures with many heads and about his companions being turned into beasts by magical spells. Among Indian travelogues must be included such accounts as Sindbad's voyages from the *Arabian Nights* or those used by Al-Qazwīnī in his *Cosmography*, and taken over by Sir John Mandeville. India remained the most remarkable, though not the only, land of fable. Similar marvels were said to exist in the far north and in Africa, especially in Ethiopia. Lucian himself, who ridiculed stories of the miraculous, was responsible for some of the most sensational, though he freely admits that they were deliberate lies. He thus initiated the long series of extravaganzas, which was to culminate in *Gulliver's Travels to Lilliput and Brobdingnag* and the *Adventures of Baron von Münchhausen*. Here are also to be found the first famous space adventures: the journeys of Lucian and Münchhausen to the moon.

Journeys to Fabulous Countries

It is in these historical – and deliberately fictional – travelogues that most composite monsters appear. Whether allegedly observed or specially invented, they play a large part in literature and above all in visual art, and we have already encountered some of them. It is interesting to find that certain types occur again and again and even find their way into scientific literature, early works of zoology or comprehensive historical works such as Schedel's *Weltchronik* (World Chronicle) or Sebastian Münster's *Cosmographia*. These provided, though not exclusively, the material for the old bestiaries. In this connection mention must be made of the *Physiologus*, which more than any other book transmitted and kept alive the ancient monster shapes for the Middle Ages and in part, too, for modern times.

'They are invincible enemies, people who come from the East. They are called Sciapods or Monocoles, since they have only one foot and what is more, they cover themselves with it when the sun is hot, and hop so fast that no one can catch up with them, and on the sea they leap even faster than on dry land', says Gustav Schwab in retelling the German folk-tale of Duke Ernst. Already mentioned by Scylax, Hecataeus and Ctesias, the Sciapods or shade-footed creatures are here, as indeed in Pliny, identified with another mythical Indian tribe mentioned by Ctesias, the one-footed. The Sciapods protected themselves from the sun with their single foot and their name can be translated, as was done by Lassen, into Hindustani because they come from India, though they do not occur in old Indian texts (211). The one-footed, however, do turn up in ancient Indian literature. In the Rāmāyana they are called Ekapāda and are fast runners. As both imaginary tribes were said to be one-footed they later were identified with each other, probably on the authority of Pliny, who relies on earlier, Greek informants, and whose writings were widely popular, highly regarded and much translated. Sciapods are found in Romanesque sculpture, especially in France (212), and also in illuminations of Gautier de Metz' manuscript *Image du Monde* from Paris, dated 1276. A woodcut illustration to Megenberg's *Puch der Natur* of 1478 (Plate 143) shows a one-footed creature together with other fabulous creatures; Schedel's *Weltchronik* includes them and so does Sebastian Münster's *Cosmographia* of 1544. In a Mandeville illustration of 1481 we find them located in Ethiopia (213). But one-legged men also occur independently of this pedigree – according to local tradition such a creature existed at one time in Madagascar, for example (214).

Megasthenes was the first to mention the Astomi, said to live on the banks of the Ganges. Like the Sciapods they are unknown from Indian writings. Pliny includes them in his *Natural History* (215) and describes them as follows: 'Towards the furthest frontiers of India in the East, around the sources of the Ganges, the Astomi are said to live, a people without mouths and with a very rough body, which they cover with foliage. They are supposed to feed on air alone and on the smell which they breathe in through their noses. They know nothing of meat and drink, but use for nourishment the most varied scents of roots, trees and wild apples, which they carry with them on long journeys in order always to have something to smell. Any more pungent smell is said to be fatal to them.' (216) Although the Astomi are here described in some detail, what distinguished them most was apparently their sense of smell and it is thus not surprising that they are hardly to be recognized in illustrations.

The case of one-eyed creatures is different. They were equally popular with Greek, Arabic and medieval writers, even if their appearance is variously described, and have been represented very frequently and in different shapes. The oldest Greek travelogue to mention them is that of Megasthenes, and therefore later than the time of Alexander. But notions of this sort had long been current in Greece and, as we know from recent archaeological discoveries, were even known in ancient Mesopotamia. There is a one-eyed Cyclops on an Uruk seal (217) and on an early dynastic

Fabulous monsters. From Schedel's *Weltchronik*

seal-impression from Fara (218). We have already spoken of the fire-headed cyclops from Khafaje. In Greek myths the Cyclopes were one-eyed giants, who made thunderbolts for Zeus. The best-known of them, Polyphemus, was blinded by Odysseus. According to Megasthenes the one-eyed people have very hairy chests and pointed canine ears, and a single eye in the middle of the forehead. The Indian equivalent are the Ekalokana in the Mahābhārata (219). No other details are usually given about their appearance. In the folk-tale of Duke Ernst they are called Arimaspians. Literary tradition about the Arimaspians and griffins seems to go back to a poem by Aristeas of Proconnesus and they are originally located in the North. Herodotus and Aeschylus seem also to rely on this source (220). Since the Arimaspi fight with griffins over gold, their home is often sought in the Altai mountains of Mongolia. In his *Cosmography* Al-Qazwīnī speaks of an island with one-eyed inhabitants: they had lost their second eye in a fight with cranes, but even so these descriptions are certainly not unconnected with the reports of older writers (221). The blinding of Polyphemus is depicted on Greek vases but, as in most depictions of this incident in modern art, it is less the one-eyedness that is emphasized than the act of blinding. Illustrations to travelogues are to be found in the books of Megenberg, Schedel and Sebastian Münster, and can be traced back to older, less well-known manuscripts, for example, the *Livre de Merveilles* in the National Library in Paris (222). Here it may be added that triocularity, that is an additional eye, is well known in Indian art. The god Shiva is often portrayed with a third eye and figures of this sort occur later in Tibetan and Mongolian cult pictures.

Among the most striking of the innumerable monstrous creatures of the travelogue are the androgynous creatures who, according to Aristotle, have a male right breast and a female left (223), and the large-lipped people, whose gigantic lower lips provide a welcome shade. These, like many other marvels already mentioned and still to be mentioned, are to be seen on Richard of Haldingham's map of Hereford of about 1280 (224). The Agrippini in the folk-tale of Duke Ernst are described as 'having pointed beaks and known also as crane-heads, but otherwise with human bodies'. In illustrations they have crane's heads and markedly long necks. Such monsters were actually advertised as genuine human freaks on broadsheets of the sixteenth and seventeenth centuries and were given names of their own. Thus a giraffe-necked man is described as follows on a Cologne broadsheet of 1664: 'This is the Tartar whom Count Nicholas of Serin took prisoner anno 1664, signed Joh. Hoffmann' (225). Holländer has shown that Hoffmann had modernized a somewhat older sheet of 1660, in which the shape and origin of the creature were fully described in Latin, German and French:

'This is the figure of a misshapen marvel found on the island of Madagascar in Africa by a ship's captain of Field Marshal von Milleraije, which is at present at Nantes in Brittany but will soon be on view in Paris . . . This misshapen wonder is mild of nature and manageable. Speaks a special language that no one understands. It has been taught to make the sign of the cross. Advice has been sought of doctors of theology and medicine to find out whether it can be baptized. These have bidden that it be taught for four months. If at the end of that time sense and reason was discovered in it, it can be baptized.'

However exact this description may sound, the print is based on copies from older travelogues, on the portrayal of crane-heads such as were found in Schedel's *Weltchronik* of 1493.

Ear-men go back to Scylax, who speaks of ears as big as shovels, and to Ctesias, who describes their ears as being so big that they can be wrapped round arms and back up to the elbows (226). Lassen gives them the Indian name of Karnaprāvarana. According to Megasthenes these people sleep on their ears. These Panoti, who are said by later classical authors to live on an island in the Northern Ocean or in Scythia, are also mentioned in the folk-tale of Duke Ernst – here as Panochi. The Fanesians, a people living in the Caspian Sea, are described as fifteen feet tall, marble-white ear-men, able to wrap the whole of their gigantic bodies in their ears (227). This shows the potential for exaggeration of such descriptions, which were capable of making the fantastic even more fantastic. Pictures of these curious figures are not wanting in old illustrated books. Dog-headed and headless or stomach-faced creatures have already been mentioned. But as these two types are among the most important marvels of fabulous lands, a little more will be said about them here. Réau traces the cynocephalics – the dog-heads – back to Egyptian notions and connects St Christopher, sometimes portrayed with a dog's head, with the jackal-headed Egyptian Anubis (228). But it is just here that literary continuity with Greek travelogues is most marked. Lassen has connected these reports of Ctesias and others with an Indian people which really existed, since they go into such detail and correspond so closely with the social conditions of primitive Indian tribes (229). He cites as a parallel the Indian expression Cunamukha and points out that the name 'dog-heads' may reflect either the contempt in which the more cultured Brahmans held such primitive peoples, or the custom of such tribes to make especial use of dogs for hunting. However such descriptions may be interpreted, the dog-heads are a distinct type of composite creature, even if they are illustrated in various forms. Later European traditions of them go back – as so often – to Pliny (230). They are sometimes pictured as consisting of two bodies, one human and one dog-headed, for instance in the books of Lycosthenes in 1557 (231) and of Aldrovandi, 1642 (232). But far more frequently, they are depicted as single-bodied and dog-headed, as in Schedel's *Weltchronik* and previously on maps such as the Hereford map and others.

Dog-heads are also, of course, to be found in the Alexander literature (233) and in Al-Qazwīnī (234). Here there is mention of dog-faced creatures with wings as well as human-bodied ones. The Franciscan monk Odorico of Pordenone claimed to have found dog-faced people on the Nicobar Islands and John Mandeville took over this

Giant demon. Illustration to 'Sindbad the Sailor' *(Arabian Nights)* by H. Häfner, 1958

story (235). In folk literature, especially in that of the Slav peoples, dog-heads are known as cannibals and were sometimes identified with the Tartars (236). Of no small interest are the headless or stomach-faced men. They, too, are rooted in popular belief, often in the shape of walking corpses. Such headless revenants occur for instance in old Icelandic sagas and in German folklore (237); one of them is the headless shepherd of East Pomerania, the spectre Wor, who carries his head under his arm (238). The numerous representations in the early manuscripts, maps and books already cited probably derive from the description in Pliny. In his *City of God* St Augustine made a statement that caused confusion for centuries (239): 'While I was still Bishop of Hippo, I went to Ethiopia with some Christian slaves to teach the gospel of Christ. There we saw many men and women who had no heads and whose eyes were fixed on their breasts but who were like us in all their other limbs.' Such 'first-hand accounts' based on clerical authority nourished the tradition afresh. Today we sometimes consider such observations as sources of scientific knowledge and interpret them as a reference to pygmies. But for centuries men believed in the existence of stomach-faced people and depicted them unmistakably as miraculous creatures from distant lands. Pygmies were regarded as just such miraculous creatures and were said to live as an independent people in Ethiopia. They were indeed believed to be only as big as a man's hand (240). This fabulous people is clearly to be distinguished from dwarfs, who were also small but could be looked upon as natural creatures.

Here we shall break off, since a detailed examination of further monsters from fabulous lands would hardly add anything to our knowledge of how such ideas were transmitted and realized pictorially. Instead we shall merely enumerate a few names and the fabulous creatures associated with them. There were the Lamias, very beautiful women, seven feet tall, with horse's feet and long hair down to their ankles; women with beards and bald heads, clad in skins; women with boar's tusks and long hair as bristly as an ostrich or a fighting cock, living in the woods of Tartary; six-handed creatures similar to the Indian deities mentioned above. Then there are the marvellous animals, many of which have already been assigned to their categories but some of which must still be mentioned: horse-like animals with lion's feet, thirty foot wide and ten foot thick; two-headed snakes whose eyes shine like lamps; animals with heads like pigs and tails like lions, but with pig's claws each three foot wide; the three-horned monster Odontotyrannus; an animal like a hippopotamus but with the thorax of a crocodile, a back like a saw, and powerful teeth, but as slow as a tortoise; and many others (241).

The *Physiologus*, the moralizing bestiary written in Caesarea presumably in the fourth century A.D. (242), also introduced some monsters so far not mentioned into the medieval repertoire: the ant-lion, with the face of a lion and the hindquarters of an ant, a creature which perhaps owes its existence to an etymological misunderstanding (243); the Antholops, a cunning animal with horns like saws; the Endrop of the Romanian *Physiologus*, half horse, half fish, ploughing through the sea like a demigod

140 The Blowers *(Soplones)*. Etching by Francisco Goya, from Los Caprichos

142 Monster. Detail from the Ramakien cycle in the Wat Phra Keo Temple, Bangkok, Thailand. Early nineteenth century

141 Monster. Detail from the Ramakien cycle in the Wat Phra Keo Temple, Bangkok, Thailand. Early nineteenth century

145 Warriors with sciapods and headless men. Illustration to the Alexander romance. Italian, thirteenth century. University Library, Leipzig

143 Monstrous humans. From Megenberg, Puch der Natur. Augsburg, 1478

144 Monstrous animals. From Megenberg, Puch der Natur. Augsburg, 1478

Deinde amoto exercitu De hominibus sine capite
venerunt ad quandam fluvium in quo erat insula ubi erant ho-
mines sine capite oculos et os habentes in pectore.
quorum longitudo erat pedes xxii latitudo et ualpitas
pedes vii. colore auro similes. Deinde abeuntes per
ipsam silvam invenerunt bestias similes equis. pedes habentes leonum. quarum altitudo erat pedes xxx. Cros-
situdo erat pedes xii.

147 Sinners in hell. Detail from a Thai manuscript, 1776. Staatliche Museen, Berlin

148 Hell. Painting by Lucas Cranach. Staatliche Museen, Berlin

146 God of the dead and demon-monsters. From Tibet. Mode collection

(244); the water serpent Hydrus, a symbol of Christ, said to come from the banks of the Nile.

Far more numerous are the monsters in Arabic sources, among which we count the *Arabian Nights* despite the considerable contributions from India and Persia. Here we must refer again to the winged spirits called Jinn, of which there were good and bad: Maimuna, the daughter of the king of the genies, for example, was a winged fairy with a most noble disposition, whereas Dahnesh was of sinister mien and terrifying appearance. Taken as a whole, however, they are malignant like the Persian Dīwe and Peri; the Peri only assume a beautiful form in order to seduce men from true belief. All these pre-Adamite creatures are ruled by 72,000 sultans, all called Suleiman. Even more malignant are the ogreish Ghuls (ghouls), mostly demons or spirits of the dead, denizens of graveyards, with a likeness to both men and animals.

Jinns and Ifrits are sometimes described in greater detail. Thus one passage reads: 'Out of the earth came an Ifrit, blind in one eye, hump-backed and scaly, with slit eyes deep in his face. On his head he had seven horns, and four locks of hair fell down to his heels; his hands were like pitchforks and his legs like masts; he had nails like lion's claws and feet like those of a wild ass.' (245) In his translation of the *Arabian Nights*, Weil gives this Kashkash six horns, the hands of a forest-devil and the feet of a werewolf (246). (Translators largely take their pictorial parallels from the folklore of the country into whose language they are translating.) As for other remarkable animal-monsters, we mention only the ass-headed fish; the sea-horse, which rises out of the sea like a rampant lion, is taller and broader than ordinary horses, but covers an ordinary mare; and lastly the raven with lion's face and eagle's claws, whose maw emits columns of fire and whose eyes also shower sparks (247). A word must also be said about the gigantic birds, which play an important role not only in the *Arabian*

Der Vogel Fenix.

Fenix soll ein Vogel sein inn der Landtschafft Arabie gegen Orient oder auffgang der Sonnen gelegen / vonn diesem Vogel schreibt man trefliche Philosophische lugen / die ein jeglicher Phantast mit heiliger Göttlicher Schrifft unterstehet zu beweren / vnnd mit diesem werck mancherlei ort heiliger geschrifft zuerkleren / vnd fürnemlich gibt man für / das dieser Vogel on alle vermischung odder zuthuung / D iij men-

Phoenix.

Deutung des Münchkalbs zu Freiberg / Doctoris Martini Luthers.

Monk-calf. Woodcut by Lukas Cranach

Nights but also in other works of Persian and Indian literature: the Roc, which in the tales of Sindbad carries a man sewn in a lamb's skin through the air; the Eorosh of the Zend-Avesta; the Persian Simurgh, the Arabian Anqā and Zāgh. These birds are not always described as composite creatures; it is mainly their extraordinary size to which they owe their unnatural appearance, although some are also said to have dagger-like claws and many eyes. Here we may recall the Stymphalian birds of Greek mythology, which have iron talons and beaks. In Mongolian legend, there is also a crow with an iron beak, a messenger of the king of the gods (248).

The famous Phoenix, the firebird, is usually fantastically described rather than depicted. Herodotus (249) speaks of it and the name is often used, too, as translation of the Chinese wonder-bird, Fêng-huang. It was believed that the Phoenix only came once every 500 years from India to Egypt, burnt itself upon a pyre, and rose once more from its own ashes. The legendary Egyptian bird Benu, worshipped in Heliopolis as the soul of Osiris, is sometimes identified with this Phoenix (250). Its natural shape is defined as being that of a wagtail, or sometimes of a heron. Al-Qazwīnī's *Cosmography* and the zoological reports of Nuzhatū-l-Qulūb, a somewhat later work by a writer of the same name (251), contain numerous accounts both of human-shaped monsters and of purely animal monsters, some of which must here be added in order to attest to the wealth of such marvellous figures in Islamic literature. There are for example winged people on the island Az-Zabig, who speak a language no one understands; there are half-men, called en-Nasnas, who have only half a head, one hand and one foot, but are capable of leaping over great distances on their one foot; the peoples Yāgug and Magug (252), so numerous that only God can count them, with teeth like those of a lion and talons instead of nails. It is said that none of them dies without seeing thousands of his descendants. These books also mention the Monsok, the Ear-men or Panoti already described; a people with two faces, human bodies and long tails; human-headed snakes like the Indian Nāgas; also a race with horse's heads and wings; the Udar, with a penis as big as a bull's horn, which they use as a lethal weapon; a water-man with a tail, and many others. These creatures are already found in the older Qazwīnī. From the zoological section of the work of the younger Qazwīnī should be added: a creature with two wings which uses its tail as a screen, like a peacock; the Fīlsār similar to an elephant but with wings; the water-man Insān with a tail; the two-faced dog-man Sagsār, comparable to the cynocephalics. Finally there are the animal-monsters like the sea-hare with a hare's head and fish's body; the Sulahfāti, tortoise-like, winged yet resembling a man; the Satan, half dog and half cat, with a long proboscis; a fast runner with the body of a lion and a scorpion's tail; Mārītū-ūn, the animal with four heads from the Indian Ocean; and lastly Dū Paikar with one body but two heads, four arms and four legs, and the voice of a bird.

This is a host of hybrid creatures, in which individual features are sometimes repeated but which is otherwise of such bewildering variety that it defies comprehensive survey. They are not all found in pictorial representations and have only been enumerated here in some detail in order to document the wealth of human imagination and to show that literature, too, even if only one kind of literature, has produced a rich variety of monsters. To return to the pictorial representations, we refer to the broadsheets, which on the one hand helped to sustain a belief in miracles and witchcraft but on the other hand castigated conditions in church and state. One such broadsheet shows the sow of Halle, a monster in upright posture, which derives from some of the creatures now familiar to us. The famous Monk's Calf, on a woodcut of 1523, also hard to describe in detail, is an outspoken attack on monks. A woodcut of 1525 shows the mouth of Hell with open jaws, and the Pope being fed into it. Here animal and human parts are mixed. Out of its back grows a tree, on which small devils, swarming everywhere, have hung a cauldron for boiling the poor souls.

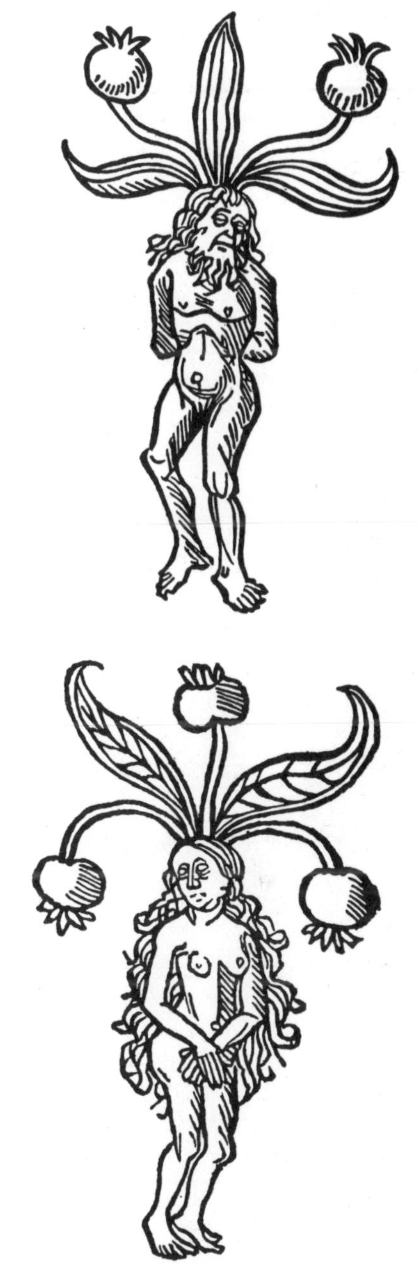

Mandrakes. Woodcuts from the *Hortus sanitatis*. Augsburg, 1486

Worth mentioning here is an oddity with an ancient tradition, which was still taken up occasionally in nineteenth-century illustrated papers. This is the belief in the mandrake and perhaps goes back to ancient notions of a female goblin. Ancient writers refer to the root of the mandragora, while in the Middle Ages its place may be taken by local herbs and roots. The abbess, Hildegard von Bingen, who died in 1178, describes mandrakes in her natural history, which was written in Latin and contained much folklore material. People thought they recognized in this plant the basic features of the human figure, male and female creatures with plant-like growths on head and limbs. A seventeenth-century illustration shows a mandrake-digger using a bugle to drown the dying wails of the exposed plant, described in the caption as the 'mandragora Alraun'. And in a letter from a reader in the Leipzig *Illustrierte Zeitung* of 11 June 1870, under the title 'A Miracle from the Plant World' there is a very remarkable passage about a whitehorn root 30 inches long, a monster known as 'the plant-man', said to be on view in Paris: 'This sport of nature realizes in its own way the fable of the man with a tail, but otherwise shows all human parts with a completeness and natural relationship which must be unique in a formation of this type. The most remarkable feature is the head, which from whatever angle it is seen always looks different; the right-hand view shows a bird of prey, the front view a wolf and the left-hand view a seal. How much of this is artificial we cannot tell, but the Paris newspapers insist on the unspoilt nature of this strange thing.'

Abraxas

Since we have devoted so much space to ancient travelogues and their extraordinary illustrations, we ought to mention also the literature of alchemy and its pictures as they include not only many of the monsters dealt with in detail above – the fish-tailed siren, the winged Mercury, the Uroborus biting its own snake-tail – but also sundry fantastic new creations of a composite character. A mass of such pictorial material has been assembled by C.G. Jung in his book *Psychologie und Alchemie*. Here monster-creation has attained the zenith of symbolic and even systematically masked expression, which makes the greatest demands on the viewer's imagination. A figure resembling the alchemistic forms but going back originally to a divinity is Abraxas, recently explained as an ancient Judaic symbol of God (253). Abraxas or Abrasax, as this tradition has it, is not a name but an 'isopsephic' term defined in Hebrew as 'genatria'. The real name of this figure, which appears on numerous late Roman gems, is Iao, a name for the deity, as is clear from inscriptions accompanying it. The figure itself is remarkable enough. On gems and amulets it has a cock's head on a human body, with lower extremities consisting of snake-bodies terminating in snake's heads. It is thus an anguipede, such as we have already met in our discussion of giants.

The witch is not a composite monster but she can have claw-feet. The 'wild man' very popular in medieval Europe, often in the company of his female counterpart and covered all over with thick hair, is also on the borderline of our subject. He is still a

Ein klag der Wildenholtzleut/ vber die vntrewe welt

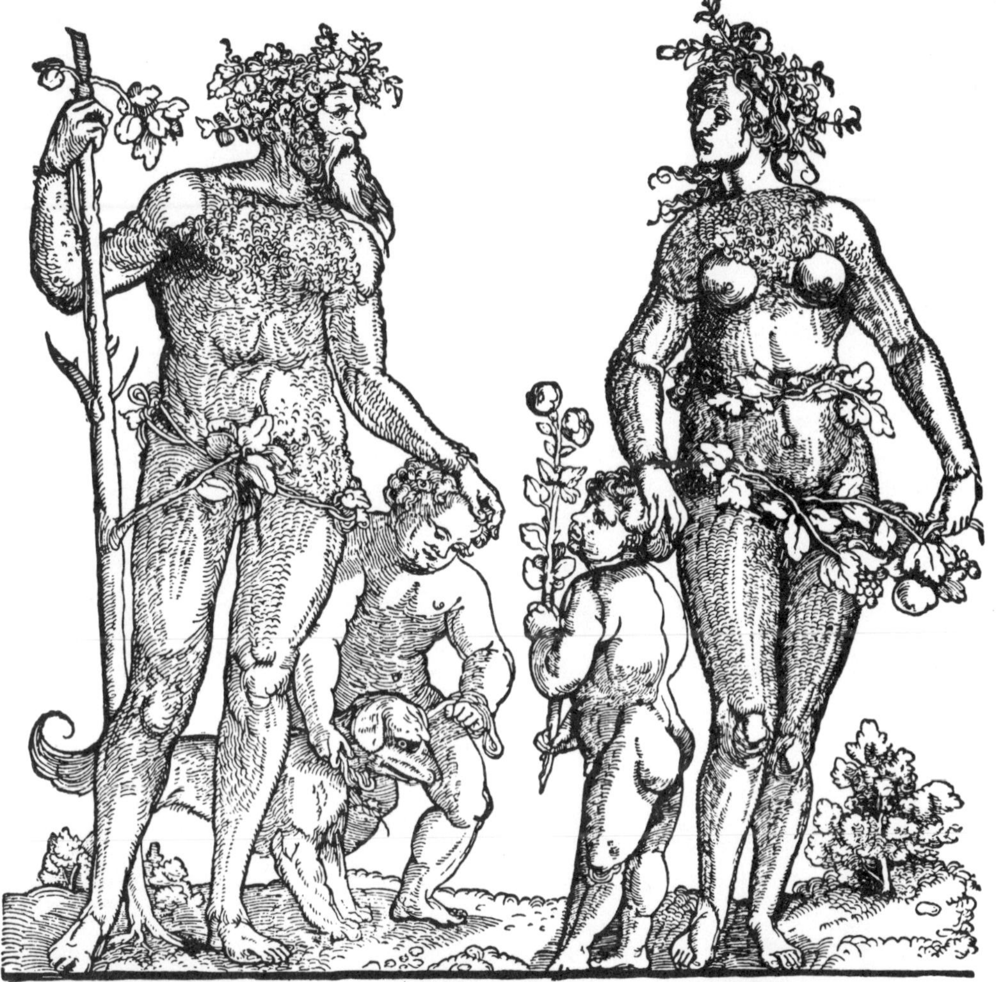

Ach Gott wie verderbt all Welt
Wie starck leyt die vntrew zufelt
Wie hart leyt gerechtigkeit gefangen
wie hoch thut vngerechtigkeit pragen/
Wie sitzt der wucher jetzt in Ehren
wie hart kan arbeit sich erneren
Wie ist gemeiner nutz so thewer
wie fült der eygen nutz sein schewer
Wie nimbt vberhandt die Finantz
wie spitzig ist der Allfantz
Wie vnuerschambt geht gwalt für recht
wie hart die warheit wird durchächt
Wie wird vnschuld mit füssen tretten
wie wenig thut man laster außjetten
Wie ring wigt man das Menschen blut
wie gar helt man kein straff für gut
Wie fürt Reichthumb so grossen pracht
wie ist Armut so gar verracht
Wie steht weißheit hinter der thür
wie dringt reychthumb vnd gwalt herfür
Wie ist Barmhertzigkeit so kranck
wie hat die Lüg ein weiten ganck
Wie regirt der Neyd mit gwalt
wie ist Brüderliche lieb erkalt
wie ist die Trew so gar erloschen
wie hat Miltigkeit außgedroschen
Wie ist Zucht so gar ein spot
wie ist Keuschheit so elend todt
wie ist Leybes wollust so mechtig
wie ist Hoffart so groß vnd prechtig
wie herscht Schmeuchlerey so gwaltig
wie ist Nachred so manigfaltig
wie gern hört man new merlin bringt
wie ist betrug in allen dingen
wie ist die Kunst so gar vnwerd/
wie groß ist die Thorheit auff Erd
wie ist die eygen Ehr so groß
wie ist der Geytz so gar grundtloß
wie ist das Spil so eygennützig
wie geschicht die Raubfrey so trützig
wie ist Diebstal also grob/
wie schwebt die Listigkeit ob
Wie ist Gottsschwern so gemein
wie rechnet man Mäyneydt so klein
wie gar ist Ehebruch mehr kein schandt
wie Fleyschlich ist der Geystlich standt
wie vngezogen ist die Jugendt
wie gar das Alter lebt ohn Tugent
wie vnuerschampt ist weiblich Bild
wie ist Mannlich person so Wild

Gedruckt zu Nürnberg bey Georg Lang Formschneider.

Wild man and wild woman. Woodcut by Hans Schäuffelein. Poem by Hans Sachs. Nuremberg, end of sixteenth century

Fabulous creatures. Seals from the workshop of the Cretan master of Zakro

prominent figure, together with griffin and lion, in the Basle Carnival processions and thus establishes a link between oriental and central European traditions; he also reminds us of notions that occur again and again all over the world, of a carefree 'golden age' when mankind lived naked and in a state of nature. In Chrétien de Troyes' *Ivain* of the twelfth century the 'wild man' is described as a giant, a shepherd with owl's eyes, boar's tusks and elephant's ears. Obviously notions that come from other cultural traditions, and that also form the basis for jinns and Indian rākshasas, have strayed into the picture of paradise and filled it with demons (254).

The so-called grylli form a category of their own. The name comes from a passage in Pliny the Elder and refers to the caricature of a certain Gryllos painted by a contemporary of Apelles, an Egyptian named Antiphilus. This collective name now covers a multitude of distortions, caricatures and deformations, which often end up as composite shapes. In the description of seals the expression is limited to monsters whose body is made up of heads or at any rate secondary to their heads (255). Baltrusaitis distinguishes two basic types: formations in which the head stands directly on the feet and those with multiple heads. We have already come across headless figures, which are here assigned to the first type, as if they had a movable head, which can either stand on its own feet or can wander around the body. Where the face appears on the chest, Baltrusaitis, following earlier scholars, thinks that it can easily become enlarged and thus take up the whole body, which then remains a head on legs. Such changes of shape lead to composite figures such as we later find in extreme form in the work of that painter of monsters *par excellence*, Hieronymus Bosch, or in the work of his equally gifted predecessor the so-called Bosch Cretensis, an extraordinarily imaginative and inventive seal-cutter who flourished at Zakro in Crete in the seventh century B.C.

A large number of seal-impressions have been discovered in a single room of a house in Kato Zakro but not a single seal, though there were several repetitions of the same impression (256). Though we know many other Cretan representations of monsters, among them many of the main oriental types such as griffin and sphinx, nowhere is there such a concentration and variety of the most fantastic creations as in this one room of a house in a small Cretan town. Whether these seal-engravings constitute attempts, made for purposes unknown to us, to vary demons' shapes dictated by religion or – as is less likely at this period – a playful fantasy as expression of creative joy, the fact remains that here we have a wealth of material packed into a small time and space, which in all probability points to a single hand. Its repertoire is unique among all the material dealt with here.

Despite the great variety of forms, few basic elements are in fact used – the human face, lower body and feet, the female breast and genitals, bird's heads and wings, goat's heads, stag's antlers, the wings of butterfly and bat, and also some inanimate objects – and the principle of contraction is often employed as with the grylli discussed above.

Unfortunately many of the tiny images are seriously damaged but they reveal the hand of an artist who was among the greatest of those who ever depicted such creatures.

With Hieronymus Bosch we come to an artist of more recent times, whose work is centred on the shapes of demons, on the combination of disparate things into new entities, on the personification of pictorially realized horror in ever new flights of fancy bordering on the grotesque. This is in no way a criticism of Bosch – though experts have so interpreted it and have described him not as a fantast, but as a profound mystic. In the course of our survey the point has been made that the creation of such monsters may not only be great art but can, in the creative invention of shapes, serve to liberate man from his secret terrors and inmost distress. With his monstrous reptiles Bosch breaks through the conventions of a gentle soothing art. He consciously creates tension but also a sense of release – contrasts which alone give meaning to his hermit and spirit figures, and which, as has long been observed, achieve a new picture of man become inwardly free, not unlike certain images in the Buddhist art of the Far East.

Unfortunately not much of the great artist's work has come down to us and even the little that has survived can hardly be touched upon in our short survey. We must content ourselves with pointing out how even such an individual artist as Bosch reaches back to forms and motifs used by his predecessors or unconsciously achieves something similar. With a little knowledge of the subject not only the monsters of alchemy but also the grylli and some of the fabulous creatures from distant countries can be detected in Bosch's work. Much of it derives from traditional folklore material which had not until then been pictorially realized. It is only possible here to indicate the general features, otherwise it would be necessary to go into every minute detail of each individual figure. At any rate it is not the large creatures such as griffins, sphinxes and centaurs that Bosch depicts, but small man-animals and animal-men created experimentally, and man-made or natural objects endowed with life. He also contracts forms like the Cretan seal-engraver, and owes his effects often more to what he leaves out than to what he adds. Sometimes heads and limbs are missing, and in most cases the neck, and yet he always succeeds in convincing us that his figures are alive.

One may regard Bosch as a solitary, an individualist; certainly he influenced many artists – quite apart from his immediate, very mediocre imitators – by putting ideas into their heads, even when they had different intentions and a different style. It is likely that even Goya was not uninfluenced by Bosch, especially as many extant works of the Netherlandish artist had long been in Spain. Though monsters in the narrow sense of the word are rarely seen in Goya's work, the demonic element pervades his conception of nature.

Fantastic figures. From ancient gems

The work of Bosch has strong affinity to folk-poetry, to the fairy-tale and to popular imagery. It is not mythological symbolism but narrative imagination, humorous

Fantastic figures. From ancient gems

despite all the horror portrayed, that constitutes the artistic charm of his work. In this he undoubtedly had followers, not only in his own country, but even among quite recent artists. The wide-ranging visual record that continues down to the present day is never at a loss for material, because – even in this age of cosmic exploration – unexplored forces and phenomena can be vividly presented both in words and in images. From children's picture books to high-quality science fiction monster-creations serve to give visual form to phenomena which are not, or not yet, found in concrete form.

It is not possible to go far into fields adjacent to our subject, but one creative process which is closely connected with it and which has proved an inspiration and a model to many modern artists, must be dealt with briefly.

Distinct from the hybrid monster, there have always been playfully combined and mixed shapes, including those made up from single figures, like a game which used to amuse our grandparents. The players had to arrange themselves in shapes and sometimes also created groups of figures in pyramid form or in twisted postures so that a new figure emerged and the audience had to guess what the figure represented. If we follow the history of such shapes composed of individual figures, we shall remember certain tendencies on ancient Mesopotamian seals which we called playfully decorative. We have already mentioned the peculiar animal-style of steppe-art, foreshadowed in early Indian and Minoan art, with its circular animals, inversions, and groups of men or animals arranged as wheels.

A highly individual artist, Giuseppe Arcimboldo, who was active before 1600 in Vienna as court painter to the Emperors Maximilian III and Rudolf II, created portraits and picture-puzzles pieced together from various kinds of fruit, vegetables, objects and so on. For instance, he painted 'Summer' as a head consisting of summer fruits, vegetables, grasses and branches; and 'Water', composed of many kinds of fishes, bizarre aquatic animals and the like. Arcimboldo was certainly not the inventor of this genre, but he was its most prominent exponent. Thus, for example, in a sixteenth-century recruiting woodcut for the army, a little devil held in the mouth is at the same time the aggressive beard of a striding warrior. From about the same period comes a man's portrait put together from agricultural implements. In later times the same method was used in caricature, as in a representation of Napoleon on a German broadsheet of 1814: an eagle serves as cap, the face is composed of naked human bodies and the robe of a cobweb-like map, a clear allusion to the Corsican's battles. This manipulation of shapes was also adopted for erotic images such as the face of an old rake made up of naked women's bodies. Quite early on this method was used to caricature technology, especially new machines or those of the future.

On a mid-seventeenth-century picture of a scene from the Mogul's court by the Dutch painter Willem Schellinks several composite figures such as are described above appear as upon a stage. A Mogul ruler is portrayed in his litter, a horse with a rider, and an elephant and a camel also with riders. Here models from India have quite

Fantastic figures

Sea creatures. From Sebastian Münster, *Cosmographia*, Basle, 1550

obviously been imitated, and some very similar Indian examples have in fact come down to us (257). For example the god of love, Kāma, rides not on a real peacock but on one made up of the bodies of three girls; Krishna rides on a horse composed entirely of Gopis, i.e. shepherdesses.

A comparatively large number of such images have come down to us, not only in illuminated manuscripts but also in carvings on ivory caskets and on the terracotta temples of Bengal, so that this type may be defined as Indian, even though no older examples have yet been found in that country. Significantly enough, however, we find the wheel-figure in medieval Indian art, and already on early Indian seals it appears contemporaneously with Mesopotamian seal-pictures. Such figure groups were also known in the neighbouring countries, Ceylon and Persia, but are only attested in more recent times.

We have included this section because a pictorial type which seems to have circulated only in more recent times provides a variant which, in complete reversal of original monster-invention, attempts to achieve an imitation of nature by the mixture of different formal elements. As so often, what was once very serious has become a game.

In his *Galgenlieder* (Songs from the Gallows) the German poet Christian Morgenstern (1871–1914) proposes 'new creations of nature': the ox-sparrow, the camel-duck, the rain-lion, the pigeon-toad, the whale-bird, the peacock-ox, the werefox, the 'daytingale', the owl-worm, the giraffe-hedgehog, the rhinopony, and others. These are partly ingenious whimsies and plays on words but at the same time they show how language itself can create composite creatures. There are more such fictional creations than one might suppose. Indeed many other compounds which describe monsters are such 'word-monsters', like wing-gate, and wing-sun. An expression like revolver-muzzle has been effectively used in political satire. This is yet another form of the mental acrobatics described in the case of those figures.

If we survey once more the long road we have travelled in so short a time, we can summarize our most significant results: the continuous train of monsters stretching across five millennia, from their birth-place in the Near East, in Egypt and in India, right up to the present day, links us with the very beginnings of our culture in a very curious way. But it should not be forgotten that they still illuminate and brighten our lives. It is in no small measure that they have contributed towards bringing primeval fears into the bright light of living reality, giving visible shape to creatures of the imagination, and thus bringing them out of mystical concealment and unfathomable eternity on to the brief stretch of earthly life, making them mortal. Even though many of these forms and images of great antiquity are still alive today, their significance, their real life is to most people now unintelligible and in need of explanation. They have long been abandoned to ridicule, but let us not forget that this was not possible until they had been given visual shape and thus made mortally vulnerable. And let us also remember that a span of human history has been preserved in these shapes which, created by the artist's hand, still offer aesthetic pleasure and intellectual enjoyment.

Sphinx. Axel Leskoschek:
'Departure'.
From the cycle 'Odysseus'.
Woodcut, 1939

1 Lucian, *The True History*, Book I.
2 Charles Gould, *Mythical Monsters*, London 1886.
3 Othenio Abel, *Vorzeitliche Tierreste im Deutschen Mythus, Brauchtum und Volksglauben*, Jena 1939.
4 *Ars Poetica*, 1sq.
5 *De architectura* VII.
6 Often quoted from a letter to the Abbé Guillaume de St Thiery. Here after A. Rosenberg, *Engel und Dämonen*, Munich 1967, p. 172.
7 Pausanias, *Description of Greece.*
8 Pausanias, op. cit.
9 Otto Keller, *Die antike Tierwelt*, vol. 2, Leipzig 1913, p. 303.
10 e.g. J. Ansbacher, *Die Abschnitte über die Geister und wunderbaren Geschöpfe in Qazwīnīs Kosmographie*, Thesis, Erlangen 1905, especially p. 29.
11 Wilhelm Wundt, *Völkerpsychologie*, vol. IV, *Mythus und Religion*, ch. 3, 'Tier-, Ahnen- und Dämonenkulte', 3rd edition, Leipzig 1920, p. 322sq.
12 Wundt, op. cit. pp. 371–2.
13 Nicolai Gogol, *Devils, Witches and Cossacks*, p. 1.
14 Advocated by H. Frankfort, *Cylinder Seals*, London 1939, p. 64sq.
15 A. Rosenberg, *Engel und Dämonen*, Munich 1967, p. 16.
16 J. Grimm, *Deutsche Mythologie*, ch. XXXIII.
17 Tobit, 3:8; Picard in *Encyclopedia of World Art*, X, p. 255.
18 Revelation of St John, 9: 11; *Handbuch des Deutschen Aberglaubens*, vol. I, p. 6.
19 Revelation of St John, 9: 7sq.
20 Most recently Otto E. Dietz, in H. W. Haussig, *Wörterbuch der Mythologie*, Stuttgart 1965, p. 46sq.
21 Bonnet, *Reallexikon der Ägyptischen Religionsgeschichte*, 1952, p. 339.
22 Picard in *Encyclopedia of World Art*, X, p. 259.
23 On this and the following names, see Bonnet, op. cit.
24 Reingart Würfel, 'Die ägyptische Fabel in Bildkunst und Literatur', *Wissenschaftliche Zeitschrift, University of Leipzig*, 1952-53, no. 3, pp. 63–77. The fable-character in no way contradicts the fact that such pictures may be looked upon as caricatures. This is supported by the term chosen by Egyptologists: 'satirical papyrus'.
25 Examples from the Middle Ages in W. von Blankenburg, *Heilige und dämonische Tiere*, Leipzig 1943; also Champfleury, *Histoire de la caricature antique*, Paris 1867, with numerous illustrations.
26 C. Netto and G. Wagener, *Japanischer Humor*, Leipzig 1901.
27 E. A. Armstrong, *The Folklore of Birds*, London 1958, p. 21.
28 loc. cit., fig. 23.
29 Eugen Holländer, *Wunder, Wundergeburt und Wundergestalt...*, Stuttgart 1921, p. 275.
30 Frequently illustrated.
31 Ovid, *Metamorphoses* III, 193–197.
32 *Encyclopedia of World Art*, vol. IV, plate 92.

Centaur. Pen drawing by Hans Baldung-Grien. About 1515

Neueingerichter und vielverbesserter
Abentheurlicher
SIMPLICISSIMUS
Das ist:
Beschreibung deß Lebens eines seltzamen Vaganten/ genant Melchior Sternfels von Fuchshaim/ wie/ wo und welcher gestalt Er neml. in diese Welt kommen/ was er darin gesehen/ gelernet/ erfahren und außgestanden/ auch warum er solche wieder freywillig quittiret hat.
Uberauß lustig/ und männiglich nützlich zulesen.
An Tag geben
Von
GERMAN SCHLEIFHEIM
von Sulsfort.
Mompelgart/
Gedruckt bey Johann Fillion
Im Jahr M DC LXIX,

Title-page: 'Abentheurlicher Simplicissimus...'
Mompelgart MDCLXIX

33 J. Moreau, *Die Welt der Kelten*, Stuttgart 1958, plates 96 and 97.

34 Assa-mukhi: Smith, V. A., *History of Fine Art in India and Ceylon*, Oxford 1911, fig. 38; Kalkyavatara of Vishnu: Jean Boisselier, *Tendances de l'art Khmer*, Paris 1956, fig. III.

35 F. S. Krauss, *Volksglauben ... der Südslaven*, 1890, p. 60.

36 E. Veckenstedt, *Wendische Sagen, Märchen und abergläubische Gebräuche*, Graz 1880, p. 106.

37 Haussig, op. cit., section 'Slaven', p. 187; cf. also Vollmer, *Vollständiges Wörterbuch der Mythologie*, Stuttgart 1836, p. 1136.

38 Haussig, op. cit., p. 131.

39 Stith Thompson, *The Types of the Folktale*, Helsinki 1964, Type 400.

40 A. Dessenne, *Le Sphinx*, Paris 1957.

41 H. Bonnet, *Reallexikon der Ägyptischen Religionsgeschichte*, Berlin 1952, p. 269.

42 Stith Thompson, *Motif-Index of Folk Literature*, vol. 3, Copenhagen 1956, sec. 761; Ludwig Leistner, *Das Rätsel der Sphinx*, Berlin 1889, 2 vols.

43 H. J. Rose, *A Handbook of Greek Mythology*.

44 Dessenne, op. cit., p. 14.

45 E. Baer, *Sphinxes and Harpies in Medieval Islamic Art*, Jerusalem 1965, part XII.

46 Chavannes, *La Sculpture sur pierres en Chine*, Paris 1893, plate XII a.

47 Rose, op. cit., p. 5.

48 Iliad I, 268; II, 743ff., etc.

49 L. Réau, *Iconographie de l'art Chrétien*, vol. I, p. 119, Paris 1955.

50 W. Neuss, *Zeitschrift des Deutschen Vereins für Kunstwissenschaft*, vol. 8, nos. 3/4, Berlin 1941, p. 113sq.

51 Baer, op. cit, p. 68sq.

52 F. Hommel, *Die Aethiopische Übersetzung des Physiologus*, Leipzig 1877, p. 60.

53 cf. *Reallexikon der Vorgeschichte*, vol. 2, plate 5.

54 Rosenberg, op. cit., p. 16; W. F. Albright, What were the Cherubim? The Biblical Archaeologist, vol. I, Feb. 1938, p. 2.

55 Réau, op. cit., vol. I, p. 124; V. H. Debidour, *Le bestiaire sculpté du Moyen Age en France*, 1961, p. 194.

56 Friedrich Alfred Schmidt Noerr, *Der Drache über der Welt*, Weimar (no date), p. 29.

57 According to the text of the oldest print of 1474, Leipzig 1923, p. 74.

58 op. cit., p. 94.

59 Kees in Bonnet, op. cit., p. 74sq.

60 Frankfort, op. cit., p. 132sq.

61 Frankfort, op. cit., p. 132sq.

62 G. Weicker, *Der Seelenvogel*, Leipzig 1902.

63 From the year 1211, cf. Réau, op. cit., vol. I, p. 121.

64 Baer, op. cit., p. 25sq.

65 J. Stephenson, *The Zoological Section of Nuzhatū-l-Qulūb*, London 1928, p. 48.

66 Baer, op. cit., plate XXVII
67 Baer, op. cit., p. 34sq.
68 Ray-Mode, *Bengalische Märchen*, Leipzig 1969, 'Der Taubenprinz', p. 369ff. and jacket title.
69 Alexander's Letter to Aristotle. Die syrische Übersetzung des Pseudo-Callisthenes, V. Ryssel, p. 365.
70 W. W. Skeat, *Malay Magic*, London 1900, p. 110, n. 2. Also the unpublished thesis by D. Sörgel, *Die Schlange in Mythos und Kult in Burma*, Leipzig 1969, e.g. p. 191.
71 Weinhold, *Zeitschrift des Vereins für Volkskunde*, 5, 1895.
72 Panzer, *Handwörterbuch des Deutschen Aberglaubens*, vol. VI, p. 71.
73 Blankenburg, op. cit., plates 22, 37, etc.
74 Blankenburg, op. cit., plate 35 from Remagen.
75 Villars, *Introduction sur les sciences secrètes*, vol. I, p. 27, edition of 1742.
76 Zimmern, *Zeitschrift für Assyriologie*, N.S., 1934, pp. 9–11; Haussig, op. cit., p. 117;
Picard in *Encyclopedia of World Art*, vol. X, p. 253.
77 A. M. Belenitski, *Arts Asiatiques*, V, 3, 1958, p. 165.
78 Stephenson, op. cit., p. 51.
79 H. Frankfort, op. cit., p. 132.
80 Sörgel, op. cit., pp. 16–7.
81 A. K. Coomaraswamy, *Geschichte der Indischen und Indonesischen Kunst*, Leipzig 1927, pp. 203–4.
82 Max von Brandt, *China*, pp. 60 and 68.
83 Bonnet, op. cit., pp. 853–4.
84 Bonnet, op. cit., pp. 455–6.
85 *Larousse Encyclopedia of Mythology*, London 1962, J. Viau, p. 41.
86 Haussig, op. cit., p. 120.
87 Hesiod, *Teogony*, 295sq. trans. A. W. Mair, Oxford 1906, pp. 41–2.
88 Keller, op. cit., p. 300.
89 C. E. Smith, *The Evolution of the Dragon*, London 1919, p. 81.
90 e.g. E. T. C. Werner, *Myths and Legends of China*, London 1924, p. 208.
91 H. Doré, *Researches into Chinese Superstitions*, trans. W. Kennelly, 1st part, vol. V, Shanghai 1922, p. 681.
92 E. Unger, *Reallexikon der Assyriologie*, 1938, 'Drachen und Drachenkämpfe'.
93 Unger, op. cit., p. 234; Haussig, op. cit., p. 259.
94 Isaiah, 27: 1; Job, 40 and 41.
95 Haussig, op. cit., p. 178; Picard in *Encyclopedia of World Art*, X, p. 255.
96 Hesiod, *Theogony*, v. 333.
97 Hesiod, *Theogony*, v. 823sq.
98 H. J. Rose, *A Handbook of Greek Mythology*.
99 *Sumerische und Akkadische Hymnen und Gebete*, by A. Falkenstein and W. von Soden, Zurich/Stuttgart 1953, p. 60.
100 Yasna 9, 7f.
101 Doré, op. cit., p. 677sq.

Title page: 'Grobianus'

Grobianus/

Von groben ſitten / vnd vnhöfflichen geberden / Erſtmals in Latein beſchriben/ durch den wolgelerten M. Fridericum Dedekindum/ vnd jetzund verteutſchet durch Caſparum Scheidt von Wormbs.

Hic nullus uerbis pudor, aut reuerentia menſæ,
Porcorum uiuit gens pecuina modo.

Liß wol diß büchlin offt vnd vil/ Vnd thů allzeit das widerſpil.

102 Translated from Doré, op. cit., pp. 691–2.
103 L. Bezacier, *Arts Asiatiques* XI, 1, 1965, p. 23.
104 loc. cit. p. 21.
105 J. Stephenson, op. cit., pp. 36–7.
106 Revelation of St John, 12,3sq.
107 Debidour, op. cit., ill. 312 and p. 220.
108 Cf. the unpublished thesis by A. Vahlen, *Mischwesendarstellungen in der kretischen Kunst*, Halle 1969, p. 15sq.
109 Pauly-Wissowa, *Real Encyklopädie der Classischen Altertumswissenschaft*, vol. 7, Stuttgart 1912, p. 1904sq.
110 Baer, op. cit., plate LVI, 99.
111 Debidour, op. cit., fig. 19, Saint Restitut, 11th century.
112 Fr. Sieber, *Sächsische Sagen*, Jena 1926, pp. 197–8.
113 Illustrations in Debidour, op. cit. and Réau, L., op. cit., pp. 113–4.
114 *Handwörterbuch des Deutschen Märchens*, vol. II, under 'Fahrzauber'.
115 Cf. the footnote in W. McCulloch, *Bengali Household Tales*, London 1912, p. 256,1.
116 Haussig, op. cit., p. 100.
117 Debidour, op. cit., figs. 411, 413.
118 Odette Viennot, *Typologie du makara* ..., I, *Arts Asiatiques* I, 3, 1954, p. 189sq.; II, *Arts Asiatiques* V, 3, 1958, p. 183ff. and V, 4, p. 272sq.
119 Frankfort, op. cit., p. 17.
120 H. Bonnet, *Reallexikon der Ägyptischen Religionsgeschichte*, Berlin 1952, pp. 373.
121 J. Baltrusaitis, *Le Moyen Age Fantastique*, Paris 1955, fig. 29.
122 Bussagli, *Encyclopedia of World Art*, X, p. 268.
123 L. Frobenius, *Volksmärchen der Kabylen*, vol. III, Jena 1921, p. 309sq.
124 Cory, *Indian Antiquary*, August 1892, p. 250sq.
125 Feilberg, 'Der böse Blick', *Zeitschrift des Vereins für Volkskunde*, 11th year 1901, p. 317.
126 Frankfort, op. cit., plate VI, c.
127 Cf. the unpublished thesis by D. Sörgel, *Die Schlange in Mythos und Kult in Burma*, Leipzig 1969, pp. 108 and 191.
128 A. Boner, Silpa Prakasa, I, v. 360–1.
129 *Arts Asiatiques* VI, 3, 1959, p. 198, Lohuizen de Leeuw.
130 Boner, op. cit., plate XVIII, 6.
131 E. Balfour, *The Cyclopaedia of India* ..., 1885, reprinted Graz 1968, vol. III, pp. 1105–6.
132 R. Ettinghausen, *The Unicorn*, Washington 1950, p. 19.
133 Boner, op. cit., II, 658.
134 A. K. Coomaraswamy, op. cit., pp. 113, 131.
135 *Arts Asiatiques*, VI, 3, 1959, p. 212.
136 *Physiologus*, German version by E. Peters, Munich 1921.
137 Doré, op. cit., p. 672.
138 Ettinghausen, op. cit., especially p. 3.
139 op. cit., p. 60.
140 op. cit., p. 64.
141 Haussig, op. cit., p. 106.

'Melusina'. Russian woodcut, first half of eighteenth century

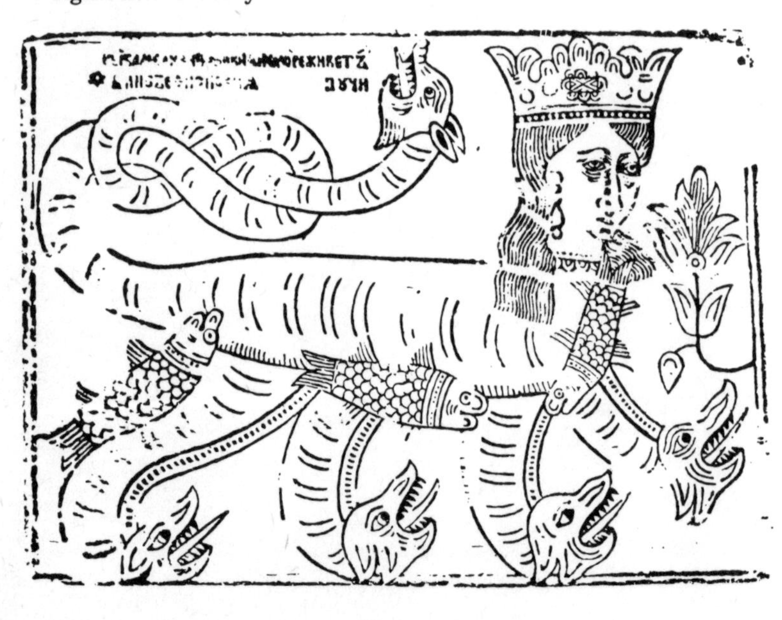

142 W. Kirfel, *Die dreiköpfige Gottheit*, 1948.
143 Réau, L., op. cit., pp. 21–2.
144 Hesiod, *Theogony*, lines 280, 311/312 and 319/324, trans. A. W. Mair, Oxford 1908.
145 H. J. Rose, *Handbook of Greek Mythology*.
146 Bittel, *Archiv f. Orientforschung*, XI, pp. 55–6.
147 J. D. S. Pendlebury, *The Archaeology of Crete*, London 1955, plate XIV, 1.
148 MS, A. Vahlen, *Kretische Mischwesen*, p. 56.
149 Bissing, *Archiv f. Orientforschung*, 5, 1928, p. 72.
150 F. Poulsen, *Der Orient und die frühgriechische Kunst*, Berlin 1912, p. 42.
151 *Athenische Mitteilungen*, 1896, plate V, 3.
152 Rose, op. cit., p. 57.
153 Both words coined by H. Frankfort, *Cylinder Seals*, p. 49 (Bullmen with double hindquarters, lion-legged men).
154 Numerous examples are given by W. v. Blankenburg, op. cit., p. 104sq., cf. also R. Grousset, *China*, fig. 41.
155 Coomaraswamy, *Journal of the American Oriental Society*, 1929.
156 Baer, op. cit., plate XVIII, 30.
157 C. Schuster, *A Perennial Puzzle*, 'Art and Thought', presented to Coomaraswamy on his 70th birthday, 1947, p. 116sq.
158 Debidour, op. cit., fig. 174.
159 Bonnet, *Reallexikon der Ägypt. Religionsgeschichte*, p. 55; *Ancient Egypt and the East*, 1934, II, p. 115sq.
160 Metten Bible, about 1414, Munich.
161 Baltrusaitis, op. cit., p. 19.
162 Pauly-Wissowa, *Altertumskunde*, 2, vol. 5, p. 647.
163 A. J. Carney, *Iranian Mythology*, Boston 1917.
164 *Arabian Nights*.
165 Rose, op. cit., pp. 110–11.
166 Schatz, *Die griechischen Götter*, p. 25.
167 *Der Rohrspatz, Ein Fabelbuch von Th. Etzel*, 1907, p. 73sq.
168 *Forschungen und Fortschritte*, 18th year, nos. 15/16, 1942.
169 Bonnet, *Reallexikon der Ägyptischen Religionsgeschichte*, Berlin 1952, p. 88sq.
170 H. W. Haussig, *Wörterbuch der Mythologie*, Stuttgart 1965, p. 196sq.
171 Frankfort, op. cit., p. 207sq.
172 E. Otto, *Egyptian Art and the Cults of Osiris and Amon*, London 1968, plate 10.
173 Sippar plaque, Frankfort, op. cit., p. 114.
174 Frankfort, op. cit., plate XX, k and text fig. 32.
175 Haussig, op. cit., p. 115–6.
176 G. Contenau, *Les Tablettes de Kerkouk*, plate X.
177 Frankfort, op. cit., plate XXI, a.
178 *Sumerische und akkadische Hymnen und Gebete* by A. Falkenstein and W. v. Soden, Stuttgart, 1953, p. 185.
179 loc. cit., p. 186.
180 Bonnet, op. cit., p. 82sq. under 'Baumkult'.
181 E. Neumann, *The Great Mother*, New York 1955, plate 103.

Dagon. Assyrian fish-god

The Woman of the Seven Deadly Sins.
From the Metten Bible, about 1414

182 K. von Spiess, *Marksteine der Volkskunst*, part 2, Berlin 1942, p. 50 sq.
183 cf. the detailed footnote in R. Burton, *1001 Nights*, Calcutta, vol. VIII, p. 60.
184 Baltrušaitis, op. cit., pp. 120 and 121, pictures.
185 J. de Mandeville, op. cit., fig. 58 B.
186 Frankfort, op. cit., p. 104.
187 H. Frankfort, *The Art and Architecture of the Ancient Orient*, plate 58 B.
188 E. Otto in *Reallexikon der Vorgeschichte*, vol. 8, plate 47 f.
189 Frankfort, *Cylinder Seals*, plate XXIV, b.
190 Frankfort, op. cit., plate XXII, e.
191 Gordon 29, BM 727.
192 Frankfort, op. cit., plate XVIII, j.
193 Frankfort, op. cit., p. 67 and p. 108.
194 Unpublished MS, D. Sörgel, *Die Schlange* ... Leipzig 1969, p. 20.
195 J. Mellaart, *Earliest Civilizations of the Near East*, London 1965, p. 25 and p. 28.
196 J. Mellaart, *Chatal Hüyük*, London 1967, p. 213.
197 Buschor, Furtwängler-Reichold, plate 161 and p. 261.
198 Unger in *Reallexikon der Vorgeschichte*, vol. 8, p. 215; Frankfort, op. cit., plate XLIV, h.
199 Unger, loc. cit., p. 210.
200 Bonnet, op. cit., p. 458.
201 Louvre relief; Pritchard, J. B., *The Ancient Near East in Pictures*, 1954, figure 144.
202 K. With, *Bildwerke Ost- und Südasiens*, Basle 1924, plate 1 and 2.
203 Stith Thompson, op. cit., vol. II under D 1150.
204 W. Heissig, *Mongolische Märchen*, 1963, no. 6 and p. 262.
205 Frankfort, op. cit., p. 128.
206 Haussig, op. cit., p. 122; *Encyclopedia of World Art*, vol. X, p. 253.
207 Haussig, op. cit., p. 161.
208 H. Damant, *Indian Antiquary*, 1875, p. 114.
209 Stith Thompson, op. cit., vol. II D 1081.
210 A. Grünwedel, *Mythologie des Buddhismus*, Leipzig 1900, fig. 24.
211 Khājāpāda, Chr. Lassen, *Indische Alterthumskunde*, 2nd ed. Leipzig 1874, vol. 2, p. 656, note 1.
212 Réau, op. cit., I, p. 125.
213 Illustrations in E. Holländer, op. cit., figs. 158, 159, 161, 162, 163.
214 Tokan-dia, cf. Cory, op. cit., p. 250 sq.
215 Pliny, book 7, ch. 2.
216 op. cit.
217 Pierpont Morgan Collection, no. 4.
218 Heinrich, *Fara*, 1931, plate 44 n.
219 Lassen, op. cit., vol. 2, p. 656, note 1.
220 E. Rohde, *Der griechische Roman*, Leipzig 1876, p. 174–5.
221 Ansbacher, op. cit., p. 31, 1905, p. 31.
222 Illustrations in E. Holländer, op. cit., figs. 156, 158, 159, 163.

223 Pliny, book 7, ch. 2.

224 *Encyclopedia of World Art*, vol. III, Cosmology and Cartography, plate 494.

225 Holländer, op. cit., fig. 151 sq.

226 Lassen, op. cit., 2nd ed., vol. 2, p. 656, note 1.

227 Weule, *Die Urgesellschaft in ihrer Lebensführung*, p. 8.

228 Réau, op. cit., vol. I, p. 124.

229 Lassen, op. cit., 2nd ed., vol. 2, p. 659.

230 Pliny, book 7, ch. 2.

231 De Prodigiorum ac Ostentorum Chronicon.

232 Monstrorum Historia, Bologna 1642.

233 J. Brummack, *Die Darstellung des Orients* . . ., Berlin 1966, p. 120.

234 Ansbacher, op. cit., pp. 31 and 36.

235 F. Kretzschmar, *Hundestammvater und Kerberos*, Stuttgart 1938, 2 vols., vol. I, p. 40 sq., etc.

236 E. Byhan, *Wunderbaum und Goldener Vogel, slovenische Volksmärchen*, Eisenach 1958, p. 149; F. S. Krauss, *Volksglaube, etc. der Südslaven*, 1890, p. 132. Here, incidentally, the one-eyed creature with the eye in the middle of its forehead: Dziganda.

237 K. Preisendanz, *Akephalos, der kopflose Gott*, 1926; *Handwörterbuch des deutschen Aberglaubens*, vol. V, p. 215 sq.

238 *Zeitschrift des Vereins für Volkskunde*, 13, 1903, p. 188/189.

239 Holländer, op. cit., p. 301.

240 Réau, op. cit., vol. I, p. 124.

241 Most of the monsters mentioned here are taken from the Alexander literature, cf. Brummack, op. cit.

242 Wellmann, *Der Physiologus*, 1931, pp. 11 and 13.

243 *Encyclopedia of World Art*, vol. X, p. 262.

244 Blankenburg, op. cit., p. 197.

245 Tale of Kamar al-Zaman: R. Burton, *1001 Nights*, vol. III, p. 235.

246 Weil, *1001 Nacht*, Leipzig, vol. I (1838), p. 806.

247 Weil, op. cit., vol. IV (1841), p. 436.

248 W. Heissig, op. cit., p. 261.

249 Herodotus, II, 73.

250 Bonnet, *Reallexikon der Ägyptischen Religionsgeschichte*, Berlin 1952, p. 594 seq.

251 Stephenson, op. cit.

252 Gog and Magog: Ezekiel, 38, 2.

253 Goodenough, *Jewish Symbolism in the Greco-Roman Period*, Pantheon Books, 1956, vol. 2, p. 245 sq.

254 R. Bernheimer, *Wild Men in the Middle Ages*, Cambridge, Mass., 1952, especially p. 28.

255 Baltrusaitis, op. cit., pp. 18/19.

256 D. G. Hogarth, 'The Zakro Sealings', *Journal of Hellenic Studies*, 1902, p. 22; cf. also A. Vahlen, *Mischwesendarstellung in der Kretischen Kunst*, unpublished MS, Halle 1969, p. 59 sq.

257 J. Auboyer, Un Maître Hollandais, *Arts Asiatiques*, 1955, vol. II, 4, p. 251 sq.

Winged snake

Dragon

Sea-dragon. From Olaus Magnus, *Monstrum in Oceano Germanica*, 1573

Abel, Othenio Vorzeitliche Tierreste im Deutschen Mythus, Brauchtum und Volksglauben. Jena 1939

Adeline, Jules Les sculptures grotesques et symboliques. Rouen 1878

Adloff, Ilse Die antiken Fabelwesen in der romanischen Bauornamentik. Thesis, Tübingen 1947

Akurgal, E. Späthethitische Bildkunst. Ankara 1949

Albright, W. F. What Were the Cherubim? The Biblical Archaeologist I, 1938, New Haven, Conn.

Aldrovandi, Ulysses Monstrorum Historia. Bologna 1642

– Serpentium et Draconum Historiae. Bologna 1640

Alföldi, A. Theriomorphe Weltbetrachtung in den hochasiatischen Kulturen. Jahrbuch des Deutschen Archaeol. Institutes, 1931/32

– Der iranische Weltriese auf archäologischen Denkmälern. Jahrbuch der Schweizerischen Gesellschaft für Urgeschichte, 1949/50

Ameisenowa, Z. Animal-headed Gods. Journal of the Warburg and Courtauld Institutes, 12, 1949

Amiet, P. Les combats mythologiques dans l'art mésopotamien du troisième et du début du second millénaire. Revue archéologique, XLII, 1953

Ansbacher, Jonas Die Abschnitte über die Geister und wunderbaren Geschöpfe aus Qazwīnī's Kosmographie. Thesis, Erlangen 1905

Anziani, D. Démonologie Etrusque. Mélanges d'Archéologie, XXX, Paris 1910

Armstrong, E. A. The Thunderbird in East and West. Thesis, Leeds University 1935

Ashiya, Mizuyo Japanische und deutsche Tiermärchen, besonders Fuchsmärchen, in ihrem Wesen und nach ihrer volkskundlichen Grundlage. Thesis, Cologne 1939

Ashmole, Elias Theatrum Chymicum Britannicum. London 1652

Ashton, John Curious Creatures in Zoology. New York, no date

Auber, Abbé Charles Auguste Histoire et théorie du symbolisme religieux avant et depuis le christianisme. Paris 1884

Ausfeld, Adolf Der griechische Alexanderroman. Leipzig 1907

Baer, Eva Sphinxes and Harpies in Medieval Islamic Art. Jerusalem 1965

Ballod Prolegomena zur Geschichte der zwerghaften Götter in Ägypten. Thesis, Munich 1912

Baltrušaitis, Jurgis La stylistique ornamentale dans la sculpture romaine. Paris 1931

– Le moyen âge fantastique: Antiquités et exotismes dans l'art gothique. Paris 1955

– Réveils et prodigues: le Gothique fantastique. Paris 1960

Bartholini, T. De unicornu observationes novas. Amsterdam 1678

Bastian, A. Das Tier in seiner mythologischen Bedeutung. Zeitschrift für Ethnologie, I, 1869

Baur, Paul Centaurs in Ancient Art. Berlin 1912

Kinnari. Thailand. Belt-buckle

Bayet, J. Le symbolisme du cerf et du centaure à la porte rouge de Notre-Dame à Paris. Revue archéologique, 44, 1954

Bayon, R. L'enfer et le diable dans l'iconographie. Revue des traditions populaires, VI, 1891

Bazin, G. Formes démoniaques, Satan. Etudes carmélitaines, 1948, Paris

Bea, A. Moloch in den Mari-Tafeln. Biblica 20, Rome 1939

Beer, Rüdiger Norbert Einhorn. Fabelwelt und Wirklichkeit. Munich 1972

Bees, N. A. Zum Thema der Darstellung des zweiköpfigen Adlers bei den Byzantinern. Repertorium für Kunstwiss. 35, 1912

Beck, A. Cl. M. Genien und Niken in der altchristlichen Kunst. Thesis, Giessen 1936

Belon, Pierre Histoire naturelle. Paris 1554

Bénédite, Georges Fantômes d'Orient. Revue archéologique V, 22, Paris 1925

Benwell, Glenn & Arthur Waugh Sea Enchantress. New York 1965

Bernhart, Joseph Heilige und Tiere. Munich 1937

Bernheimer, R. Romanische Tierplastik und die Ursprünge ihrer Motive. Munich 1931

– Wild Men in the Middle Ages. Cambridge, Mass. 1952

Berruerius, Joseph Bestiarius. Savona 1524

Besig, H. Gorgo und Gorgoneion. Berlin 1937

Bisi, A. M. Il Grifone. Studi Semitici 13, 1965, Univ. di Roma

Bissing Ein indirekter Beweis für das Alter der Hyksossphingen. Zeitschrift für Ägyptische Sprache und Altertumskunde, 65, 1930

– Bes-Kabeiros. Archiv f. Orientforschung, 13

Blake, William Book of Job. London 1825

Blankenburg, W. von Heilige und dämonische Tiere. Leipzig 1943

Bloch, Th. Über bildliche Darstellungen einiger altindischer Gottheiten. Zeitschrift der Deutschen Morgenländischen Gesellschaft, 62, 1908

– Duldul als Centaur. Zeitschrift der Deutschen Morgenländischen Gesellschaft, IV, 63, 1909

Bloomfield, M. Cerberus, the Dog of Hades. Chicago 1905

Boaistuau, Pierre Histoires prodigieuses. Paris 1597/98

Böhl, F. M. Th. Zegel met Zentaur als Boogschutter. Ex Oriente Lux, 3, Leiden 1935. Jaarbericht van het vooraziatisch-egyptisch Gezelschap

– De vermeende Cyclop op een terracotta uit Chafadje. Ex Oriente Lux, 4, Leiden 1936. Jaarbericht van het vooraziatisch-egyptisch Gezelschap

Boisselier, J. Garuda dans l'art khmer. Bulletin de l'Ecole française d'Extrême Orient. XLIV, 1951, Paris

Bonner, B. M. Amulets Chiefly in the British Museum. Hesperia XX, 1951

Boschius Ars Symbolica. Augsburg 1702

Bossert, H. Th. Janus und der Mann mit der Adler- oder Greifenmaske. Istanbul 1959

Bhāranda. Illustration by C.O. Peterson to Th. Etzel, *Der Rohrspatz*, a Book of Fables, 1907

Bredt, E.W. Amoretten und Putti. Ravensburg 1913
Breydenbach, Bernhard von Reise ins Heilige Land. Spires 1495
Bridaham, Lester Burbank Gargoyles, Chimaeras, and the Grotesque in French Gothic Sculpture. New York 1969
Brown, Robert The Unicorn, a Mythological Investigation. 1881
Brown, W.J. The Gods had Wings. London 1936
Brummack, Jürgen Die Darstellung des Orients in den deutschen Alexandergeschichten des Mittelalters. Berlin 1966
Brunfels, Othmar Herbarium. Strasbourg 1530
Bulle, Heinrich Die Silene in der archaischen Kunst der Griechen. Thesis, Munich 1893
Bunt, Cyril G.R. The Lion and the Unicorn. Antiquity, 4, 1930
Bunyan, John The Holy War made by Shaddai upon Diabolus. London 1682
Buren, E.D. van The Flowing Vase and the God with Streams. Berlin 1933
– Further Note on the Burney Relief. Archiv f. Orientforschung, XI, 1937
– The Dragon in Ancient Mesopotamia. Orientalia, 15, 1946
– Akkadian Sidelights on a Fragmentary Epic (Zu). Orientalia N.S. 19, 1950
Buschor, Ernst Kentauren. American Journal of Archaeology, XXXVIII, 1934
– Die Musen des Jenseits (Sirenen). Munich 1944
Buytendijk, F.J.J. Mensch und Tier. Hamburg 1958

Canaan, T. Dämonenglaube im Lande der Bibel. Leipzig 1929
Carrington, Richard Elefanten. Stuttgart 1962
Carter, Dagny The Symbol of the Beast. Animal-Style Art of Eurasia. New York 1957
Castelli, E. Il demoniaco nell'arte. Milan 1952
Champollion-Figeac L'Univers Pittoresque. Paris 1848
Christensen, A. Essai sur la démonologie iranienne. Copenhagen 1941
Clébert, J.P. Bestiaire fabuleux. Paris 1971
Clement, Clara Erskine A Handbook of Legendary and Mythological Art. Boston 1897
Cohn, Carl Zur literarischen Geschichte des Einhorns. Wiss. Beilage d. Jahresberichts d. XI. Städt. Realschule Berlin 1, 1896
Collins, A.H. Symbolism of Animals and Birds Represented in English Church Architecture. London 1913
Columna, Franciscus Hypnerotomachia Poliphili. Venice 1499
Combaz, C. L'Inde et l'Orient classique. Paris 1937
Comestor, Petrus Historia Scholastica. 13th century
Conway, M.D. Demonology and Devil Lore. New York 1889
Coral-Rémusat, G. de Animaux fantastiques de l'Indochine. Bulletin de l'Ecole française d'Extrême Orient, XXXVI 1, 1936
Cumont, F. Recherche sur le symbolisme funéraire des Romains. Paris 1942
– Les religions orientales dans le paganisme romain. 4th ed. Paris 1929

Garuda with snake

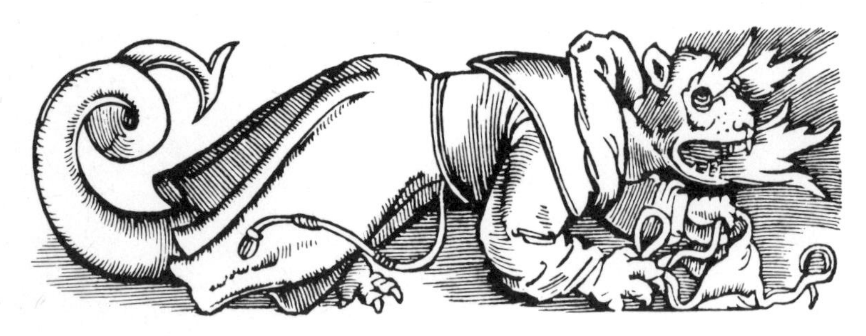

Dragon-monster. From Matthaeus Guidius, *Dialogy*, 1521

Dam, Peter Fabulous Beasts. London 1952

Daniélou, G. Les symboles chrétiens primitifs. Paris 1961

Danzel, Th. W. Symbole, Dämonen und heilige Tiere. Hamburg 1930

Dati, Giuliano de Il seconda cantare dell'India. Rome 1494

David-Neel, A. Heilige und Hexer. Leipzig 1936

Debidour, V. H. Le bestiaire sculpté du Moyen Age en France. Paris 1961

Deonna, W. La sirène femme-poisson. Revue archéologique, 27 (1928), pp. 18–25

– Etres monstrueux à organes communs. Revue archéologique, XXXI, 1930

Deshoulières, F. Le Mercure tricéphale de Soissons. Bulletin Monumental, 1931

Dessenne, A. Le griffon créto-mycénien. Bulletin de la correspondance hellénique, LXXXI, 1957

– Le sphinx, étude iconographique. I. Des origines, I. Paris 1957. Biblioth. Ecoles Franç. d'Athènes et de Rome

Detienne, M. Sur la démonologie de l'ancien pythagorisme. Annales du Musée Guimet. Revue de l'histoire des religions, CLV, 1959

Dhorme, P. & Vincent L. H. Les chérubins. Revue Biblique 35, 1926

Donaldson, B. A. The Wilde Rue. London 1939

Doré, Henry Researches into Chinese Superstitions. Shanghai 1914–1926

Dorfles, C. Bosch. Milan 1953

Dürr, L. Ezechiels Vision. Thesis, Leipzig 1917

Dumézil, G. Le problème des Centaures. Paris 1929

Duval, P. M. Les dieux de la Gaule. Paris 1957

Egede, Bishop Hans The New Survey of Old Greenland. London 1734

Eichler, P. A. Dschinn, Teufel und Engel im Qoran. Leipzig 1928

Eissfeldt, Otto Die Flügelsonne als künstlerisches Motiv und als religiöses Symbol. Forschungen und Fortschritte, 18, 1942

Eleazar, Abraham Uraltes Chymisches Werk. Leipzig 1760

Endter, A. Die Sage vom wilden Jäger und der wilden Jagd. Gelnhausen 1933

Erich, O. Die Darstellung des Teufels in der christlichen Kunst. Berlin 1931

Ettinghausen, Richard The Unicorn. Washington 1950

Evans, E. P. Animal Symbolism in Ecclesiastical Architecture. London 1896

Eygun, François Ce qu'on peut savoir de Mélusine et de son iconographie. Bull. des Antiquaires de l'Ouest, 1949

Falke, O. von Romanische Drachenleuchter. Zeitschrift für Bildende Kunst, 60, 1926/27

Faral, Edmond La Queue de poisson des Sirènes. Eomania, 1953

Feil, V. Vögelin Praktik. Vienna 1534

Fenten, E. Certain Secret Wonders of Nature. London 1569

Ferettus, Nicolaus De structure compositionis. Forli 1495
Finch, F. G. The Winged Bulls of the Nergal Gate of Nineveh. 'Iraq', 10, 1948
Findeisen, Hans Das Tier als Gott, Dämon und Ahne. Stuttgart 1956
Fish, T. The Zu Bird. Bull. John Rylands Library 31, 1948
Floury, Phil. Compendiosa. Paris 1510
Focillon, H. Art d'Occident. Le moyen âge, roman et gothique. Paris 1938. English edition, Art of the West. London 1963
Fränkel, Ludwig Altes und Neues zur Melusinensage. Zeitschrift d. Vereins f. Volkskunde, 4, 1894
Fraipont, Max de Les origines orientales du type de Saint Michel debout sur le dragon. Revue belge d'archéologie et d'histoire de l'art, 1937
Frank, Carl Babylonische Beschwörungsreliefs. 1908
– Lamastu, Pazuzu und andere Dämonen. Mitt. Alt Orient. Gesellschaft, 14, 1941
Frankfort, Henry Cylinder Seals. London 1939
– Gods and Myths on Sargonid Seals. 'Iraq' I, 1934
– Notes on the Cretan Griffin. Bulletin of the British School of Archaeology in Jerusalem, XXXVII, 1936/37
– The Burney Relief. Archiv f. Orientforschung, XII.
Franko, J. Die Einhornsage und ihre bulgarische Variante. Sbornik na narodni umetvorenija, Sofia 1896
Fraser, J. G. The Golden Bough. 12 volumes. London 1907–1915
Frothingham, A. L. The Babylonian origin of Hermes, the Snakegod and of the Caduceus. American Journal of Archaeology, 20, 1916
Furlani, Guiseppe Dei e demoni bifronti et bicefali dell'Asia occidentale antica. Analecta Orientalia, Deimel dedicata, XII

Garbini, G. Gilgames. Encycl. dell' arte antica III, Rome 1960
– Etana. Op. cit.
Gaster, M. Rumanian Bird and Beast Stories. London 1915
Gaster, T. H. Thespis; Ritual, Myth and Drama in the Ancient Near East. New York 1961
Gesner, Konrad De quadrupedibus viviparis. Basle, 16th century
Getty, Alice Ganesa. Oxford 1936
– On the Serpent God. Archivum Asiae, 1940
Gill, M. A. V. The Minoan Dragon. Institute of Class. Studies, University of London, 10, 1963
– The Minoan 'Genius'. Mitteiln. d. Deutschen Archäol. Institutes, Athens, 79, 1964
Glück, H. Eine seldschukische Sphinx im Museum von Konstantinopel. Jahrb. d. Asiat. Kunst II, 1925
Godbey, Allen H. The Unicorn in the Old Testament. American Journal of Semitic Languages and Literatures, 56, 1939
Goldman, B. The Development of the Lion-Griffin. American Journal of Archaeology, 64, 1960
Goldziher, I. Der Seelenvogel im islamischen Volksglauben. Globus, III. Zs. f. Länder- u. Völkerkunde, 83, 1903
Goodenough, Erwin R. Jewish Symbols in the Greco-Roman Period. Pantheon Books 1953

Ch'i-lin. Ancient Chinese drawing

Melusinas. From Abraham Eleazar,
Uraltds Chymisches Werk, 1760

Graf, R. Die Darstellungen der sakralen Einhorn-Jagd in der altdeutschen Kunst. Münster 1928

Gould, Charles Mythical Monsters. London 1886

Greifenhagen, A. Griechische Eroten. Berlin West 1957

Grenfell, A. Iconography of Bes and of Phoenician Bes-Head Scarabs. Proceedings of the Society of Biblical Archaeology, 24

Grimal, P. Dictionnaire de la mythologie grecque et romaine. Paris 1951

Gubernatis, Angelo de Mythologie zoologique ou les légendes animales. Paris 1874

Güntert, H. Kalypso. Halle 1919

Gueroult, Guillaume Le Blason des Oyseaux. Lyons 1550

Güterbock, H.B. The Hittite Version of the Hurrian Kumarbi Myth. American Journal of Archaeology, 1948

Hafner, G. Neue Mischwesen des 4. Jahrh. Wiener Jahreshefte, XXXII, 1940

Hahn, H. Demeter und Baubo. Lübeck 1896

Hambis, Louis Le mythe de l'aigle et ses représentations artistiques en Eurasie septentrionale. Arts Asiatiques, VI, 1959

Harlez, C. de Le Tscheou-li et le Shan-hsi-king. Toung Pao, V, 1894, Leiden

– The Four-Eyed Dog of Yama. The Babylonian and Oriental Record, I, 1886/87

Hartmann, A. Silenos und Satyros. Pauly-Wissowa, 2,5. 1927

Hassan, S. The Sphinx, its History in the Light of Recent Excavations. Cairo 1949

Haussig, Hans Wilhelm (ed). Götter und Mythen im Vorderen Orient. I. Stuttgart 1965

Hegemann, H.W. Der Engel in der deutschen Kunst. Munich 1950

Helck, H.W. Die liegende und geflügelte weibliche Sphinx des Neuen Reiches. Mitteiln. d. Inst. f. Orientforschung, III, 1955

Hentze, C. Bronzegeräte, Kultbauten, Religion im ältesten China der Shang Zeit. Antwerp 1951

Herbert, Thomas Some Yeares Travels into Africa and Asia. London 1677

Herbig, R. Götter und Dämonen der Etrusker. Berlin 1948

Hertz, W. Der Werwolf. Stuttgart 1862

Heuzey Les deux Dragons sacrés de Babylon. Revue d'assyriologie et d'archéologie orientale, VI, 1906

Hinke, R. P. Myth and Allegory in Ancient Art. London 1939

Hogarth, D.G. Excavations at Zakro, Crete. Bulletin of the British School of Archaeology in Jerusalem, VII, 1900/01

– The Zakro Sealings. Journal of Hellenic Studies, 22, 1902

Holländer, Eugen Wunder, Wundergeburt und Wundergestalt in Einblattdrucken des 15. bis 18. Jahrhundert. Stuttgart 1921

Holmström, H. Studier over Swanjungfrumotivet I volundarkvida och annorstädes. Lund 1919

Hommel, Fritz Die Aethiopische Übersetzung des Physiologus. Leipzig 1877

Hopfner, Th. Der Tierkult der alten Ägypter. Denkschrift Akad. d. Wiss. LVII, 1913, Vienna

Hopkins, O. Assyrian elements in the Perseus-Gorgon Story. American Journal of Archaeology, XXXVIII, 1934
Horapollo Selecta Hierogryphica. Rome 1597
Howe, T. P. The Origin and Function of the Gorgon Head. American Journal of Archaeology, LVIII, 1954
Howey, M. Oldfield The Horse in Magic and Myth. London 1923
– The Encircled Serpent. New York 1955
Hrozny, Bedrich Der Babylonische Fischgott Oannes in den Keilinschriften. Archiv Orientalni, 7, 1935
Hunger, H. Lexikon der griechischen und römischen Mythologie. 3rd ed. Vienna 1953
Hyginus Poeticon Astronomicon. Venice 1482

Ilberg, Johannes Die Sphinx in der griechischen Kunst und Sage. Abhandl. u. Jahresber. d. Königl. Gymn. Leipzig 1895/96
Ingersoll, E. Dragon and Dragon-Lore. New York 1928
Isaac, D. Les démons minoens. Annales du Musée Guimet. Revue de l'histoire des religions, 118, 1938

Jacoby, A. Der hundsköpfige Dämon der Unterwelt. Archiv für Religionswiss. XXI, 1922
Jalabert, Denise Les Sirènes. Bulletin Monumental. 1936
– Le Sphinx. Bulletin Monumental. 1935
Jamsthaler, H. Viatorium Spagyricum. Frankfurt 1625
Jouon, P. Le grand Dragon, l'ancien Serpent. Recherches de science relig., 17
Jubainville, d'Arbois de Les druides et les dieux celtiques à forme d'animaux. Paris 1906
Jullian, Philippe Mythen und Phantasmen in der Kunst des Fin de Siècle. Berlin West 1971

Kanpel, H. Die Dämonen im Alten Testament. Augsburg 1930
Kircher, Athanasius Mundus Subterraneus. 17th century
– Oedipus Aegyptiacus. Rome 1652
Kirfel, W. Die dreiköpfige Gottheit. Bonn 1948
Klein, D. Einhorn. Jahrbuch f. Histor. Volkskunde, 3/4, 34
Köhne, B. von Vom Doppeladler. Berliner Blätter f. Münz-, Siegel- und Wappenkunde, 6
Kohn, Carl Zur Literaturgeschichte des Einhorns. Berlin 1896
Kramer, S. N. (ed.) Mythologies of the Ancient World. New York 1961
Kreeling, Emil G. A Unique Babylonian Relief. Bull. American School of Oriental Research, 67, 1937
Kreftig, A. St. Michael und St. Georg. Jena 1930
Kühn, H. Romanisches Drachenornament in Bronze- und Architekturplastik. Strasbourg 1930
Kühnel, Ernst Drachenportale. Zeitschrift für Kunstwissenschaft, 4, 1950
Künstle, K. Ikonographie der christlichen Kunst. I/II. Freiburg 1926/28
Kuntze, F. Die Jagd des Einhorns in Wort und Bild. Archiv für Kulturgesch., 5, 1907

Phoenix. Ancient Chinese pen drawing

Illustration to the *Arabian Nights*, Urdu edition

Lafond, P. Hieronymus Bosch. Brussels 1914

Lanckorenski, L.M. Mythen und Münzen. Munich 1958

Langbehn, J. Flügelgestalten der ältesten griechischen Kunst. Munich 1881

Langdon, S. Babylonian and Hebrew Demonology. Journal of the Royal Asiatic Society, 1934

Lange, K. Der Pabstesel. Berlin 1891

Langlet Dragons and Genies. Paris 1928

Langlotz, E. Perseus. Heidelberg 1951

Langton, E. Essentials of Demonology. London 1949

– Satan. A Portrait. London 1945

– Eine eteokretische Sphinx. Corella Ludwig Curtius. 1937

Lassus, Jean La mosaïque du phénix... d'Antioch. Monum. Piot 1938

Lauchert, Fr. Geschichte des griechischen Physiologus. Strasbourg 1889

Leeu, Gerhard Meluzyne. Antwerp 1491

Lehner, Ernst and *Johanna* A Fantastic Bestiary. New York 1969

Leibovitch, J. Le Griffon. Cairo 1946

– La sphinge. Cairo 1947

Leubuscher, R. Über die Werwölfe und die Tierverwandlungen im Mittelalter. Berlin 1850

Levron, I. Le diable dans l'art. Paris 1935

Levy, Rachel The Oriental Origin of Herakles. Journal of Hellenic Studies, LIV, 1934

Licetus, Fortuna De Monstrorum Natura. Padua 1634

Lommel, Andreas Schlange und Drache in Hinterindien und Indonesien. Thesis, Frankfurt 1937. Gräfenhainichen 1939

Lucas, Frederic A. The Unicorn and His Horn. 'Natural History', 20, 1920, New York

Lüders, Heinrich Die Sage von Rsyaśrága. Gesellsch. d. Wissenschaften Göttingen, Phil. Hist. Nachr. 1897; 1901

Lycosthenes, Conrad Wolfhardt Prodigiorum ac ostentorum chronicon. Basle 1557

Mähly Die Schlange in Mythus und Cultus der klassischen Völker. 1867

Maeterlinck, Louis Le genre satirique, fantastique et licencieux dans la sculpture flamande et wallone. Paris 1910

Magnus, Olaus Monstrum in Oceano Germanica. Rome 1573

– Historia de Gentibus Septentrionalibus. Bologna 1555

Major, M. Secretorum Chymicum. Frankfurt 1687

Mâle, Emile L'art religieux du XII e siècle en France. Paris 1947

– L'art religieux de la fin du moyen âge en France. Paris 1920

Mandeville, Sir John Itinerarius. Augsburg 1482

Marinatos, S. Gorgones und Gorgoneia. Archaiologike Ephemeris. 1927/28

Massé, H. L'imagerie populaire de l'Iran. Arts Asiatiques, VII, 1960

Masson, J. La religion populaire dans le canon bouddhique pali. Louvain 1942

Matz, F. Göttererscheinung und Kultbild im minoischen Kreta. Abhandl. d. Akad. Mainz, 7, 1958

Mayer, Maximilian Giganten und Titanen in der antiken Sage und Kunst. Berlin 1887

Megenberg, Conrad von Puch der Natur. Augsburg 1478

Mendelssohn, H. Die Engel in der bildenden Kunst. Berlin 1907

Merlin, A. Pégase et Chrysaor sur un pyxide attique. Mélanges G. Glotz, II, 1922

Metivet, Lucien Contribution à l'étude de la caricature, la physionomie humaine comparée à la physionomie des animaux. Paris 1917

Michel, Wilhelm Das Teuflische und Groteske in der Kunst. Munich 1911

Molsdorf, W. Christliche Symbolik der mittelalterlichen Kunst. Leipzig 1926

Moltheim, W. Die Darstellung der mythischen Einhornjagd. Zeitschrift f. Kunst und Kunsthandwerk, 10

Müller, W. von Das Einhorn vom geschichtlichen und naturwissenschaftlichen Standpunkt betrachtet. Stuttgart 1892

Münster, Sebastian Cosmographia Universalis. Basle 1544

Murray, Alexander S. Manual of Mythology. New York 1954

Murray, M. A. Ritual Masking. Melanges Maspero. 66

Neuss, W. Die Apokalypse des Hl. Johannes in der altspanischen und altchristlichen Bibelillustration. Münster 1931

Nilsson, M.P. The Minoan-Mycenean Religion and its Survival in Greek Religion. 2nd ed. Lund 1950

– Greek Popular Religion. New York 1940

– The Anguipede of the Magical Amulets. Harvard Theol. Review, XLIV, 1951

Nykrog, P. Les fabliaux: étude d'histoire littéraire et de stylistique médiévale. Copenhagen 1957

Oesterley, W.O.E. Persian Angelology and Demonology. Gaster Anniversary Volume, London 1936

Oldham, C.P. The Nagas, a Contribution to the History of Serpent-Worship. Journal of the Royal Asiatic Society, 1901

Opitz, D. Die vogelfüßige Göttin auf dem Löwen. Archiv für Orientforschung, XI

Osten, H.H. von der Zwei neue Labartu Amulette. Archiv für Orientforschung, 4, 1927

– The Snake Symbol and the Hittite Twist. American Journal of Archaeology, 30, 1926

Otto, Franz Wunderglaube und Wirklichkeit. Leipzig, no date

Panchamukhi Vidvaratna, R.S. Gandharva and Kinnara in Indian Iconography. Dharwar 1951

Panofsky, E. Idea. Florence 1952

Paré, Ambroise Des monstres tans terrestes. Paris 1573

Parmentier, H. Animaux fantastiques. Ars Asiatica, IV

Parrot, A. Glyptique de Māri et Mythologie Orientale. S. Mariana I, 1950

Peri, Noel Hāriti, la mère des démons. Bulletin de l'Ecole française d'Extrême Orient, XVII, 1917; XVIII, 1918

Petersdorff, E. von Dämonologie. 2 vols. Munich 1956/57

Hie fleügt Cupido Psyches man in die lüfft do hin/stürtzt sich Psyche vor layde vom gestat in den nechste bache/erhelt sie dennocht der bach Cupidini zü liebe/trest sie Pan der gaiß got/mit lieblichen worten.

Pan rescuing Psyche

Pettazoni, R. The Pagan Origins of the Threeheaded Representatives of the Christian Trinity. Journal of the Warburg and Courtauld Institutes, IX, 1946

Pfister, K. Hieronymus Bosch. Potsdam 1922

Philipoff, K. von Wissenschaft, die lügt. 'Atlantis', Oct. 1932

Picard, Charles Les origines du polythéisme hellénique. Paris 1930/32

– Les religions préhelléniques: Crète et Mycènes. Paris 1948

Poppen, Hans Alexander am Freiburger Münster und die mittelalterlichen Kunsttypen von Alexanders Greifenfahrt. 'Cimbria', Dortmund 1926

Porzig, W. Illyankas and Typhon. Kleinasiatische Forschungen 1

Praz, M. La carne, la morte e il diavolo nella letteratura romantica. Florence 1948

Preisendanz, M. K. Akephalos, der kopflose Gott. Beihefte Alter Orient, 8, Leipzig 1926

Prinz, H. Der Greif in den Orientalischen Kulturkreisen. Pauly's Real Encycl. vol. 7. Stuttgart 1912

Pritchard, J.B. The Ancient Near East in Pictures Relating to the Old Testament. Princeton 1954

Procopé-Walter, A. Iao und Set. Archiv f. Religionswiss., XXX, 1933

– Geflügelte doppelköpfige Sphinx. Archäol. Anzeiger, 1928

Przyluski, J. Dragon chinois et Nāga indien. Monumenta Serica, III, 1938

Réau, Louis Iconographie de l'art Chrétien. I/II. Paris 1955/56

Régamey, R.P. Anges. Paris 1946

Renz, R. Der orientalische Schlangendrache. Augsburg 1930

Robbins, Russell Hope The Encyclopedia of Witchcraft and Demonology. New York 1959

Robinson, M.W. Fictitious Beasts. London 1961

Roeck, P. Skorpionmenschen. 'Mitra', I, 1914

Roeder, G. Eine große Bronzefigur des falkenköpfigen Gottes Horus. Ex Oriente Lux, 6, Leiden 1939. Jaarbericht van het vooraziatisch-egyptisch Gezelschap

Roes, A. The Representation of the Chimaera. Journal of Hellenic Studies, 54, 1934

Róheim, Géza Drachen und Drachenkämpfer. Berlin 1912

Roscher, W.H. Die Gorgonen und Verwandtes. Leipzig 1879

Rose, H.J. Handbook of Greek Mythology. 3rd ed. London 1953

Rosenberg, Alfons Engel und Dämonen. Munich 1967

Rosenberg, A. Die Erinyen. Berlin 1874

Rosskoff, G. Geschichte des Teufels. Leipzig 1869

Rowe, A. Winged Monsters – Some Tentative Suggestions. Palestine Explorations Quarterly, 1933

Rudenko, S.J. The Mythological Eagle. The Gryphon. The Winged Lion and the Wolf in the Arts of Northern Nomads. Artibus Asiae, XXI, 1958

Rudwin, M. The Devil in Legend and Literature. Chicago 1931

Ruyt, F. de Charun: Démon étrusque de la mort. Rome 1934

Woman with many arms and woman with one eye. Broadsheet, 1475

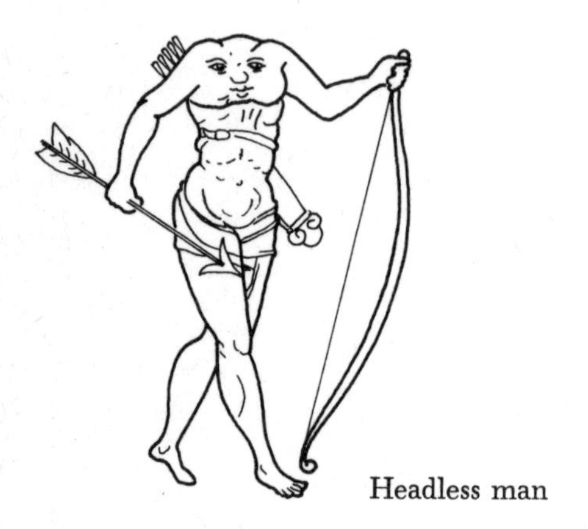

Headless man

Sälzle, K. Tier und Mensch, Gottheit und Dämon. Munich 1965
Salerno, L. Il demoniaco nell'arte. Exhibition catalogue, Rome 1952
Sarasin, F. Über Löwe und Flügellöwe in der Kunst. Verhandl. d. Naturforsch. Gesellsch. Basle 52, 1941
Scaliger, Paulus Explanatio Imaginum. Cologne 1570
Schade, H. Dämonen und Monstren. Regensburg 1962
Schatz Die griechischen Götter und die menschlichen Mißgeburten. Lecture, Wiesbaden 1901
Schefold, Karl Das Dämonische in der griechischen Kunst. Festschrift Otto Regenbogen, Heidelberg 1952
Scheil, V. Fragments de la légende du dieu Zu. Revue Assyr., 35, 1938
– Mythe d'Etana. Revue d'assyriologie et d'archéologie orientale, XXIV, 1927
Schenk, J. G. Monstrorum Wunderbuch 1610
Schmidt, E. The Evolution of the Dragon. London 1919
Schönberger, Guido Narwal 'Einhorn'. Staedel Jahrb. IX, 1935/36
Schrader, E. Die Vorstellung vom Monokeros und ihr Ursprung. Abhandl. d. Preuss. Akad. d. Wiss., 1892
Schrader, H. Die Sirenen. Berlin 1868
Schreyer, Lothar Bildnis der Engel. Freiburg 1939
Schuster, C. A Perennial Puzzle. The Motive of Three Fishes with a Common Head. A.K. Coomaraswamy 70th birthday. London 1947
Schweitzer, Ursula Löwe und Sphinx im alten Ägypten. Ägyptol. Forschungen, XV, Glückstadt 1949
Sébillot, P. L'enfer et le diable dans l'iconographie. Revue des traditions populaires, IV; V; IX. 1889; 1890; 1894
Seeburg, Ludwig Die Sage von dem Gryps bei den Alten. Thesis, Göttingen, no date
Seligman, Kurt Mirror of Magic. New York 1948
Shepard, Odell The Lore of the Unicorn. London 1930
Siecke, E. Indra's Drachenkämpfe. Jahresbericht Lessing Gymnasium, Berlin 1905
Simonett, Ch. Die geflügelten Löwen aus Augst. Basle 1944
Smith, C. Elliott The Evolution of the Dragon. London 1919
Smith, Sidney Demons of Sickness. Journal of the Royal Asiatic Society, 1926
Sörgel, Dagmar Die Schlange im Mythus und Kult in Burma. Thesis, Leipzig 1969
Spenser, Edmund The Faerie Queene. London 1590
Spiess Die Darstellung der Trinität mit drei Gesichtern. Vienna 1927
Spiess, Karl von Marksteine der Volkskunst (Einhorn, Fischjungfrau). Part 2. Berlin 1942
Stabius, Johann De Labyrintho. Nuremberg 1510
Stephenson, J. The zoological section of the Nuzhatū-l-Qulūb of Hamdullāh Al-Mustaufi Al-Qazwīnī. London 1928
Stoye, K. Die Geschichte vom Einhorn. Natur und Heimat, Dresden 1957
Stuhlfauth, G. Der Einhorn-Altar in Dambeck. Marburger Jahrbuch, 13, 1944

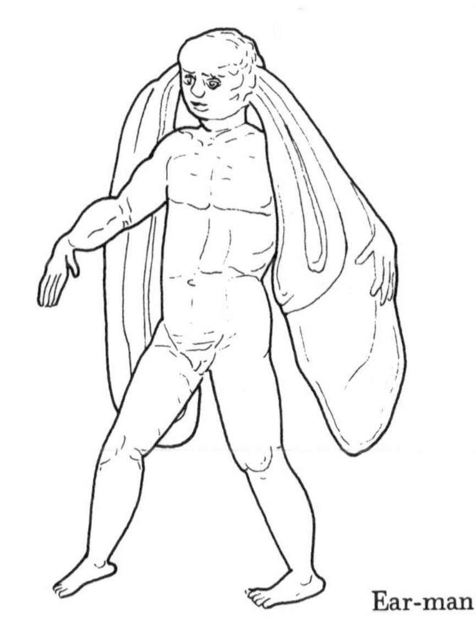

Ear-man

Double-man, half dog, half human

Witches. Woodcut from Augsburg, 1508

– Die Engel in der altchristlichen Kunst. Freiburg 1897

Summers, Montague The Vampire, his kith and kin. London 1928

– The History of Witchcraft and Demonology. London 1926

Thompson, C.J.S. The Mystery and Lore of Monsters. London 1930

Thompson, R. Campbell The Devil and Evil Spirits of Babylonia

Thureau-Dangin, F. Rituel et Amulettes contre Labartu. Revue d'assyriologie et d'archéologie orientale, XVIII, 1921

– Le voyage de Lamastu aux enfers. Revue d'assyriologie et d'archéologie orientale, XXXI, 1934

Tolnay, Ch. de Die Zeichnungen Pieter Bruegels. Zurich 1952

– Hieronymus Bosch. Basle 1937

Topsell, Edward A History of Four-Footed Beasts. London 1658

Toscanne Le lion cornu. Revue d'assyriologie et d'archéologie orientale, XIII, 1916

– Skorpionmenschen. Revue d'assyriologie et d'archéologie orientale, XIV, 1917

Trilles, R.P.H. Les Pygmées. Paris 1944

Trower, C. The Dog-Bird. Leningrad 1938

Tritton, A.S. Spirits and Demons in Arabia. Journal of the Royal Asiatic Society, 1934

Tucci, G. The Demoniacal in the Far East. East and West, IV, 1953

– Tibetan Painted Scrolls. 3 vols. Rome 1949

Turnel, J. Histoire du diable. Paris 1931

Unger, E. Mischwesen. Reallexikon der Vorgeschichte (ed. Max Ebert) 8, 1927

Valton, Edmond Les monstres dans l'art. Paris 1905

Verdélis, N. L'apparition du sphinx dans l'art grec aux VIIIe et VIIe siècles av. J. C. Bulletin de la correspondance hellénique, 1951

Vetter, E. Der Schlangendrache auf Abor. Jahrbuch für Prähistorische und ethnographische Kunst, 1935

Vian, G. Répertoire des Gigantomachies figurées dans l'art grec et romain. Paris 1952

Viennot, Odette Le makara dans la décoration des monuments de l'Inde Ancienne. Arts Asiatiques, V, 1958

Villeneuve, R. Le diable dans l'art. Paris 1957

Visser, M.A. de The Ten-gu. Transactions of the Asiatic Society of Japan, XXXI, 1908

– The Dragon in China and Japan. Amsterdam 1913

Visser, W. de Die nicht menschengestaltigen Götter der Griechen. Leiden 1903

Waddell, H. Beasts and Saints. London 1934

Wainwright, G. A. The Ram-Headed god at Hermopolis. Journal of Egyptian Archaeology, 19

Waser, O. Skylla und Charybdis in der Literatur und Kunst der Griechen und Römer. Thesis, Zurich 1894

Weber, Otto Dämonenbeschwörung bei den Babyloniern und Assyrern. Alter Orient, vol. 7

Wegner, Ingeborg Studien zur Ikonographie des Greifen im Mittelalter. Fribourg 1928

Weicker, G. Der Seelenvogel in der antiken Literatur und Kunst. Leipzig 1902

Weinhold, Karl Beitrag zur Nixenkunde auf Grund schlesischer Sagen. Zeitschrift des Vereins für Volkskunde, 5, 1895

Werbrouck, M. Les multiples formes du dieu Bes. Bulletin des musées royaux d'art et d'histoire, Brussels, 11

Werner, E. T. C. Myths and Legends of China. London 1924

White, T. H. The Book of Beasts, being a Translation from a Latin Bestiary of the 12th Century. New York 1954

Wiebel, R. Drachenbilder und Drachenkampfdarstellungen in der romanischen Kunst. Deutsche Gaue, XXV, 1924

Wield, F. Drachen in Beowulf und andere Drachen. Vienna 1962

Wild, F. Gryps – Greif – Gryphon. Vienna 1963

Williams, C. A. S. Outlines of Chinese Symbolism. Peiping 1931

Winkler, A. Die Darstellung der Unterwelt auf unteritalischen Vasen. Breslau 1888

Wit, de Le rôle et le sens du lion dans l'Egypte Ancienne. Leiden 1951

Wittkower, Rudolf Marvels of the East. A Study in the History of Monsters. Journal of the Warburg and Courtauld Institutes, V, 1942

Wood, E. J. Giants and Dwarfs. 1868

Woolley, Leonard Babylonian Prophylactic Figures. Journal of the Royal Asiatic Society, 1926

Wright, Thomas A History of Caricature and Grotesque in Literature and Art. London 1875

Würfel, Reingart Die ägyptische Fabel in Bildkunst und Literatur. Wissensch. Zeitschr. Univ. Leipzig, 1952/53. No. 3

Wulff, C. Cherubim, Throne und Seraphim. Ikonographie der ersten Engelshierarchie. Thesis, Leipzig/Altenburg 1894

Wundt, Wilhelm Völkerpsychologie. IV. Mythus und Religion. 3rd ed. Leipzig 1920

Zajadacz-Haslenzath, Salome Fabelwesen. Reallexikon zur Deutschen Kunstgeschichte, part 66/67, Stuttgart 1971

Zbinden, E. Die Djinn des Islam und der altorientalische Geisterglaube. Bern 1953

Zimmer, H. Myths and Symbols in Indian Art and Civilisation. New York 1946

Snake with the head of a woman. Chinese

Yu-lung. Ancient Chinese drawing

Sources of illustrations: The page numbers in italics refer to the text illustrations.

Alinari, Florence 46; Anton, Munich 61, 70, 173; Arch. Survey of India, Asutosh Museum, Calcutta 39, 93, 95 (below), 96 (above); Beyer, Weimar 62, 96 (below); Bibliothèque Nationale Paris 72, 84, 135; Birnbaum, Halle 19, 24, *73*, *92*, *101*, 110, *114*, *130*, 137, *153*, 162, 164, *170*, 177, 180, *205*, 216, 218, *211*, *222*, *224*, *239*, *241*, *242*, *246*, *248*, *250*, *252–256*, *258*, *259*, *260*, *264–267*, *273*; Chandra, Calcutta 40 (below), 42, 86, 112, 189; Corvina Publishers, Budapest 48; Deutsche Fotothek, Dresden 167; Foto Marburg 122; Grahl, Meissen 93; Häfner, Düsseldorf 99; Hansmann, Munich *6*, 8, 21, 25, 26, *29*, 37, 47, 51, *54*, *59*, 64, 68, 82 (below), 83, 98, 100, *102*, *103*, 106, 107, 110, 111, *117*, 124, *127*, 133, 138, 139, 146, 147, 149, *155*, 161, 165, 166, 179, 180, *185*, 195 (on the right), 214, 215, *208*, 221, *225*, *238*, *246* (below), *248*, *259* (below), 269; Hirmer-Bildarchiv, Munich 50, 66, 81, 82 (above), 88, 94, 168, 173, 193; Kunstgewerbeschule Zürich 137, 174, 178; Kunsthistorisches Institut, Halle 131; Musée de l'Homme, Paris 69; Museum für Islamische Kunst, West Berlin 136; Museum für Völkerkunde/Weidel, Dresden 192; Nickel, Halle 28; Nyssen, Cologne 38; Oriental Institute Chicago 195; Preiss, Albaching near Munich 65, 108; Prestelverlag, Munich 98 (on the left): Reinhold, Mölkau, 62, 134, 145, 148, 176; E.A. Seemann, Leizig 10, 100 (below); Staatliche Museen zu Berlin 220; Strobel, Leipzig 22, *34*, 63 (above), 151, 191, 213; T.A.P. Service, National Arch. Museum, Athens 43; Thorau, Leipzig 22 (on the left), 40 (above), 50, 67 (above), 95, 122 (above), 150 (above), 162 (above), 163, 174 (above), 194; Topkapi-Museum, Istanbul 87; Verlag der Kunst, Dresden 20, 27 (below), *35*, 45, *60*, *77*, 109, 196, *233*; Verlagsarchiv 23, 44, 49, 52, 63 (below), 67, 71, 85, 97, 121, 140, 152, 190; Universitätsbibliothek, Leipzig 217

The text illustrations named below were drawn by Gerhard Rühmann, Halle *12–15*, *54*, *55*, *57*, *79*, *80*, *89*, *91*, *102*, *113*, *125*, *126*, *128*, *129*, *131*, *141*, *142*, *143*, *144*, *160*, *171*, *172*, *181*, *182*, *186*, *187*, *188*, *199*, *203*, *226*, *228*, *229*, *230*, *243*, *245*, *246*, *247*, *249*, *250*, *251*, *254*, *255*, *257*, *259*, *260*, *262*, *270*, *271*

The publishers wish to thank Ernst and Johanna Lehner, authors of 'A Fantastic Bestiary', New York 1969, for the illustrations on the following pages of our book *5*, *18*, *92*, *101*, *103*, *114*, *130*, *132*, *170*, *183*, *222*, *224*, *239*, *241*, *242*, *244*, *246*, *248*, *250*, *252*, *253*, *254*, *255*, *256*, *258*, *260*, *264–267*, *273*

Text illustrations have also been taken from the following publications:

Archaeol. Mittg. aus Iran 1938: *257*; Arts Asiatiques: *160*; Baer, Eva, Sphinxes and Harpies in Mediaeval Islamic Art: *113*, *172*; Baltrušaitis, Jurgis, Le moyen âge fantastique: Antiquités et exotismes dans l'art gothique. Paris 1955: *229*, *230*; Bossert, Altanatolien: *172*, *197*, *203*; Champfleury, Histoire de la Caricature: *57*; Champollion, Monuments de l'Egypte: *102*; Christian, Altertumskunde des Zweistromlandes: *254*; Coomaraswamy, A.K., Mediaeval Sinhalese Art: *143*; Contenau, Tablettes de Kerkouk: *187*; Debidour, V.H., Le bestiaire sculpté du Moyen Age en France. Paris 1961: *251*, *259*; Ettinghausen, Richard, The Unicorn. Washington 1950: *243*, *251*; Frankfort, Henry, Cylinder Seals. London 1939: *57*, *91*, *102*, *128*, *141*, *144*, *171*, *186*, *197*, *199*, *247*, 260; Frommhold, Erhard, Kunst im Widerstand. Dresden 1968: *35*, *60*, *77*, *233*; Grünwedel, Buddhistische Kunst. 1900: *113*; Harcourt-Smith, Persian Sculptures from Persepolis: *186*; Hogarth, D.G., The Zakro Sealings. Journal of Hellenic Studies 22, 1902: *226*; Holländer, Eugen, Wunder, Wundergeburt und Wundergestalt in Einblattdrucken des 15. bis 18. Jahrhunderts. Stuttgart 1921: *79*, *91*, *143*, *243*; Hulsius, L., Erste Schiffart ... Nuremberg 1599: Klassiker der Kunst, Moritz von Schwind: *205*; Moor, Hindu Pantheon: *249*; Perrot-Chipier, Histoire de l'Art II: *255*; Poeschel, Die romanischen Deckengemälde von Zillis: *131*; Reallexikon für Vorgeschichte: *188*; Reau, Louis, Iconographie de l'art Chrétien. I/II. Paris 1955/56: *181*; Rosenberg, Alfons, Engel und Dämonen. Munich 1967: *120*; Singh, M., Himalayische Kunst: *143*; Strommenger, Fünf Jahrtausende Mesopotamien: 188; Strzygowski, Asiens Bildende Kunst: *181*.

Abaddon Prince of the Furies, King of the Demon Locusts, Angel of the bottomless pit. Revelation 9:11. 34

Abgal/Apkallu Seven Sumerian spirits, subjects of Enki, probably connected with legendary, antediluvian kings; sometimes shown in monster shapes. 104

Abraxas Gnostic divinity. Monster with human torso, cock's head and snake-feet, see Anguipede. According to Goodenough originally called Iao. 172, 224, *224*

Acephali Headless. In old Icelandic sagas, headless spirits of the dead, often returning to earth; also known as 'living corpses'.

Acheloïds Daughters of Greek river god Achelous and the muse Melpomene: Sirens. 102

Actaeon Theban hero and hunter, transformed by Artemis into a stag, sometimes depicted as a man with stag's antlers. 58, 59 197, Plate 37

Adami Adamite descended from mythical Adam, described as sea-man.

Aegir Nordic sea-giant.

Aeternitas Roman personification of eternity. One of her attributes is the Phoenix.

Agathos daimon 'Good spirit' of the Greeks, sometimes conceived as winged serpent hovering invisibly around men. 141

Agrippini In the folk-tale of Duke Ernst, a people in human form but with pointed beaks. Also called crane-heads. 209

Agrus Greek giant with snake-feet.

Airāvata Mount of the Indian god Indra, an elephant, sometimes with three heads.

Aker Ancient Egyptian god embodied in the Earth. Depicted with lion's paws, also as double sphinx with lion's head.

Alborak Silver horse of the Archangel Gabriel, on which Mohammed made his night-ride from Mecca to Jerusalem and back so quickly that he was able on the return journey to catch up a pitcher which he had overturned on leaving. Plate 59

Alcyoneus Greek giant with dragon's feet, sprung from the blood of the emasculated Uranus.

Al-mi'raj Monster in Islamic poetry, a yellow hare with a single black horn on its head. 158

Alopex Huge fox in Greek mythology, sent by Themis into the region of Thebes, to which a boy had to be given every month as food.

Amat Ancient Syrian winged fertility goddess, sister of Baal.

Ammon God of Egyptian Thebes, with the head of a ram.

Amoretti Children of Amor and the Nymphs, winged love-gods (Cupids) of late classical times. 55, 74

Amphisbaena Serpent with a head at each end. According to Pliny, it gives protection in pregnancy, when alive, a cure for rheumatism, when dead.

Anchius Centaur living in Thessaly, overcome by Hercules using flaming brands.

Androgynes Men-women (but not Hermaphrodites), which combine male and female features. Original ancestors of men. When Zeus found them troublesome, he divided them into halves, making them into ordinary men and women.

An Agrippine

Actaeon. Alexander Colin, Munich

Al-mi'raj

Two-headed Amphisbaena. From a twelfth-century bestiary

An Arimaspian. After Lycosthenes, *Prodigiorum*. Basle, 1557

Androsphinx Human-headed Sphinx of Egypt. According to Herodotus erected by Amasis in male form. Sphinxes are frequently shown as female with breasts.

Angel Collective term for winged beings in human form, of both sexes; in Christian art mostly female or of indeterminate sex. 18, 34, Plate 24

Anguipede See also Abraxas. An expression first used in scientific literature for this monster. 102, 172, 224

Anqā Also known as Simurgh, an enormous bird, which lived before Adam. Al-Mas'udi describes it as having a human face. 227

Antaeus Greek giant, son of Poseidon and Ge. He was invincible so long as he remained in contact with the earth. Hercules lifted him off the ground and killed him.

Antholops Animal in the *Physiologus* with large horns in the shape of a saw, but with the body of a bull.

Ant-Lion Monster-figure in bestiaries, because of a linguistic misunderstanding pictured as a lion with the hind quarters of a gigantic ant. Described in detail in the *Physiologus*. It can neither eat meat (because its mother is entirely herbivorous) nor live a vegetarian life (because its father is entirely carnivorous).

Anubis Jackal-headed Egyptian god. 53, 210

Apocalyptic Animal Has seven heads and ten horns, bear's feet and lion's mouth. Revelation of St John 13:1ff.

Apophis Dragon Huge Egyptian serpent, overcome by Osiris. 118

Arba Monster in Islamic literature, of human appearance but with wings and a long tail, which it uses to protect itself.

Archer Sign of the Zodiac, sometimes portrayed as centaur. Also called Sagittarius. 90, 169

Argus Son of Agenor, the hundred-eyed giant watchman of Greek myth. After he had been killed by Hermes, his eyes were placed on the peacock's tail.

Arimaspi Mythical people living on the shores of the Caspian Sea and having only one eye in the middle of the forehead. They fought over gold against the griffins. 209

Arius Centaur, killed in the battle with the Lapiths.

Arke Sister of Iris, the messenger of the Greek gods, and like her possessing coloured wings.

Asakku Assyrian figure with human body and animal's head. 36

Asbsār Supposed to live in Chinese waters, to have the body of a man but with wings and a horse's head. Perhaps identical with the horse-headed Assa-mukhi of India.

Ash Egyptian god, 'Lord of Libya', often portrayed with a falcon's head, later as a triple-headed demon. 181

Asmodeus Hebrew demon, akin to the Mesopotamian Pazuzu. Tobit 3:8. 34

Aspis Small dragon, supposed to be very musical, often portrayed in the religious art of the Middle Ages. 126

Assa-mukhi Horse-headed, man-eating female Indian demon (Yakshini). 73

Ass-headed Fish Mentioned by Pliny, later also in the *Arabian Nights*. 221

Astomi The 'mouthless' people, said to live near the sources of the Ganges. First mentioned by the Greek Megasthenes. 207

Asura Indian demigods, often represented as demons and composite in shape. 73

Atargatis Hellenistic-Syrian goddess, the Dea Syria of Lucian, worshipped in Ascalon in the shape of a fish, under the name Derkete.

Athos Snake-footed giant of the Greeks, son of Earth, begotten from the blood of Uranus.

Ba 'Soul'. Portrayed in Egypt as a bird with a woman's head and human hands. 102, 184

Baal Chief god of Phoenicia, sometimes represented with a bull's head.

Bahri Human-headed bird of Islam.

Balaena Giant fish with a sabre on its back. Seamen used it as an island and cut up meat on the sabre.

Balarāma Described in the Indian epic Mahābhārata as a snake-monster or Nāga.

Baphemet In early literature, the image of an idol or devil of female shape but with the head of a bearded man.

Bardewitt Wendish god of peace, commerce and the five senses, with five heads.

Basilisk King of serpents, gigantic monster with the body of a cock, iron claws and beak, and a triple snake's tail. Its stare, like that of the Medusa head, is fatal. Killed by holding a mirror up to it. Also named Cockatrice. 31, 129, 130, 141, *132*, Plate 5

Bastet Egyptian goddess with the head of a lion or cat. 53

Baubo Female demon or demi-goddess of Priene in Asia Minor. 182
Headless, or with head on legs, but without trunk. Important in fertility cult.

Beelzebub See Devil. 35

Behedti Egyptian sun-deity worshipped in Behedti, portrayed as winged sun's disc, or as falcon-headed god. 184

Behemoth Gigantic animal, similar to a hippopotamus or a huge water-buffalo. Job 40, 15–24. *153*

Benu Sacred bird of the Egyptians, sometimes equated with the Phoenix as a symbol of resurrection. 223

Berchta See Sedim.

Berstuk A forest divinity of the Slavs, often thought of as a half-man with goat's feet.

Bes A demon or dwarf-sized 'wild man', with a large lolling tongue; his image wards off evil spirits; of Egyptian origin (Beset). 53, 181, 182, Plate 124

Bhāranda Two-headed bird of Indian fairy-tales. 183, *262*

Bicha Similar to the Lamassu. Best known from large zoomorphic stone sculptures found in Spain, probably made under Greek influence. 94

Blemmyes Headless people, with eyes and mouth on the thorax. They were believed to live in Africa. See also Acephali.

Boramez Legendary Scythian lamb. Plate 5

Ba. From an Egyptian Book of the Dead

Baubo. Ancient clay figure

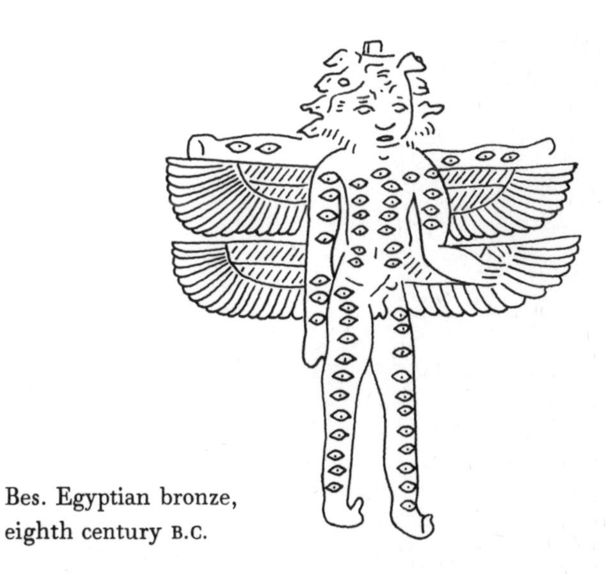

Bes. Egyptian bronze, eighth century B.C.

Cernunnos. Museum of St.Germain-en-Laye

Ch'i-lin. Ancient Chinese drawing

Cecrops. Ancient vase painting

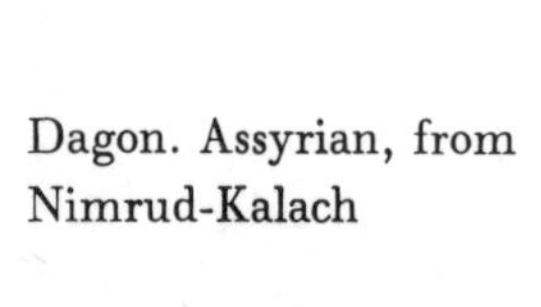

Dagon. Assyrian, from Nimrud-Kalach

Bucentaur Centaur with bull's body. 90

Cacus Fire-breathing giant, slain by Hercules.

Catoblepas Ethiopian bull-monster feeding on poisonous herbs. Its breath killed all adversaries. Mentioned by Pliny.

Cecrops Supposed to have been the first autochthonous King of Attica and founder of the Acropolis. He had a snake's body below the waist. 114

Centaurs Greek men-horses, symbols of brute strength, and in the Middle Ages: of unbridled passion and paganism. As collective term, name for animal-bodied monsters with human upper body, such as ass-centaurs, lion-centaurs, sea-centaurs, etc. 11, 17, 18, 31, 76, 79, 80, 89, 90, 92, 169, 228, *60, 89, 91, 92, 235*, Plates 3, 8, 57, 60, 62, 122

Cerberus Three-headed watchdog of the underworld (Hades), taken by Hercules into the upper world. 115, 160, 169

Cernunnos Celtic deity with stag's antlers. 73, Plate 50

Cetus Greek whale constellation, derived from the mythological sea-monster which Poseidon sent to devour Andromeda; sometimes depicted with lion's head and feet, fish-tail and wings. 90

Charybdis Greek sea-monster, which wrecked ships and devoured sailors. 182

Cheiron Centaur, son of Kronos; prophet and healer. 84

Chentechtai Egyptian god with the head of a falcon and sometimes with horns. 53

Chenti-irti Egyptian god with the head of a falcon but without eyes. 53

Chepre Egyptian god: scarab beetle. 53

Cherub Winged guardian of Paradise, angel. The name is sometimes etymologically connected with the Greek '*gryps*' (griffin). 33. 90, Plate 19

Cherufe Fabulous gigantic creature among Araucanians, living in volcanoes and feeding on young girls.

Ch'i-lin Chinese male-female form of unicorn; symbolic of grandeur, felicity, noble offspring and good administration. 126, 157, *265*

Chimaera Ancient Greek monster in Homer, with the head of a lion, the body of a goat, the tail of a serpent. In Hesiod, it has not a triple body, but three heads – of lion, goat, and snake. Begot by Typhon and Echidna and defeated by Bellerophon. 115, 130, 160, 169, Plates 3 and 106

Chnum Ram-headed god of the cataracts in Upper Egypt. 53

Chors Slav deity, has a dog's head with horns.

Cidipes Corrupt form for sciapods, one-footed creatures.

Cinnamastakā Horrific manifestation of an Indian goddess who holds her severed head in her hand, the mouth open to catch the blood flowing from the neck. 182, *182*

Cockatrice See Basilisk.

Corpse-Eater Monster in the Egyptian Book of the Dead, with the head of a crocodile, the hindquarters of a hippopotamus, and the torso of a lion. Other names of such demons are: Blood-Sucker, Bone-Breaker, Gut-Eater.

Crane-heads See Agrippines.
Cupids See Amoretti.
Cyclopes Giants of Greek mythology with one round eye. One of them was Polyphemus, son of Poseidon. 18, 197, 207, 209
Cynocephalics Dog-heads. Located by Ctesias in India, by Herodotus in Ethiopia. Fire-spewing, with horse's necks. Sometimes explained in the Middle Ages as dog-headed monkeys. In East European folklore they are man-eating monsters. 210, 223

Dābbe-i-chahār-sar Four-headed monster of Islamic legend, living in the Indian Ocean, winged and making horrifying sounds.
Dagon God of the Philistines, later of the Phoenicians; half man, half fish.
Dahnesch Son of Shamurash, an unbelieving winged spirit in the *Arabian Nights*. 221
Dakinī Man-eating female Indian-Tibetan monster; similar to the Arabian Ghulah.
Dekan The soul freed from sin; in human form but with bird's head and feet.
Demeter Greek goddess, pursued by Poseidon, turned herself into a mare and was portrayed in Phigeleia with a horse's head.
Derkete See Atargatis.
Devil A collective term for the ruler of hell, mostly depicted in human form with minor animal features such as horns, tails goat's foot, etc. The Wendish Zart also has bat's wings, horse', feet, and a monkey's tail or a horse's. Lucifer, the fallen rebel angel, is also equated with the devil, and so is Beelzebub. See also Satan. 18, 32, 54, *34*, Plates 15, 28, 30
'*Devourer*' He and the 'Devastator' are an old Syrian demonic pair. Human face, but with horns and hump of a buffalo. 36
Dīwe So-called after the Daivas in the Avesta. In Persian fairy-tales they are gigantic cannibals, with animal faces and massive tusks and horns, and can turn themselves into any shape. 221
Djinn See genies; winged spirits.
Dog-Heads See Cynocephalics.
Dou Dou Dragon-monster of the Church of St George in Mons.
Dragon Collective term for a monster type, usually snake-like, to be found in various civilizations in different forms. The name goes back to the Greek 'drakon' via Latin 'draco'. The figure goes back to early Mesopotamian myth. Most forms in East Asia and in the Christian Middle Ages. Depicted especially in connection with Saints Margaret, George, Sylvester and Michael. The winged two-legged form with barbed tail is sometimes called a wivern. 14, 17, 18, 31, 116, 118, 120, 125, 126, 132, 141, 157, 160; *117*, *127*, *131*, *170*, Plates 5, 9, 43, 84, 85, 87, 88, 89, 92
Drud (or Trud). Vampire, witch with bat's wings, sucks its victims' blood.
Dū Paikar Two-faced monsters in the China Sea, generally with animal body. 223
Durga Great Indian goddess, spouse of Shiva, appears sometimes as woman with bull's head. Mostly, however, depicted as com-

Dīwe. Islamic miniature, seventeenth century

Cynocephalic. From Vézelay

Dragon. After Hans Thoma

Ea. Akkad seal

Goat-fish. From Vézelay

Fêng-huang. Early Chinese

Foot-Shade Man (sciapod)

pletely human, but with several pairs of arms, like other Indian divinities.

Ea Or Enki, water-god of Eridu in Sumer. Human in form, with streams of water flowing out of his shoulders. One of his attributes is the goat-fish. 104, 118, 132, 159, 198, *197*

Ear-Men See Monsok and Panochi. 210, 223, *277*

Echidna Snake-maiden of the Greeks, half woman, half serpent; bore Cerberus and the Hydra to Typhon. 114, 115, 169

Ekaśringa 'Unicorn', name of an Indian seer. His legend has influenced Islamic and Christian versions of the unicorn stories, but is derived from the Mesopotamian Enkidu/Gilgamesh story. 158, 160

Elephant-Headed Tiger Mentioned in the *Arabian Nights*. 142, *143*

Elves In ancient Germanic mythology, beings of small stature, like dwarfs.

Endrop In the Rumanian *Physiologus*, a creature half horse and half fish.

Enki See Ea.

Enkidu The ancient Mesopotamian bull-man and compagnion of Gilgamesh. In literature not described as monstrous, but represented in human posture or as a monster. 32/3, 156

Ephialtes Or Epiales, nightmare demon, horror figure of Greek tales.

Erechtheus Greek tribal hero and earth-god, in the form of a snake. See also Cecrops. 114

Erotes See Amoretti.

Fafner Dragon-watchman of the Nibelungs' treasure. 126

Fama Reputation or Rumour, Roman allegorical deity, with a thousand eyes and wings, sees and hears everything, can grow to infinite size.

Fanamin-Pitoloha Seven-headed hydra from Madagascar.

Fanesians Said to live on an island in the Caspian Sea, fifteen feet high, marble-white; their ears are so large that they can wrap their enormous bodies in them. 210

Faun Roman forest deity, cf. the Greek satyr. Has a goat's tail, pointed ears and a flattened nose. 36

Fêng-huang The Chinese phoenix, male-female, with the head and comb of a pheasant and the plumes of a peacock. 222

Fīlsār Elephant-man, who according to Islamic accounts lives in the region of the China Sea and has wings in addition to a trunk. 223

Fire-Bird See Phoenix.

Fish-Man Sumerian and Akkadian: Kululu. Has a fish-body and fins.

Foot-Shade-Men A wondrous people, who have a single gigantic foot, which they can lift over their heads to provide shade.

Four-Eyed Bitch A figure in gipsy folklore predicting rain with her howling.

Fu-hsi Chinese ruler of the mythical third age. He has the body of a serpent, an ox-head or human head and horn-like growths.

He teaches men the domestication of animals, fishing and writing. 113, 125

Gajasimha A monster, with an elephant's head and a lion's body; it occurs in later Sinhalese art but also in India, e.g. in Orissa. 144

Gajavirāla Indian monster-type consisting of lion and elephant components. 148

Gallu Mesopotamian demons of the air, mostly symbolizing diseases. Men with animal heads.

Galon Giant bird of Burmese mythology, corresponding to the Indian Garuda.

Gandharva Indian demigods, sometimes depicted with wings. 103

Ganesha Indian elephant-headed god of erudition, son of Shiva and Parvati. 58, 142, *143*, Plate 60

Gargoyle A dragon-monster in Rouen, France, carried around in processions.

Garuda Mythical giant bird of India, representative and king of the animals and mortal enemy of the Nāgas. Sometimes depicted as a winged man with a beak. 56, *269*, Plate 27

Genies Arabic Jinn or genies (hence the French and English names). Mostly giants of the pre-Adamitic period, often depicted winged and having parts and characteristics of animals. 221, 227, Plate 35

Geryoneus Three-headed giant of Greek mythology, who fought against Hercules. 169

Ghormuha Sanskrit: ghotamukha, a horse-faced Indian demon with one leg, but otherwise human in shape. See also the female Assa-mukha.

Ghul (Female: Ghulah) English: ghoul. An Arabian desert monster, blood-sucker and man-eater. It resembles both man and animal. 221

Giant Fairy-tale and mythical figure, can also occur as monster, e.g. 'with five heads, five forelocks and five necks', like the giant in the Irish fairy-tale of Diarmuid Redbeard. Jinns are almost always of gigantic size. 29, Plates 4 and 73

Gigantes Giants of Greek mythology, often of composite shape. See also Agrus, Alcyoneus, etc.

Girtablulu See Scorpion-man.

Glycon Gnostic-Mithraic demon, with human head and a snake's body. Sometimes a many-headed snake. 115

Goat-Fish Sumerian monster, the carp-goat, Suhur mas, in the Middle Babylonian emblem of Nabu. 132

Gog and Magog See Yagug.

Gorgon See also Medusa, lewd female figure in Greek mythology, whose look was fatal. 74, *74*

Graouilli Dragon-monster in Metz.

Griffin, griffon, gryphon Huge bird, often portrayed as a monster. Actually a collective term covering a large variety of components. Still popular as a heraldic device. Also a favourite figure in Carnival processions, e.g. in Basle. 14, 17, 18, 31, 54, 116, 127, 128, 129, 132, 141, 157, 209, 227, 228, *6*, *125*, *126* *128*, *133*, Plates 4, 10, 83, 86, 90, 91 94, 98, 100

Gandharva. Indian fresco. Ajanta

Ganesha

Gargoyle

Hanuman

Harpy. From a sixteenth-century German bestiary

Janus-head. Roman

Jinn. Illustration to the *Arabian Nights*. Pforzheim edition, 1838

Grylli Fantastic creatures found frequently on engraved Graeco-Roman gems and later in medieval art. Made up of heads, or consisting only of heads and feet; also in other forms. 18, 227, 228, Plate 3

Gula Winged dog-headed man in a late Assyrian text.

Hanuman King of monkeys, figure from the Indian epic Rāmāyana, depicted with monkey's head and long tail. 73, Plate 46

Harish Unicorn figure in Islamic literature. 157

Harmachis Greek name for the Egyptian sun-god. Also proper name of the Great Sphinx of Gizeh.

Harpies Greek spirits of sudden death. Head and breasts of a woman, bird-body and lion's claws. 102, 202, Plates 4, 69, 71

Hathor Cow-headed Egyptian goddess. 53, *55*

Headless Men Men without heads are mentioned by St Augustine as inhabitants of Ethiopia. They appear often in folklore, e.g. the headless shepherd, or the Wor, who carries his head under his arm. *276*

Hecate Greek mistress of ghostly spectres. Depicted as a bitch, or as a giant-woman with snake-locks and snake-foot, or with a horse's head, or triple-headed: cow, bitch, woman. 115

Hedamnu Hurrite snake-demon, amphibious snake-dragon living in the sea.

Herishef Egyptian god with the head of a ram. 53

Hippocamp Sea-centaur. 132, *144*, Plates 97 and 99

Hippogryph Horse-griffin (horse's body) with eagle's head and wings.

Hor-Hekenu A Horus, worshipped in Egyptian Bubastis. Sometimes depicted as a griffin with a lion's body and the head of a falcon.

Horse-headed Fiddle Morin toluyai-tu quyur. Accompanying instrument of Mongolian singers, mostly a one-stringed fiddle, with a horse's head at the top of the stem. Its origin is explained in a Mongolian fairy-tale.

Horse-heads People in Islamic cosmography, of tall stature, with blue eyes, wings, horse's heads and human bodies. A horse-like people is also mentioned in the Alexander romance.

Horus Egyptian sun-god in the form of a falcon. 53, 114, 184, *55*

Hrungnir The noisy one, a giant in Nordic mythology.

Humbaba A demon figure in the ancient Mesopotamian Gilgamesh epic.

Hydra The Lernaean snake of Argos, a monster with nine heads, slain by Hercules. 115, 118, 160, 169

Iblis The Arabian Satan, a fallen angel driven out of heaven because he refused to bow the knee to Adam. In the Koran, he is one of the Jinns, and like them, winged.

Ifrit Demon figure in the *Arabian Nights*, with horns, lion's claws and ass's hoofs, and of gigantic size. 221

Ihāmriga Indian monster, with human head and animal parts.

Illuyanka Hittite dragon-figure, similar to the Greek Hydra. 118, 160

Imdugud Ancient Mesopotamian lion-headed bird, symbol of the nature-god (Tammuz); later the petrel. 102, 132, 170, *142*
Insān Water-man of Islamic literature. 104, 223
Ipi Early Egyptian goddess with the head of a hippopotamus. 53
Iron-Billed Crow Figure from the folklore of Tibet and Mongolia, messenger of Khormusta, King of the Gods.
Ishtar Goddess of love (chief deity) in Mesopotamia, often portrayed with wings.
Irsan Water-man of Islamic literature, usually said to have human form, but also a tail.

Janus Ancient Italian god of doors and gates, two-faced. Two-headed figures had existed already in ancient Mesopotamia. 159, 170, 171
Jinn See Genies.
Jvaradeva See three-legged deity.

Kabandha Highest of the demons in the Indian Rāmāyana epic, consisting of a massive torso with one large yellow eye and an all-devouring mouth on the chest.
Kalināga A monstrous thousand-headed snake in Indian mythology.
Kāmadhenu Indian sphinx with the body of a cow. 78, 92
Kardopion Or Kardys, one of the dwarf-like smiths of Mount Ida in Crete. He maltreated the mountain-mother Rhea and was cast into fetters of iron.
Karkaddan Arabian name for a unicorn, often winged and having the body of an antelope. 157
Kashkash A hump-backed half-blind spirit in the *Arabian Nights*, with six horns on its head and tufts of hair hanging down to its feet. Its hands and feet are like those of animals. 221
Kautūhala Indian term for animals of combined forms. One kind has the head of an elephant and the body of a lion, another has the head of a deer. 144
Keinnara Burmese term for Indian Kinnara.
Kerub See Cherub.
Kinnara Bird-monster of Indian mythology, with body of a bird and face of a man. 18, 103, *113*, *268*, Plate 75
Kinoly Demonic corpse, mythical figure from Madagascar. 141
Kiu-lung Chinese hornless dragon.
Kuhulu See Fish-Man. 125
Kumbhandha A class of demonic beings, whose testicles are potlike, in Sanskrit-Buddhist literature. Dwarfs.
Kutrub Fabulous animal in the *Arabian Nights*, with long forefeet.
Kutshedra Demonic figure in Albanian folk-poetry: a gigantic, grey woman with face and body covered in hair, a long tail and nine tongues.

Labartu Labbu, the Babylonian female fever-demon, with lion's head and pointed ass's ears, with a wolf or dog sucking at her breasts. 36

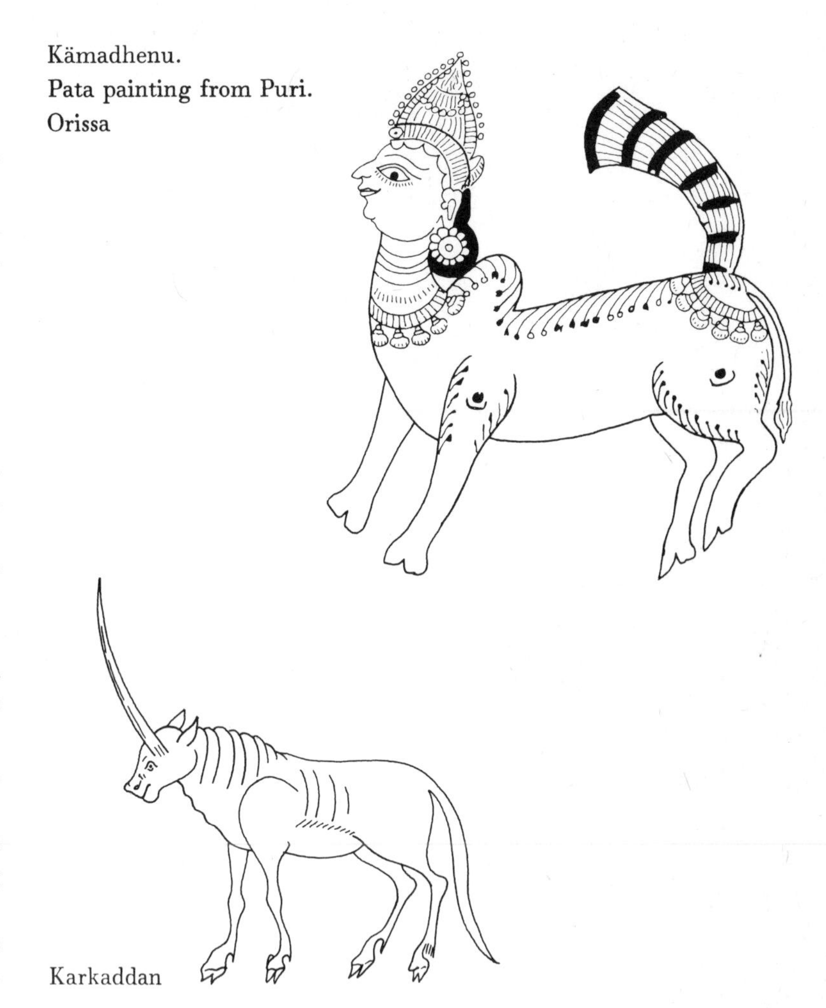

Kämadhenu.
Pata painting from Puri.
Orissa

Karkaddan

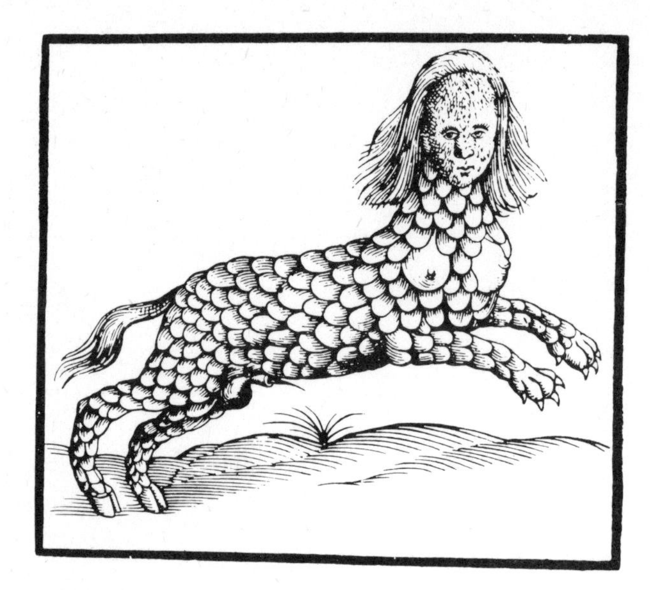

Lamia. London, 1658

Manticora. From a seventeenth-century bestiary

Lacertine A two- or four-footed eel-like creature in medieval book-illumination.

Lahamu Fish-like monster in Akkadian creation myth; offspring of Apsu and Tiāmat. 118

Lamassu Winged lion, or winged bull with human head of late Assyrian times. Guardian spirit of the city of Assur. 33, 90, 113, *18*, Plate 63

Lamia Greek witch who devours children, also called Mormolicoe. She has cow's feet and cat's claws.

Lamias In the Alexander romance, very beautiful women, larger than life, with long hair and horse's feet.

Lapiths 'Stone men' of Greek legend. Enemies of the centaurs. They were believed to have built the Thessalian rock fortresses. 89, Plate 60

Large-lipped People Mentioned in early travelogues. They use their enormous underlip to shade themselves. 209

Lasi Etruscan winged demons. 36

Laskowice Leschia, satyr-like forest-spirits of Slav mythology. 74

Leongalli Live in the forests of Tartary and combine the features of the lion and the cock.

Leviathan Biblical dragon, many-headed like the Greek Hydra. Isaiah, 27,1. 118, 119, 120, *153*

Licorne French name for unicorn, with horse's body.

Lilith The biblical snake, mostly conceived as a monster with snake's body and woman's head. 114, *114*

Lindwurm Winged snake-dragon monster of Germanic and Nordic folklore.

Lion-Dogs Dogs of Fo, portrayed often in China with lions' bodies and a bushy tail. 141

Locust-Demons In the Revelation of St John (9, 7–10), described as monsters: similar to horses, with human face and a scorpion's tail. 34, 141

Long-mā Vietnamese horse-dragon, probably taken over from China and sometimes identified with the unicorn. 126

Lorelei Semi-human water-maiden of Rhenish folklore. 104

Lu See Thu'bān.

Luachsh Wild animal in monster-form in Cabyle legend. 142

Lucifer See Devil. 34, 182

Lung Fire-spewing, scaly, horned dragon of Chinese mythology. 120

Mafedet Ancient Egyptian snake-necked lion.

Mahr Goblin or domestic spirit in Slav legend, can appear in the shape of an object, a hair or a straw.

Maimuna Daughter of the king of the genies, a winged fairy in the *Arabian Nights*. 221

Makara Indian monster, with features of a crocodile, an elephant and a snake; sacred to the river-goddess Gangā. 132, 141, 142

Māmītu Demon or underworld god of late Assyrian literature, with goat's head. 36

Manticora Monster mentioned in bestiaries, probably of Indian provenance, according to a report by Ctesias. It has four feet, a woman's head and a scorpion's tail. Runs faster than a bird can fly. Likes to feed on human flesh. Also called Martikhora. 92

Mārītū-ūn The Manticora of Islamic literature, of similar form. 223

Masculine Women In wonder-tales like the Alexander romance. With beards and bald heads; also with boar's tusks and bristles, of gigantic size and with a bull's tail.

Medusa Greek, one of the Gorgons. Originally depicted as a horse with wings, later as a woman with equine hind quarters. Her head (on Athena's shield) has snakes for hair. Her sight was fatal to the beholder. 73, 74, 114, 130, 182

Melusina European mermaid, who in the legend married the nephew of the Count of Poitiers. Her descendant, Guy de Lusignan, was King of Jerusalem and Cyprus in the twelfth century. 92, 104, 115, *101*, *272* Plate 80

Menhit Lion-headed Egyptian goddess. 53

Meresger Or Merit-seger, snake-bodied monster. Goddess of the Necropolis in Egyptian Thebes. 114

Mermaid Collective name for various figures. She is very beautiful and has full breasts, which she can throw over her shoulders and thus suckle babies on her back. The human trunk ends in a fish-tail. 107, *107*, Plate 17

Meschenet Egyptian goddess of childbirth, sometimes represented in the form of a tile with a human head. The tile was intended to accelerate parturition. 201

Midas King of Phrygia, who turned everything he touched into gold. For disparaging the god Apollo he received a pair of ass's ears. 58

Midgard Serpent Gigantic demon-snake of Nordic mythology, which bites its own tail. 126

Milse Mermaid rising by night out of the dark waves.

Minotaur Bull-man, lived in the Cretan Labyrinth, slain by Theseus. 18, 58, Plates 42 and 45

Miysis Or Mios, Greek version of the Egyptian sun-god as 'wild-eyed lion'. Lion-headed human figure.

Moghur See Thu'bān.

Moloch Divinity of the Ammonites in the Bible, bull-headed monster. 35

Monoceros See Unicorn.

Monocoles See Sciapods. 206

Monsok In Islamic literature, peoples of the Orient, of human form but with ears like those of a female elephant. The ears serve as a covering during sleep. See Panochi. 223

Montu Or Menthu, god of war in Egyptian Thebes, identified by the Greeks with Apollo. Human form with falcon's head.

Mormolicoe Also Mormo, Mormolykeion. See Lamia.

Murakumo-No-Taurugi Dragon-sword of Japanese legend.

Murgh-i ādami Islamic human-headed birds. 103

Mušhuššu Fire-red dragon in Babylonian mythology, created by Tiāmat. 116, Plate 82

Mut Egyptian goddess with head of lion or vulture. 55, 184

Mūtu Personification of death with the head of a serpent-dragon, in late Assyrian literature. God of the underworld.

Moloch. From Athanasius Kircher, *Oedipus Aegyptiacus*, Rome, 1652

'Nāga' couple.
After a late Egyptian portrayal:
Isis and Harpocrates

Ningyo. Ancient Japanese portrayal

Nisaba. Relief from Lagash,
3rd millennium B.C.

Nāga Indian demigods, part snake, part man. Compare also human-headed snake of the temptation in Paradise, similar to snake-monsters of Islamic and European legends. 18, 76, 104, 113, 144, 170, 200, 223, Plate 81

Naiads Greek water-nymphs. 102

Nārasingha The Indian god Vishnu in human form with lion's head. 58, 73, 92, Plate 20

Nāravirāla Indian monster, combination of lion's body with human head.

Nereids Greek sea-nymphs, daughters of Nereus. 102, *131*, Plates 4 and 29

Nessus Centaur of Greek mythology, shot with a poisoned arrow by Heracles. 89, Plate 61

Nidhogar Nordic serpent-monster, representing the volcanic forces of the earth.

Ningirsu Sumerian god, ruler of Girsu. Appears with wings to King Gudea in a dream. His emblem is Imdugud. 102, 132, 203

Ningyo Mermaid of Japanese folklore; she wards off evil and protects the peace.

Nisaba Sumerian goddess of fertility. Corn-deity. Plants grow out of her shoulders.

Nu-kwa Chinese goddes and creator of mankind. Usually depicted with a serpent-like tail. 113

Nixies Water-elves. In later European art sometimes portrayed as winged maidens with bird's feet and tails, but generally as mermaids with fish-body and tail-fins. See e.g. Melusina. In Wendish folklore they have foxes' tails and hoofs on their forefeet and waylay young girls.

Nut Egyptian giantess, whom the Greeks identified with Rhea, goddess of the heavens. Sometimes portrayed with wings. 188

Oannes Hellenized name for a Mesopotamian primeval being represented in the shape of a fish but with human head and feet. 104

Odontotyrannus Three-horned monster of the Alexander romance.

One-Eyed See Arimaspi and Cyclopes.

One-Legged Deity In Indian iconography, the divine figure in Ekapādatrimurti; see also Sciapods. 18

Onocentaurs Ass-centaurs. See Centaurs. 188

Pachet 'The Scratcher', Egyptian lion-goddess.

Pan Greek god of shepherds and hunters. Leader of the satyrs. He was born horned, bearded, hook-nosed, hairy, with tailand with goat's feet, so that his horrified mother ran away. *275*, Plate 25

Panochi Or Panoti. People with gigantic ears, the lobes hanging down to the ground. According to Ctesias they had eight fingers on each hand and eight toes on each foot. See also Monsok. 210, 223

Pazuzu Assyrian demon with four wings, terrible bringer of diseases, represents the south-eastern storm wind. Gargoylelike, horned head, lion's forepaws, eagle's feet and scorpion's tail. 34

Pegasus Divine winged horse of the Greeks, mount of Bellerophon. Supposed to have sprung from the blood of Medusa. 18, 90, 114, 130, *29*

P'eng-Niao Enormous bird of Chinese mythology.

Peri Persian witches of great beauty who attempt the sensual temptation of the faithful. Like the Dīwe they like to feed on human flesh, but in general they are well-disposed towards men. 221

Phantom In Arabic, Tayf, the shadow of a dead person. Ghost.

Phoenix A wonder-bird, which according to Herodotus flies once every five hundred years from India to Egypt, burns itself there on a pyre and arises renewed from the ashes. In medieval art shown surrounded by a ring of fire. Also known in East Asia. In Vietnam (phung) it has monster-shape, with snake-neck and fish-tail, like the horse-dragon. 31, 157, 222, 223, *221*, *273*, Plate 5

Pi-hsi River deity of Chinese mythology in form of a tortoise.

Plague-Women In Croatian folklore women of small stature, without noses or ears, with tiny snake's eyes, cat's paws and goat's feet. 74

Polyphemus Cyclops of Greek mythology, blinded by Odysseus. 182, 197, 198, 209

Poqhirāj Pakshirāja, originally a gigantic Indian bird, king of the birds, mount of Vishnu. In Bengali folklore a flying horse similar to Pegasus; like the horse of Achilles or the horse Falada in German tales, it speaks and advises its rider.

Porovit Porenutius, god of Slav myth, with four heads on a neckless body, and a fifth on the breast.

Psezpolnica 'Midday woman' of Wendish legend, covered all over in black hair, with horse's feet, but with human face. Whoever cannot talk to her for a whole hour, between midday and one, about flax or millet has his head cut off by her with a sickle. 74

Ptah Dwarf-like Egyptian protector of craftsman and artists.

Python Dragon-like monster at Delphi. Killed by Apollo. 120

Quetzalcoatl Mexican divinity. Quetzlal, the feathered Aztec snake, a symbol of air. 113

Rākshasa Class of Indian demons, hostile to man, fire-breathing, with massive tusks and of gigantic size. 227

Rāmagāyatri Indian monster, a cow with a human face.

Raven-Genius Has a lion's face, an eagle's talons and spark-showering eyes. In the *Arabian Nights*.

Re Egyptian sun-god, sometimes with the head of a falcon. 53

Roc Or Rukh. Enormous bird, probably of Persian origin, said to live in India, having two horns and four humps on its back; best known from the tales of Sindbad the Sailor. 129, 130, 222, Plates 5

Ryu Japanese dragon, which can live and move in air, in water and on land.

Sachmet Lion-headed Egyptian goddess. 53

Pazuzu

Bellerophon and Pegasus. Greek vase painting

Quetzlal. Aztec. From Palenque, Mexico

Satyr. Vase painting from Duris, fifth century B.C.

Senmurv. Sassanid-Persian

Sagittarius See Archer.

Sagsār Dog-like, see Cynocephalics. In Islamic legend sometimes having two heads, a man's and a dog's. 223

Sarabha Deer-like animal with eight feet, living on snow-covered mountains. Appears in the Indian epic *Mahābhārata*. 144

Sardula Horned lion in Indian art. 144

Satan The devil. In Islamic tradition he had a wife (Haww'a) and nine sons. In the *Cosmography* described as half-dog and half-cat, with a long trunk. 34, 35

Satyr Greek monster, originally perhaps partly horse-shaped and not, as in later art, with goat's legs. He has a flat nose and a brutish expression. A forest-demon of voluptuousness and unbridled lust. See Faun. 34, 36, 89, 90, *54*, Plates 4 and 26

Schaitan See Satan.

Sciapods One-footed beings, whose gigantic foot serves as a sunshade, see Foot-Shade-Men. They move at great speed, even hopping over the surface of the sea. Also called Monokoles. 206, 207, Plate 145

Scorpion-Man Sumerian and Akkadian monster-figure, Girtablulu, created by Tiāmat to do battle with the gods. Gilgamesh meets him on his wanderings. 115

Scylla Like Charybdis, a Greek sea-monster, which wrecks ships. Has twelve shapeless feet, six extraordinary long necks, and on each a hideous head with three rows of deadly teeth. 182, *179*

Sea-Horse Rises up like a wild lion out of the water and covers an ordinary mare. (Sindbad's first voyage in the *Arabian Nights*) 132, 221, Plate 4

Sedim Babylonian demons with cocks' feet. Compare the goose-footed Berchta.

Senmurv The seed-scatterer, a mythical Persian bird-monster, symbolizing the union of earth, air and water.

Seraph Angel with six wings.

Sesa Gigantic thousand-headed Indian serpent, upon which Vishnu rests. 170

Seth Egyptian god of uncertain animal shape. 53

Sharav See Sarabha.

Shedu Human-headed, winged bull-monster of Assyrian-Babylonian mythology.

Shen-nung Chinese ruler with human body and ox's head. Said to have invented the plough and agriculture in primeval times.

Sickle-Man In Wendish legend and fairy-tale, male pendant to Psezpolnica and, like her, appears at midday. He has spark-showering eyes, one horse-leg and one cow-leg and long talons.

Simurgh See Anqā. Gigantic bird of Persian mythology. It is so old that it has already seen the world destroyed three times. 102, 129, 130, 222

Sinād A unicorn similar to Karkadann.

Siqq In Islamic cosmography a devilish creature in the shape of a half-man.

Shesemtet Lion-headed Egyptian goddess.

Sirabich tandjung Bird-like spirits of Indonesian women who have died in childbirth. They correspond to the Pontianak of the Malays. To take their revenge they cause the deaths of other women in childbed.

Sirens Greek mermaids with fish-tails, who sing on Mediterranean cliff-tops and so lure sailors to their deaths. See also Acheloïds. 18, 31, 76, 89, 92, 101, 102, 103, 104, 224, *102*, *103*, *113*, *131*, Plates 3, 10, 69
In the *Physiologus* these sirens are described as women above the waist and birds below.

Skoffin Icelandic monster corresponding most closely to the Basilisk. According to some sources, hatched from an egg, according to others the offspring of a tomcat and a vixen. Its look is deadly. 142

Sobek See Suchos.

Somā Cambodian Nāgini. See Nāga. 113

Spahlen-Tier Dragon-like spectral animal in the folklore of Basle.

Sphinx Originally an Egyptian monster, taken over by various civilizations in East and West and given a more general application. Mostly, however, a lion with a human head, male or female. See also Harmachis. 14, 17, 18, 54, 76, 78, 79, 80, 90, 115, 128, 157, 181, 202, 227, 228, *79*, *80*, *233*, Plates 3, 9, 52, 53, 54, 55, 56

Stomach-Faces Headless beings, or portrayed with second face on stomach, on ancient gems and in medieval art. 210

Stymphalian Birds Giant birds with iron talons and beaks, driven away by Heracles with a rattle. 222

Suchos Egyptian crocodile god, also known as Sobek. 54, Plate 34

Sulafātī Islamic figure with human characteristics combined with a turtle's body and two long wings. 223

Swan Maidens Term for the Valkyries in Nordic mythology. In fairy-tales they are supernatural beings, who fly down to earth, mostly to bathe, laying aside their winged or feathered garb. 75

Sword-Man Personified weapon depicted in Yazilikaya. In India, too, the sword can serve as embodiment of a deity. In fairy-tales there are self-moving and other miraculous swords. 29

Sz Sword-ox, Malayan unicorn.

Stomach-face

Scorpion-man.
From a Kassite boundary-stone of the 2nd millennium B.C.

Taksaka Indian snake-demon in service of the demon-king Ravana. 113

Tannin Many-headed Syrian dragon slain by El's daughter, Anath. 126

Tarasque The dragon of Tarascon, a massive, famous monster.

Tāyir The 'Flyer', a two-winged, human-shaped animal in Islamic tradition; it speaks a language no one understands.

Tatzlwurm Winged, fire-breathing dragon of Germanic legends.

Tefnut Lion-headed Egyptian goddess. 53

Telchines Type of demon in the Southern Aegean. Partly fish, partly snake.

Tenes Greek figure with two faces. See also Janus.

Ten-gū Winged Japanese mountain and forest sprites with long noses or beaks. Sometimes they steal children, but mostly they play harmless tricks. 56

Ten-gū

Teviel Man-eating monster of the Cabyles, a witch.

Thot Egyptian god with the head of an ibis. 53

Three-legged monsters Indian deity named Jvaradeva or Jvaraha-reśvara. Three-legged donkey with six eyes in Indian mythology.

Thu'bān Dragon in Islamic literature, called 'Tinnīn' by the Arabs, 'Moghur' by the Mongols, and 'Lu' by the Turks. In all probability, originally a snake, which later grew into a gigantic fire-breathing dragon. 126

Tiāmat In Akkadian, the sea; an ancient Mesopotamian dragon-figure. 115, 116, 118

Tinnīn See Thu'bān.

Toe Nayo Burmese unicorn with horse's body.

Toeris Egyptian goddess with the head of a hippopotamus. 53

Tokan-dia One-footed creature on Madagascar. 142

Trauku Giant in Araucanian fairy-tales, the Old Man of the Mountain. In Chile he is exactly the opposite, a malignant dwarf.

Triglaw Three-headed deity of Serbs, Wends, Poles, and other Slav peoples. Mostly with three goat's heads.

Triple-Head Or Triple-Face, in Indian, Greek and Christian medieval art.

Triton Son of Poseidon and Amphitrite. He has a human body with a fish-tail. 11, 102, *5*, Plate 79

Trud See Drud.

Tuchulka Etruscan figure of the underworld, in human form but with a vulture's beak and animal ears.

Two-Foot Halved quadruped body in medieval art; later depicted by Bosch in endless variations.

Typhon Greek giant with a hundred snake-heads, son of Ge and Tartarus. Echidna is his mate, Hydra and Cerberus his children. 120, Plate 68

Uroboros. From Abraham Eleazar, *Uraltes Chymisches Werk*, 1760

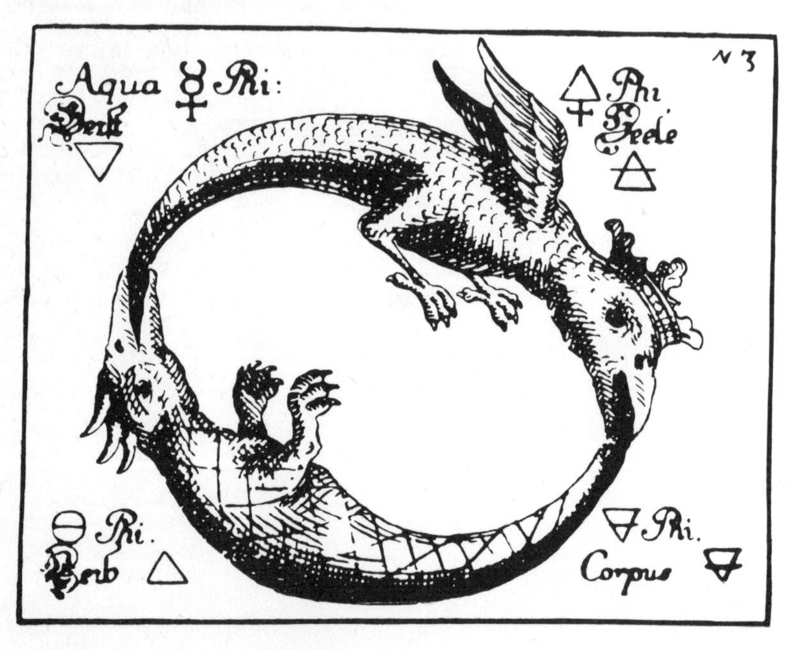

Udaramukha Indian gryllus-like monster, face on stomach.

Undine Legendary female water-sprite, see Mermaid. 104

Unicorn Found in the legends of many countries. Often derived from the rhinoceros and explained as a real animal, or interpreted as the profile view of a two-horned animal, with one horn hidden behind the other. But in the literature of many peoples unicorns occur clearly as fabulous animals. The name is a collective term for a monster which, like the dragon, can assume many forms. 17, 18, 31, 126, 144, 154, 155, 156, 157, 158, 169, *30*, *155*, Plates 5, 104, 107, 108

Upuaut Jackal-headed Egyptian god. 53

Uroboros Serpent biting its own tail, an ancient symbol of eternity. 224

Usmu Mesopotamian predecessor of two-headed figures (see Janus and Tenes), minister of the water-god Ea. 159, 170

Uto Egyptian snake-headed goddess of Buto. 113

Utukku Late Assyrian god of underworld, with a human body and a lion's head. 36

Varāha The Indian god Vishnu in his manifestation as boar-headed liberator of the earth-goddess. 73

Vetāla Indian class of demons, which take possession of corpses, enter into them and revivify them.

Vouivre One-eyed dragon in French-speaking Switzerland. His eye is formed by a garnet and promises riches, but also danger.

Vyālaka A lion-like monster in India. 144

Wak-Wak Tree A tree whose fruits consist of human and animal heads, on the eastern island of Wakwak in the *Arabian Nights*. See also the Hell-Tree Zakkum in the Koran. In some medieval tales birds also grow on trees.

Walimana Malayan monster; in ancient Javanese poetry it has a bird's body and a human face.

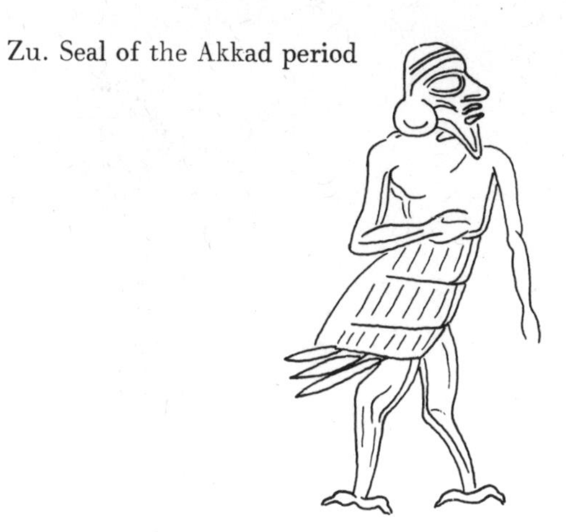

Zu. Seal of the Akkad period

Werewolf

Varāha. North Indian stele. Calcutta, Museum

Wild men

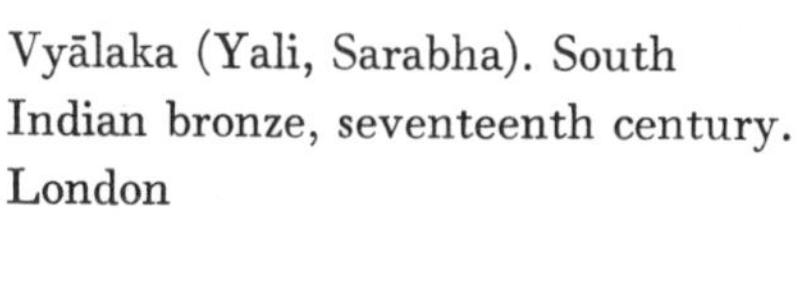

Vyālaka (Yali, Sarabha). South Indian bronze, seventeenth century. London

Water-Elephant In Burmese folklore an elephant as small as a mouse, but so strong that it threatens real elephants and likes to feed on their brains. 144

Werewolf Nocturnal strangler, sometimes in monster-shape as a wolf-man. 221

Wild Men Figures in medieval poetry and art; often they are giants with owl's eyes, boar's tusks and elephant's ears. They have survived, like the griffin, in the Carnival processions in Basle. 224, 227, *30*, *225*

Winged Animals Collective term. Almost all quadrupeds can be provided with wings and so appear as monsters. Especially famous in the ancient world was Pegasus, the winged horse, which also occurs in folklore. 18, 55, 130, 132, *141*, Plate 101

Witch Not really of composite shape, but sometimes depicted with clawed feet. 29, 224, *272*

Wivern Or wyvern. See Dragon. 116

Wor See Headless men.

Wuarsen Or Warseniu, man-eating giant of the Cabyles.

Yakshas Indian group of demons or demigods, who in poetry are said to have been the original inhabitants of Ceylon and are even today portrayed there in masked dances, mostly associated with snakes, but with human and animal characteristics mixed.

Yagug and Magug Gog and Magog (Ezekiel 38–39). Legendary peoples, very numerous. According to Qazwīnī they are half the size of a man and stocky, with lion's fangs and claws. It was said that hardly one of them died without having thousands of descendants. 223

Yali Like the Sarabha, a type in Indian art, mostly shown with a lion's body and the trunk and tusks of an elephant.

Yü-lung Chinese water-monster, half fish, half dragon.

Zägh Human-faced, speaking crow in Islamic poetry, sometimes identified with the Roc bird. 222

Zart Wendish name for the Devil.

Zu Mesopotamian petrel, a bird-centaur, but also a descendant of Imdugud. 102, 132